MARTIAL ARTS SUDOKU ★ NOT-SO-EASY ®

# SECOND-DEGREE
# GREEN BELT
# SUDOKU®

## Frank Longo

PUZZLE
WRIGHT
PRESS
New York

# CONTENTS

**PUZZLE**
WRIGHT
**PRESS**

New York

An Imprint of Sterling Publishing Co., Inc.
1166 Avenue of the Americas
New York, NY 10036

ISBN 978-1-4027-3715-2

Distributed in Canada by Sterling Publishing Co., Inc.
c/o Canadian Manda Group, 664 Annette Street
Toronto, Ontario, Canada M6S 2C8
Distributed in the United Kingdom by GMC Distribution Services
Castle Place, 166 High Street, Lewes, East Sussex, England BN7 1XU
Distributed in Australia by NewSouth Books
45 Beach Street, Coogee, NSW 2034, Australia

For information about custom editions, special sales, premium and corporate purchases, please contact Sterling Special Sales at 800-805-5489 or specialsales@sterlingpublishing.com.

*Manufactured in Canada*

16  18  20  19  17  15

www.sterlingpublishing.com

# INTRODUCTION

To solve sudoku puzzles, all you need to know is this one simple rule:

**Fill in the boxes so that the nine rows, the nine columns, and the nine 3×3 sections all contain every digit from 1 to 9.**

And that's all there is to it! Using this simple rule, let's see how far we get on this sample puzzle at right. (The letters at the top and left edges of the puzzle are for reference only; you won't see them in the regular puzzles.)

|   | A | B | C | D | E | F | G | H | I |
|---|---|---|---|---|---|---|---|---|---|
| J |   |   |   |   |   |   |   |   |   |
| K |   |   |   |   | 2 |   | 1 | 8 | 4 |
| L | 9 |   | 5 |   | 7 |   | 2 |   | 6 |
| M | 1 |   | 4 | 3 | 9 | 2 |   | 7 |   |
| N |   |   |   | 7 |   | 6 |   |   |   |
| O |   | 7 |   | 1 | 4 | 8 | 9 |   | 2 |
| P | 3 |   | 2 |   | 6 |   | 8 |   | 5 |
| Q | 8 | 4 | 9 |   | 3 |   |   |   |   |
| R |   |   |   |   |   |   |   |   |   |

The first number that can be filled in is an obvious one: box EN is the only blank box in the center 3×3 section, and all the digits 1 through 9 are represented except for 5. EN must be 5.

The next box is a little trickier to discover. Consider the upper left 3×3 section of the puzzle. Where can a 4 go? It can't go in AK, BK, or CK because row K already has a 4 at IK. It can't go in BJ or BL because column B already has a 4 at BQ. It can't go in CJ because column C already has a 4 at CM. So it must go in AJ.

Another box in that same section that can now be filled is BJ. A 2 can't go in AK, BK, or CK due to the 2 at EK. The 2 at GL rules out a 2 at BL. And the 2 at CP means that a 2 can't go in CJ. So BJ must contain the 2. It is worth noting that this 2 couldn't have been placed without the 4 at AJ in place. Many of the puzzles rely on this type of steppingstone behavior.

We now have a grid as shown.

Let's examine column A. There are four blank boxes in column A; in which blank box must the 2 be placed? It can't be AK because of the 2 in EK (and the 2 in BJ). It can't be AO because of the 2 in IO. It can't be AR because of the 2 in CP. Thus, it must be AN that has the 2.

|   | A | B | C | D | E | F | G | H | I |
|---|---|---|---|---|---|---|---|---|---|
| J | 4 | 2 |   |   |   |   |   |   |   |
| K |   |   |   |   | 2 |   | 1 | 8 | 4 |
| L | 9 |   | 5 |   | 7 |   | 2 |   | 6 |
| M | 1 |   | 4 | 3 | 9 | 2 |   | 7 |   |
| N |   |   |   | 7 | 5 | 6 |   |   |   |
| O |   | 7 |   | 1 | 4 | 8 | 9 |   | 2 |
| P | 3 |   | 2 |   | 6 |   | 8 |   | 5 |
| Q | 8 | 4 | 9 |   | 3 |   |   |   |   |
| R |   |   |   |   |   |   |   |   |   |

3

By the 9's in AL, EM, and CQ, box BN must be 9. Do you see how?

We can now determine the value for box IM. Looking at row M and then column I, we find all the digits 1 through 9 are represented but 8. IM must be 8.

This brief example of some of the techniques leaves us with the grid at right.

You should now be able to use what you learned to fill in CN followed by BL, then HL followed by DL and FL.

As you keep going through this puzzle, you'll find it gets easier as you fill in more. And as you keep working through the puzzles in this book, you'll find it gets easier and more fun each time. The final answer is shown below.

This book consists of 300 puzzles of medium level of difficulty.

—Frank Longo

|   | A | B | C | D | E | F | G | H | I |
|---|---|---|---|---|---|---|---|---|---|
| J | 4 | 2 |   |   |   |   |   |   |   |
| K |   |   |   |   | 2 |   | 1 | 8 | 4 |
| L | 9 |   | 5 |   | 7 |   | 2 |   | 6 |
| M | 1 |   | 4 | 3 | 9 | 2 |   | 7 | 8 |
| N | 2 | 9 |   |   | 7 | 5 | 6 |   |   |
| O |   | 7 |   | 1 | 4 | 8 | 9 |   | 2 |
| P | 3 |   | 2 |   | 6 |   | 8 |   | 5 |
| Q | 8 | 4 | 9 |   | 3 |   |   |   |   |
| R |   |   |   |   |   |   |   |   |   |

|   | A | B | C | D | E | F | G | H | I |
|---|---|---|---|---|---|---|---|---|---|
| J | 4 | 2 | 1 | 6 | 8 | 3 | 5 | 9 | 7 |
| K | 7 | 3 | 6 | 5 | 2 | 9 | 1 | 8 | 4 |
| L | 9 | 8 | 5 | 4 | 7 | 1 | 2 | 3 | 6 |
| M | 1 | 5 | 4 | 3 | 9 | 2 | 6 | 7 | 8 |
| N | 2 | 9 | 8 | 7 | 5 | 6 | 4 | 1 | 3 |
| O | 6 | 7 | 3 | 1 | 4 | 8 | 9 | 5 | 2 |
| P | 3 | 1 | 2 | 9 | 6 | 7 | 8 | 4 | 5 |
| Q | 8 | 4 | 9 | 2 | 3 | 5 | 7 | 6 | 1 |
| R | 5 | 6 | 7 | 8 | 1 | 4 | 3 | 2 | 9 |

**1**

| 5 | 4 | 7 | 6 | 3 | 2 | 8 | 9 | 1 |
|---|---|---|---|---|---|---|---|---|
|   |   |   | 7 | 4 | 8 |   | 3 |   |
| 3 | 8 | 2 | 9 | 1 | 5 | 4 | 6 | 7 |
| 6 | 5 | 1 | 8 | 2 | 4 | 9 | 7 | 3 |
| 7 | 3 | 4 | 5 | 9 | 1 | 6 | 2 | 8 |
| 2 | 9 | 8 | 3 | 6 | 7 | 1 |   |   |
| 8 | 6 |   | 2 | 7 | 9 | 3 | 1 |   |
|   | 7 |   | 1 | 8 | 3 |   |   | 6 |
| 1 | 2 | 3 | 4 | 5 | 6 | 7 | 8 | 9 |

**2**

| 9 |   |   |   |   | 3 |   | 8 |   |
|---|---|---|---|---|---|---|---|---|
|   | 2 |   |   |   |   | 4 | 5 | 9 |
|   | 1 |   |   |   |   |   |   |   |
|   |   | 2 |   | 3 | 5 |   | 4 |   |
|   |   |   | 9 |   | 2 |   |   |   |
|   | 6 |   | 1 | 7 |   | 9 |   |   |
|   |   |   |   |   |   |   | 6 |   |
| 8 | 4 | 9 |   |   |   |   | 2 |   |
|   | 7 |   | 5 |   |   |   |   | 8 |

**3**

| | | 9 | | 7 | | 4 | | 3 |
|---|---|---|---|---|---|---|---|---|
| | | | 9 | | | | 6 | |
| | 1 | 4 | 2 | | | | 8 | |
| | | | | 2 | | 6 | | |
| | | 5 | 1 | | 8 | 3 | | |
| | | 1 | | 3 | | | | |
| | 8 | | | | 2 | 9 | 7 | |
| | 2 | | | | 4 | | | |
| 1 | | 7 | | 6 | | 8 | | |

**4**

| | | 8 | | | 4 | | | |
|---|---|---|---|---|---|---|---|---|
| 2 | 1 | | | 8 | | | 6 | |
| | | | | 6 | 1 | | 4 | |
| | | | | | | 3 | 5 | 7 |
| | 5 | 6 | | 7 | | 1 | 2 | |
| 7 | 9 | 2 | | | | | | |
| | 2 | | 1 | 3 | | | | |
| | 6 | | | 2 | | | 7 | 3 |
| | | | 5 | | | 2 | | |

**5**

| | | | | | 4 | | 6 | |
|---|---|---|---|---|---|---|---|---|
| 1 | | 7 | | | | 4 | 5 | 2 |
| | 2 | 4 | | | 8 | 7 | | |
| | | | 9 | 5 | | | | |
| 7 | | 8 | | | | 6 | | 9 |
| | | | | 8 | 6 | | | |
| | | 1 | 8 | | | 3 | 4 | |
| 8 | 3 | 5 | | | | 9 | | 1 |
| | 7 | | 3 | | | | | |

**6**

| | 3 | 5 | | | | | | 9 |
|---|---|---|---|---|---|---|---|---|
| | | | | 5 | 7 | 1 | | |
| | | | 4 | | | | 6 | 5 |
| | 1 | | | 8 | | 4 | | |
| | 4 | 8 | | 2 | | 6 | 9 | |
| | | 9 | | 7 | | | 2 | |
| 9 | 2 | | | | 3 | | | |
| | | 4 | 7 | 6 | | | | |
| 6 | | | | | | 8 | 4 | |

**7**

| | | | 2 | | | | | |
|---|---|---|---|---|---|---|---|---|
| 6 | 7 | 4 | | 8 | | | | |
| | | | | 5 | 1 | 7 | | |
| | 1 | 6 | | | | 4 | 5 | |
| | 4 | | | | | | 2 | |
| | 5 | 3 | | | | 9 | 6 | |
| | | 8 | 1 | 4 | | | | |
| | | | | 7 | | 5 | 4 | 3 |
| | | | | | 2 | | | |

**8**

| | | | | 2 | 7 | | | |
|---|---|---|---|---|---|---|---|---|
| 9 | | 1 | | 3 | | 8 | | |
| | 2 | | 1 | | | | | |
| | 9 | | 4 | | | 3 | 2 | |
| 6 | | 7 | | | | 4 | | 9 |
| | 4 | 2 | | | 9 | | 1 | |
| | | | | | 2 | | 8 | |
| | | 4 | | 1 | | 7 | | 3 |
| | | | 3 | 5 | | | | |

9

| | | | | | | | | |
|---|---|---|---|---|---|---|---|---|
| 6 | | 5 | | 9 | | 7 | | 2 |
| | | | 5 | | | 1 | | 4 |
| | | | 6 | | | | | |
| | 3 | | | | 5 | | 2 | 9 |
| 4 | | | | 7 | | | | 8 |
| 1 | 9 | | 2 | | | | 7 | |
| | | | | | 6 | | | |
| 5 | | 1 | | | 9 | | | |
| 9 | | 7 | | 1 | | 8 | | 6 |

10

| | | | | | | | | |
|---|---|---|---|---|---|---|---|---|
| 7 | | 8 | | 9 | 1 | | | |
| | 5 | 1 | | | | 6 | | |
| | 9 | 4 | | | | | | 1 |
| 5 | | | | 4 | 8 | | | |
| | 4 | | | 7 | | | 1 | |
| | | | 2 | 5 | | | | 6 |
| 1 | | | | | | 3 | 6 | |
| | | 7 | | | | 9 | 5 | |
| | | | 7 | 3 | | 1 | | 2 |

Puzzle 1:

| 7 |   |   |   |   | 5 | 4 | 8 |   |
|---|---|---|---|---|---|---|---|---|
|   |   |   | 9 | 3 |   | 2 | 5 |   |
|   | 2 |   |   |   |   | 9 |   |   |
|   |   |   |   |   | 2 |   |   | 8 |
|   | 1 | 6 |   |   |   | 3 | 4 |   |
| 8 |   |   | 3 |   |   |   |   |   |
|   |   | 2 |   |   |   |   | 7 |   |
|   | 6 | 7 |   | 8 | 9 |   |   |   |
|   | 9 | 5 | 4 |   |   |   |   | 6 |

Puzzle 2:

|   |   | 4 |   |   |   | 3 |   |   |
|---|---|---|---|---|---|---|---|---|
|   | 8 |   | 2 |   |   |   |   | 6 |
| 1 |   | 7 |   | 5 |   |   |   |   |
| 6 |   |   |   | 1 | 2 |   | 3 |   |
|   |   | 5 |   |   |   | 9 |   |   |
|   | 4 |   | 6 | 7 |   |   |   | 1 |
|   |   |   |   | 6 |   | 5 |   | 8 |
| 4 |   |   |   |   | 8 |   | 1 |   |
|   |   | 9 |   |   |   | 6 |   |   |

**Puzzle 1·3**

| 9 |   | 7 |   |   |   |   |   |   |
|---|---|---|---|---|---|---|---|---|
|   |   |   | 6 |   |   |   |   | 1 |
| 1 |   | 8 |   | 9 |   |   | 3 | 4 |
|   | 2 |   | 1 |   |   | 6 |   |   |
| 4 |   |   |   |   |   |   |   | 9 |
|   |   | 9 |   |   | 4 |   | 8 |   |
| 2 | 9 |   |   | 8 |   | 4 |   | 7 |
| 5 |   |   |   |   | 7 |   |   |   |
|   |   |   |   |   |   | 2 |   | 5 |

**Puzzle 1·4**

|   |   |   | 1 | 4 |   | 3 |   |   |
|---|---|---|---|---|---|---|---|---|
|   | 1 |   | 9 | 8 |   | 7 | 2 | 6 |
|   |   | 5 |   |   |   |   |   |   |
| 9 |   |   |   |   | 4 | 6 |   |   |
| 2 |   |   |   | 7 |   |   |   | 8 |
|   |   | 7 | 8 |   |   |   |   | 4 |
|   |   |   |   |   |   | 1 |   |   |
| 5 | 6 | 9 |   | 1 | 7 |   | 3 |   |
|   |   | 8 |   | 3 | 9 |   |   |   |

|   |   |   |   |   |   |   |   |   |
|---|---|---|---|---|---|---|---|---|
| 3 |   |   |   |   |   |   |   | 4 |
| 9 |   |   | 7 | 6 | 2 |   |   |   |
|   |   |   |   | 3 |   |   | 8 | 7 |
|   |   |   |   |   |   | 1 | 3 |   |
|   | 1 | 8 | 6 |   | 3 | 4 | 2 |   |
|   | 3 | 9 |   |   |   |   |   |   |
| 7 | 9 |   |   | 5 |   |   |   |   |
|   |   |   | 4 | 2 | 6 |   |   | 1 |
| 4 |   |   |   |   |   |   |   | 5 |

|   |   |   |   |   |   |   |   |   |
|---|---|---|---|---|---|---|---|---|
| 4 |   |   |   |   |   | 7 | 9 |   |
|   | 1 |   |   |   |   | 8 |   | 5 |
|   |   |   | 1 |   | 8 |   |   |   |
|   | 4 |   |   | 2 |   |   | 8 | 7 |
|   |   |   | 5 |   | 3 |   |   |   |
| 7 | 2 |   |   | 1 |   |   | 5 |   |
|   |   |   | 7 |   | 1 |   |   |   |
| 1 |   | 9 |   |   |   |   | 6 |   |
|   | 5 | 6 |   |   |   |   |   | 8 |

**17**

| | 1 | | | 6 | | | | 9 |
|---|---|---|---|---|---|---|---|---|
| | 2 | 4 | | 7 | | | | |
| | | | | | 5 | | 3 | 1 |
| | | | | | 6 | 1 | 2 | 3 |
| | | | | | | | | |
| 2 | 9 | 5 | 8 | | | | | |
| 6 | 5 | | 7 | | | | | |
| | | | | 1 | | 3 | 8 | |
| 8 | | | | 2 | | | 6 | |

**18**

| 1 | | | | | 7 | 9 | 3 | |
|---|---|---|---|---|---|---|---|---|
| | | | | | 8 | | | 1 |
| | | 6 | | 3 | | | | |
| | 2 | 3 | | | 6 | 1 | 4 | |
| 7 | | | | | | | | 2 |
| | 4 | 1 | 5 | | | 8 | 9 | |
| | | | | 8 | | 4 | | |
| 5 | | | 9 | | | | | |
| | 3 | 7 | 6 | | | | | 9 |

13

**19**

|   |   | 2 | 5 |   |   |   |   |   |
|---|---|---|---|---|---|---|---|---|
|   | 6 | 5 |   |   |   |   | 3 |   |
| 8 |   |   |   | 6 | 9 |   |   |   |
|   |   | 1 |   | 4 |   |   | 5 | 9 |
|   | 5 | 6 |   | 2 |   | 8 | 1 |   |
| 9 | 8 |   |   | 1 |   | 3 |   |   |
|   |   |   | 4 | 9 |   |   |   | 5 |
|   | 2 |   |   |   |   | 6 | 9 |   |
|   |   |   |   |   | 2 | 1 |   |   |

**20**

|   |   | 6 |   |   | 9 |   |   | 8 |
|---|---|---|---|---|---|---|---|---|
|   | 8 |   | 2 |   | 1 | 6 |   |   |
| 9 | 1 |   | 3 |   |   | 2 |   |   |
|   |   |   |   |   |   | 5 |   |   |
|   |   | 5 |   | 7 |   | 9 |   |   |
|   |   | 3 |   |   |   |   |   |   |
|   |   | 2 |   |   | 8 |   | 9 | 6 |
|   |   | 8 | 4 |   | 7 |   | 5 |   |
| 3 |   |   | 6 |   |   | 4 |   |   |

## 2-1

| | 6 | | 2 | 4 | | | | 8 |
|---|---|---|---|---|---|---|---|---|
| | 1 | | | 5 | | | | 9 |
| | | | | | | 5 | | |
| 3 | | 4 | | | 1 | | | |
| | | 7 | 4 | | 8 | 6 | | |
| | | | 7 | | | 9 | | 2 |
| | | 1 | | | | | | |
| 7 | | | | 9 | | | 8 | |
| 2 | | | | 1 | 6 | | 7 | |

## 2-2

| 7 | 5 | | 4 | | | 1 | | |
|---|---|---|---|---|---|---|---|---|
| | | | | | | | 8 | 6 |
| 6 | | 2 | | 5 | | | | |
| | 9 | 8 | | | 5 | | 4 | |
| | | 6 | 8 | | 3 | 2 | | |
| | 3 | | 1 | | | 6 | 5 | |
| | | | 3 | | 9 | | | 2 |
| 3 | 2 | | | | | | | |
| | | 9 | | | 8 | | 6 | 5 |

| | | | 3 | 1 | | | | |
|---|---|---|---|---|---|---|---|---|
| | | | 6 | | 2 | | | |
| 5 | | | 7 | | | 8 | | 1 |
| | 2 | | | | 7 | | 5 | |
| | 5 | 9 | | | | 6 | 8 | |
| | 6 | | 5 | | | | 7 | |
| 3 | | 1 | | | 6 | | | 4 |
| | | | 4 | | 8 | | | |
| | | | | 5 | 3 | | | |

Puzzle 2/4

| 6 | | | 4 | | | | | 9 |
|---|---|---|---|---|---|---|---|---|
| | | 5 | | | | 1 | 4 | 3 |
| | | | 7 | | | | | 6 |
| | 4 | 2 | 3 | 1 | | | | |
| | | | | | | | | |
| | | | | 9 | 4 | 5 | 7 | |
| 1 | | | | | 6 | | | |
| 2 | 9 | 7 | | | | 8 | | |
| 8 | | | | | 7 | | | 5 |

| | | | | | | | | |
|---|---|---|---|---|---|---|---|---|
| | | 6 | 3 | 9 | | | | |
| 5 | 9 | | | 7 | | 8 | | |
| | 2 | | | 5 | | | | |
| 4 | 7 | 9 | | | | | | 8 |
| | | 8 | | | | 2 | | |
| 1 | | | | | | 7 | 9 | 4 |
| | | | | 1 | | | 8 | |
| | | 5 | | 2 | | | 3 | 6 |
| | | | | 3 | 6 | 4 | | |

| | | | | | | | | |
|---|---|---|---|---|---|---|---|---|
| | | | | | 5 | | | 9 |
| 5 | | 7 | | | | | 8 | 6 |
| 9 | | | 1 | | | 4 | | |
| | | | | | 3 | | | 5 |
| | 2 | 6 | | | | 9 | 7 | |
| 1 | | | 9 | | | | | |
| | | 1 | | | 2 | | | 8 |
| 3 | 9 | | | | | 7 | | 4 |
| 6 | | | 5 | | | | | |

**2 / 7**

| 7 |   |   |   |   | 9 | 8 |   |   |
|---|---|---|---|---|---|---|---|---|
|   | 9 |   |   |   | 6 |   | 5 |   |
|   |   | 8 | 1 |   | 4 | 3 | 9 |   |
|   | 2 | 5 |   |   |   | 1 |   | 9 |
|   |   |   |   |   |   |   |   |   |
| 4 |   | 9 |   |   |   | 7 | 2 |   |
|   | 3 | 2 | 7 |   | 1 | 9 |   |   |
|   | 8 |   | 2 |   |   |   | 7 |   |
|   |   | 7 | 6 |   |   |   |   | 5 |

**2 / 8**

|   |   | 2 | 3 |   |   |   |   |   |
|---|---|---|---|---|---|---|---|---|
| 4 |   |   | 7 |   | 6 | 8 | 5 |   |
|   |   | 8 | 5 |   |   |   | 3 |   |
|   |   |   |   |   |   | 7 | 2 | 6 |
|   |   |   |   |   |   |   |   |   |
| 9 | 6 | 4 |   |   |   |   |   |   |
|   | 9 |   |   |   | 4 | 3 |   |   |
|   | 7 | 5 | 6 |   | 8 |   |   | 9 |
|   |   |   |   |   | 5 | 6 |   |   |

| | | 7 | | | | | | |
|---|---|---|---|---|---|---|---|---|
| | | 8 | 5 | | 2 | | 6 | 9 |
| | | 2 | | 7 | | | 5 | |
| 8 | | | 1 | | | | | 7 |
| | 3 | 6 | | | | 4 | 1 | |
| 5 | | | | | 3 | | | 6 |
| | 6 | | | 9 | | 5 | | |
| 9 | 8 | | 4 | | 7 | 2 | | |
| | | | | | | 6 | | |

| | | | 5 | | | | | |
|---|---|---|---|---|---|---|---|---|
| | | | 7 | | | | 9 | 4 |
| 5 | 3 | 8 | | 4 | | | | |
| | | 3 | 4 | 9 | | | | 6 |
| 6 | | | | | | | | 1 |
| 9 | | | | 2 | 3 | 7 | | |
| | | | | 1 | | 3 | 6 | 2 |
| 2 | 9 | | | | 7 | | | |
| | | | | | 6 | | | |

Puzzle 3/1:

| | 8 | | | | | 6 | 5 | 1 |
|---|---|---|---|---|---|---|---|---|
| | | 3 | 5 | | | | | 7 |
| 6 | | | | | 1 | | | |
| | 7 | | 1 | | | 4 | | |
| 2 | 1 | | | 4 | | | 3 | 6 |
| | | 6 | | | 9 | | 8 | |
| | | | 9 | | | | | 5 |
| 5 | | | | | 4 | 1 | | |
| | 6 | 4 | 7 | | | | 9 | |

Puzzle 3/2:

| | | | | | 8 | 3 | | 5 |
|---|---|---|---|---|---|---|---|---|
| 2 | | | | 3 | | | 7 | |
| | | | | | 6 | | | 2 |
| | 4 | | | | | 1 | | 6 |
| | | 6 | 5 | | 1 | 7 | | |
| 1 | | | 2 | | | | 8 | |
| 5 | | | 1 | | | | | |
| | 7 | | | 6 | | | | 8 |
| 8 | | | 1 | 4 | | | | |

| | | | 3 | | | | | |
|---|---|---|---|---|---|---|---|---|
| | 4 | 7 | | 5 | | 3 | 2 | |
| 2 | | | | 7 | | 6 | | 5 |
| | 5 | 8 | | | | | 4 | |
| | | 2 | | | | 1 | | |
| | 6 | | | | | 2 | 9 | |
| 9 | | 1 | | 6 | | | | 2 |
| | 7 | 5 | | 2 | | 9 | 6 | |
| | | | | | 9 | | | |

| | | | | 5 | 6 | | | 7 |
|---|---|---|---|---|---|---|---|---|
| 5 | 2 | | | | 1 | 4 | 8 | |
| | 9 | | | | | 6 | | 2 |
| | | 4 | 7 | | | | | |
| | | | | 9 | | | | |
| | | | | | 4 | 5 | | |
| 9 | | 2 | | | | | 1 | |
| | 8 | 1 | 5 | | | | 6 | 9 |
| 7 | | | 1 | 4 | | | | |

Puzzle 3/5:

| | 1 | | | | 7 | 2 | | |
|---|---|---|---|---|---|---|---|---|
| | | | | 8 | | | | 3 |
| 4 | 2 | 7 | 9 | | | 8 | | |
| | | | 6 | | | | 2 | |
| 2 | | 6 | | | | 3 | | 5 |
| | 4 | | | | 5 | | | |
| | | 2 | | | 1 | 4 | 3 | 9 |
| 7 | | | | 6 | | | | |
| | | 9 | 3 | | | | 7 | |

Puzzle 3/6:

| | | | 5 | 8 | | | 4 | |
|---|---|---|---|---|---|---|---|---|
| 2 | | | | | | | 3 | |
| | | | | 9 | | | | 8 |
| 4 | 3 | | | | 6 | 1 | | |
| | | 7 | 4 | | 8 | 5 | | |
| | | 5 | 9 | | | | 6 | 4 |
| 5 | | | | 6 | | | | |
| | 8 | | | | | | | 6 |
| | 1 | | | 7 | 2 | | | |

## 3/7

| | | 3 | | | | | 7 | |
|---|---|---|---|---|---|---|---|---|
| 4 | | | | | 5 | 3 | | |
| | | | 8 | | 2 | | 4 | |
| | | 5 | 3 | 1 | | | 2 | 9 |
| | | | | | | | | |
| 9 | 8 | | | 4 | 6 | 1 | | |
| | 5 | | 9 | | 3 | | | |
| | | 6 | 2 | | | | | 3 |
| | 1 | | | | | 8 | | |

## 3/8

| | | 8 | | 5 | 1 | | | 4 |
|---|---|---|---|---|---|---|---|---|
| 1 | | | | 9 | | | | |
| | 9 | 3 | | | | | | 1 |
| | 7 | | 4 | 3 | | | | |
| | | 6 | | 2 | | 3 | | |
| | | | | 1 | 5 | | 6 | |
| 7 | | | | | | 4 | 5 | |
| | | | | 6 | | | | 2 |
| 5 | | | 9 | 4 | | 1 | | |

**39**

| | | | | | | | | |
|---|---|---|---|---|---|---|---|---|
| | | | | | | | | |
| | 8 | | 5 | | | 6 | | |
| | 1 | 2 | | 3 | | 5 | | |
| | 6 | | | | 8 | 1 | 9 | |
| | | 8 | 1 | | 7 | 3 | | |
| | 3 | 5 | 6 | | | | 4 | |
| | | 7 | | 9 | | 4 | 6 | |
| | | | 8 | | 5 | | 7 | |
| | | | | | | | | |

**40**

| | | | | | | | | |
|---|---|---|---|---|---|---|---|---|
| | 4 | | | 9 | 1 | | | |
| | 9 | | 8 | | | 4 | | 5 |
| | | | | | 6 | 1 | 7 | |
| | 6 | | | 4 | | | | |
| | 7 | 4 | | | | 6 | 9 | |
| | | | | 8 | | | 3 | |
| | 3 | 7 | 1 | | | | | |
| 1 | | 9 | | | 5 | | 4 | |
| | | | 9 | 6 | | | 1 | |

## 4-1

| | | | | | | | | |
|---|---|---|---|---|---|---|---|---|
| 3 |   | 1 | 6 | 8 |   |   | 5 |   |
| 5 |   |   |   |   | 3 |   |   |   |
|   |   |   |   |   |   |   | 2 |   |
| 1 |   |   |   |   | 8 | 2 |   |   |
|   | 3 |   | 7 |   | 5 |   | 8 |   |
|   |   | 5 | 4 |   |   |   |   | 7 |
|   | 5 |   |   |   |   |   |   |   |
|   |   |   | 2 |   |   |   |   | 4 |
|   | 7 |   |   | 1 | 9 | 5 |   | 6 |

## 4-2

| | | | | | | | | |
|---|---|---|---|---|---|---|---|---|
|   |   | 8 |   |   | 2 |   |   |   |
|   | 7 |   |   |   |   |   | 8 |   |
|   | 2 | 4 |   | 1 | 5 | 3 |   |   |
|   |   | 9 | 7 |   |   |   | 5 |   |
|   | 1 |   | 5 | 3 | 4 |   | 6 |   |
|   | 4 |   |   |   | 9 | 8 |   |   |
|   |   | 6 | 4 | 9 |   |   | 7 | 3 |
|   | 3 |   |   |   |   |   | 9 |   |
|   |   |   | 1 |   |   | 5 |   |   |

**4 / 3**

| 6 |   | 1 |   |   |   |   |   |   |
|---|---|---|---|---|---|---|---|---|
|   |   | 3 |   |   | 4 |   | 8 | 7 |
|   |   |   | 1 | 7 |   |   | 3 |   |
| 2 |   |   |   |   | 7 |   | 5 |   |
|   |   | 7 |   |   |   | 8 |   |   |
|   | 5 |   | 4 |   |   |   |   | 3 |
|   | 2 |   |   | 4 | 1 |   |   |   |
| 7 | 4 |   | 5 |   |   | 9 |   |   |
|   |   |   |   |   |   | 3 |   | 4 |

**4 / 4**

| 9 | 4 |   |   |   | 8 |   |   |   |
|---|---|---|---|---|---|---|---|---|
|   |   | 5 |   |   |   |   |   |   |
| 3 |   |   |   | 5 |   | 1 | 8 | 9 |
|   | 5 |   |   | 8 | 2 |   | 9 |   |
|   |   | 9 |   |   |   | 3 |   |   |
|   | 1 |   | 3 | 7 |   |   | 4 |   |
| 6 | 3 | 7 |   | 9 |   |   |   | 2 |
|   |   |   |   |   |   | 5 |   |   |
|   |   |   | 8 |   |   |   | 6 | 4 |

**4/5**

| | | 1 | 7 | 8 | | 5 | | |
|---|---|---|---|---|---|---|---|---|
| | 8 | 3 | 1 | | 6 | | | 7 |
| | 7 | 6 | | | | | | |
| | | | | | 8 | | 1 | |
| 4 | | 9 | | | | 6 | | 2 |
| | 1 | | 4 | | | | | |
| | | | | | | 4 | 9 | |
| 7 | | | 6 | | 4 | 8 | 2 | |
| | | 4 | | 1 | 5 | 3 | | |

**4/6**

| | | | 3 | | | 9 | 6 | 8 |
|---|---|---|---|---|---|---|---|---|
| | | | 2 | 7 | | 3 | | 1 |
| | | | | | | | 2 | |
| 6 | | | | | 8 | 7 | | 4 |
| | 4 | | | 6 | | | 1 | |
| 1 | | 5 | 4 | | | | | 9 |
| | 5 | | | | | | | |
| 7 | | 1 | | 8 | 9 | | | |
| 3 | 9 | 8 | | | 4 | | | |

| | | 2 | | 3 | | 4 | | |
|---|---|---|---|---|---|---|---|---|
| | 8 | | 4 | | | 5 | | |
| 4 | | | 8 | | | 9 | | 6 |
| | | 7 | | | 5 | | | |
| | 6 | | 1 | | 3 | | 5 | |
| | | | 6 | | | 7 | | |
| 5 | | 9 | | | 8 | | | 7 |
| | | 3 | | | 1 | | 4 | |
| | | 6 | | 4 | | 8 | | |

| | | 8 | 4 | | 7 | | 6 | |
|---|---|---|---|---|---|---|---|---|
| | | 5 | | 8 | | | 2 | |
| 6 | | | 5 | | | | 3 | |
| | | | | | 3 | | 1 | 4 |
| 3 | | | | | | | | 7 |
| 4 | 5 | | 2 | | | | | |
| | 4 | | | | 5 | | | 6 |
| | 2 | | | 3 | | 1 | | |
| | 8 | | 6 | | | 1 | 3 | |

## 49

| | | 9 | | | | | | |
|---|---|---|---|---|---|---|---|---|
| | 3 | 8 | 5 | | 1 | | | |
| | | 2 | 3 | 8 | | | | 9 |
| 9 | | 7 | | | | 6 | 5 | |
| | | | | 2 | | | | |
| | 8 | 5 | | | | 9 | | 3 |
| 6 | | | | 5 | 3 | 7 | | |
| | | | 1 | | 6 | 2 | 9 | |
| | | | | | | 5 | | |

## 50

| | | | 2 | | | | | |
|---|---|---|---|---|---|---|---|---|
| 9 | 8 | | 6 | | | | | 3 |
| | 1 | | | 8 | 3 | 6 | 7 | |
| 5 | | | | 6 | | | | |
| | | 3 | | 7 | | 4 | | |
| | | | | 4 | | | | 8 |
| | 4 | 9 | 1 | 5 | | | 2 | |
| 2 | | | | | 6 | | 1 | 5 |
| | | | | 9 | | | | |

## 5/1

| 4 | 8 |   |   |   | 6 |   |   |   |
|---|---|---|---|---|---|---|---|---|
|   |   | 9 |   |   | 4 |   |   |   |
|   |   | 6 |   |   | 8 |   | 5 | 2 |
|   | 6 |   |   | 5 |   |   |   | 9 |
| 2 |   |   | 8 |   | 1 |   |   | 7 |
| 1 |   |   |   | 4 |   |   | 2 |   |
| 6 | 3 |   | 7 |   |   | 5 |   |   |
|   |   |   | 4 |   |   | 2 |   |   |
|   |   |   | 2 |   |   |   | 1 | 3 |

## 5/2

| 6 | 5 | 2 | 1 |   |   |   |   |   |
|---|---|---|---|---|---|---|---|---|
|   |   | 1 |   |   | 7 |   |   | 2 |
|   |   |   | 2 |   |   |   | 5 | 3 |
| 1 |   |   | 8 | 4 |   |   | 3 |   |
| 3 |   |   |   |   |   |   |   | 4 |
|   | 4 |   |   | 1 | 5 |   |   | 9 |
| 5 | 6 |   |   | 7 |   |   |   |   |
| 4 |   |   | 9 |   |   | 6 |   |   |
|   |   |   |   |   | 6 | 9 | 2 | 5 |

**5 3**

| 4 |   |   |   | 8 |   | 5 |   |   |
|---|---|---|---|---|---|---|---|---|
|   | 8 | 3 | 5 |   |   |   | 1 | 9 |
|   |   |   |   |   | 2 |   | 7 |   |
| 8 |   |   | 2 |   |   | 7 |   |   |
|   |   |   |   | 7 |   |   |   |   |
|   |   | 7 |   |   | 9 |   |   | 2 |
|   | 1 |   | 7 |   |   |   |   |   |
| 2 | 6 |   |   |   | 5 | 3 | 9 |   |
|   |   | 5 |   | 9 |   |   |   | 6 |

**5 4**

| 0 |   | 8 | 2 | 9 |   |   |   |   |
|---|---|---|---|---|---|---|---|---|
| 6 |   |   |   |   |   | 1 | 2 |   |
| 4 |   |   |   |   | 6 | 3 |   |   |
|   | 1 |   |   | 8 | 3 |   | 4 |   |
|   |   |   |   |   |   |   |   |   |
|   | 4 |   | 1 | 2 |   |   | 7 |   |
|   |   | 4 | 8 |   |   |   |   | 9 |
|   | 7 | 3 |   |   |   |   |   | 2 |
|   |   |   | 4 | 9 | 5 |   |   |   |

## Puzzle 55

| 1 |   |   |   | 2 | 3 |   |   |   |
|---|---|---|---|---|---|---|---|---|
|   | 8 |   |   |   |   |   | 7 |   |
| 7 |   |   | 6 |   |   | 3 |   | 4 |
|   |   | 1 | 8 | 3 |   |   |   |   |
| 8 |   |   |   | 9 |   |   |   | 3 |
|   |   |   |   | 6 | 2 | 5 |   |   |
| 6 |   | 2 |   |   | 4 |   |   | 1 |
|   | 4 |   |   |   |   |   | 5 |   |
|   |   |   | 3 | 8 |   |   |   | 2 |

## Puzzle 56

|   | 7 |   |   |   |   | 1 | 2 | 6 |
|---|---|---|---|---|---|---|---|---|
| 8 |   |   |   |   |   |   |   |   |
| 1 |   |   |   | 4 | 7 | 9 |   | 3 |
|   | 5 |   |   |   | 4 |   |   |   |
| 9 |   | 8 |   |   |   | 3 |   | 5 |
|   |   |   | 1 |   |   |   | 6 |   |
| 4 |   | 9 | 7 | 3 |   |   |   | 2 |
|   |   |   |   |   |   |   |   | 4 |
| 7 | 2 | 6 |   |   |   |   | 3 |   |

Puzzle 5/7:

| | 3 | | | 9 | | 1 | | |
|---|---|---|---|---|---|---|---|---|
| | 4 | | | | | | 9 | |
| 6 | | | | 3 | | | 8 | |
| | 2 | 3 | 9 | | | | 1 | |
| 9 | | | | | | | | 7 |
| | 8 | | | | 7 | 3 | 6 | |
| | 7 | | | 4 | | | | 6 |
| | 9 | | | | | | 2 | |
| | | 8 | | 5 | | | 4 | |

Puzzle 5/8:

| | 8 | | | | | | | |
|---|---|---|---|---|---|---|---|---|
| | | 6 | | 3 | 9 | | | 5 |
| | | | | 2 | | | | 7 |
| | | 7 | | | | | 6 | 4 |
| 2 | | | 4 | | 3 | | | 1 |
| 8 | 1 | | | | | 3 | | |
| 4 | | | | 5 | | | | |
| 7 | | | 1 | 9 | | 6 | | |
| | | | | | | | 7 | |

**59**

| 8 |   | 4 |   | 1 |   |   |   | 5 |
|---|---|---|---|---|---|---|---|---|
|   |   |   | 5 |   |   | 3 |   |   |
| 6 |   |   |   |   |   |   |   |   |
| 1 |   |   |   |   | 7 | 8 | 5 |   |
| 5 |   |   | 1 |   | 2 |   |   | 4 |
|   | 6 | 8 | 4 |   |   |   |   | 2 |
|   |   |   |   |   |   |   |   | 3 |
|   |   | 7 |   |   | 1 |   |   |   |
| 4 |   |   |   | 9 |   | 6 |   | 1 |

**60**

|   |   | 9 |   |   |   | 6 |   |   |
|---|---|---|---|---|---|---|---|---|
|   | 3 |   | 9 |   | 7 | 2 |   |   |
| 1 | 8 |   |   |   |   |   | 3 |   |
|   |   | 6 |   |   | 9 |   |   | 5 |
|   |   |   | 7 | 4 | 3 |   |   |   |
| 2 |   |   | 5 |   |   | 7 |   |   |
|   | 9 |   |   |   |   |   | 5 | 1 |
|   |   | 3 | 4 |   | 5 |   | 6 |   |
|   |   | 2 |   |   |   | 3 |   |   |

**6-1**

| 8 |   | 7 |   | 9 |   | 4 |   | 1 |
|---|---|---|---|---|---|---|---|---|
| 1 |   |   |   |   | 7 |   | 3 | 8 |
|   |   |   |   |   |   |   |   | 9 |
|   | 6 |   | 1 |   |   | 9 |   |   |
|   |   |   |   | 4 |   |   |   |   |
|   |   | 1 |   |   | 6 |   | 7 |   |
| 5 |   |   |   |   |   |   |   |   |
| 9 | 7 |   | 3 |   |   |   |   | 4 |
| 4 |   | 8 |   | 5 |   | 6 |   | 3 |

**6-2**

| 3 |   |   | 9 |   |   | 8 |   | 4 |
|---|---|---|---|---|---|---|---|---|
|   |   |   |   |   |   | 1 |   |   |
| 4 |   | 8 |   |   | 3 |   |   |   |
| 1 | 5 |   |   | 6 |   |   |   |   |
| 8 |   |   |   | 2 |   |   |   | 5 |
|   |   |   |   | 8 |   |   | 4 | 7 |
|   |   |   | 1 |   |   | 4 |   | 2 |
|   |   | 2 |   |   |   |   |   |   |
| 9 |   | 5 |   |   | 7 |   |   | 8 |

| 5 |   |   | 2 |   |   |   |   | 4 |
|---|---|---|---|---|---|---|---|---|
|   |   | 8 |   |   |   | 3 |   | 2 |
|   |   |   |   |   | 6 |   | 8 |   |
| 7 |   |   | 6 |   | 8 |   |   |   |
|   | 4 | 9 |   |   |   | 5 | 3 |   |
|   |   |   | 3 |   | 5 |   |   | 6 |
|   | 7 |   | 9 |   |   |   |   |   |
| 1 |   | 2 |   |   |   | 7 |   |   |
| 8 |   |   |   |   | 2 |   |   | 3 |

| 3 |   | 1 | 9 | 7 |   |   | 4 |   |
|---|---|---|---|---|---|---|---|---|
|   |   |   |   |   |   | 9 |   |   |
|   |   | 6 |   |   | 3 |   | 2 |   |
|   | 9 | 5 |   |   | 2 |   | 1 |   |
|   |   |   |   | 9 |   |   |   |   |
|   | 6 |   | 1 |   |   | 4 | 5 |   |
|   | 1 |   | 3 |   |   | 5 |   |   |
|   |   | 4 |   |   |   |   |   |   |
|   | 5 |   |   | 2 | 9 | 8 |   | 1 |

| | | | | | | 2 | | |
|---|---|---|---|---|---|---|---|---|
| | | | 9 | 3 | | 1 | 4 | |
| | | | 7 | 5 | | | | 6 |
| | 9 | 5 | | | 8 | | 2 | |
| 8 | 2 | 7 | 6 | | 5 | 4 | | 1 |
| | 6 | | 2 | | | 9 | | |
| 9 | | | | 2 | 7 | | | |
| | 1 | 3 | | 6 | 9 | | | |
| | | 4 | | | | | | |

| | | 3 | | | | | 7 | |
|---|---|---|---|---|---|---|---|---|
| | | 9 | 2 | | 6 | | | |
| | | 7 | | | | | | 8 |
| | | | 8 | | | 2 | 3 | |
| 3 | | 1 | | 9 | | 8 | | 5 |
| | 6 | 5 | | | 2 | | | |
| 9 | | | | | | 7 | | |
| | | | 3 | | 8 | 9 | | |
| | 1 | | | | | 5 | | |

**6/7**

| | | 7 | | | 5 | | | |
|---|---|---|---|---|---|---|---|---|
| | | | 2 | | | 1 | 7 | |
| 8 | | | | 1 | 4 | 3 | | |
| 5 | | 9 | | | | | 1 | |
| | 6 | | | 4 | | | 5 | |
| | 7 | | | | | 2 | | 6 |
| | | 4 | 1 | 3 | | | | 9 |
| | 8 | 1 | | | 7 | | | |
| | | | 9 | | | 5 | | |

**6/8**

| | | | | 2 | 5 | 4 | | |
|---|---|---|---|---|---|---|---|---|
| | 6 | 1 | | | | 9 | | 2 |
| | | | | | 6 | | 8 | |
| | | 8 | 5 | 6 | | | 9 | 4 |
| | | | | | | | | |
| 4 | 9 | | | 8 | 7 | 5 | | |
| | 5 | | 4 | | | | | |
| 8 | | 3 | | | | 7 | 4 | |
| | | 4 | 9 | 7 | | | | |

**69**

| | | | 5 | | | | 8 | |
|---|---|---|---|---|---|---|---|---|
| | | | 1 | | 3 | 4 | 6 | |
| 4 | | | | 2 | | 3 | | 1 |
| 2 | | | | | | | 9 | |
| | 9 | | | 8 | | | 5 | |
| | 7 | | | | | | | 8 |
| 3 | | 9 | | 4 | | | | 7 |
| | 2 | 6 | 9 | | 7 | | | |
| | 4 | | | | 5 | | | |

**70**

| 1 | | | | | | 3 | | 4 |
|---|---|---|---|---|---|---|---|---|
| | | 6 | | | 4 | 1 | | |
| | 7 | | 6 | | | | | 5 |
| | | | | | 1 | | 4 | |
| | | 9 | | 2 | | 7 | | |
| | 5 | | 9 | | | | | |
| 6 | | | | | 8 | | 1 | |
| | | 1 | 2 | | | 4 | | |
| 3 | | 7 | | | | | | 2 |

| 5 | 3 |   |   |   | 2 |   |   |   |
|---|---|---|---|---|---|---|---|---|
|   |   | 1 |   |   |   | 9 |   |   |
|   |   |   | 6 | 9 |   | 2 |   | 5 |
|   |   |   | 4 | 8 |   |   | 1 |   |
|   |   | 5 |   |   |   | 8 |   |   |
|   | 2 |   |   | 7 | 6 |   |   |   |
| 1 |   | 4 |   | 6 | 9 |   |   |   |
|   |   | 3 |   |   |   | 5 |   |   |
|   |   |   | 5 |   |   |   | 4 | 1 |

| 8 | 5 |   |   |   |   |   | 9 | 6 |
|---|---|---|---|---|---|---|---|---|
| 1 |   |   | 5 |   |   |   | 8 |   |
|   |   |   |   |   | 2 |   |   |   |
|   |   |   | 6 | 3 |   | 8 |   | 1 |
|   | 1 |   |   |   |   |   | 7 |   |
| 7 |   | 5 |   | 1 | 9 |   |   |   |
|   |   |   | 9 |   |   |   |   |   |
|   | 4 |   |   |   | 1 |   |   | 5 |
| 5 | 6 |   |   |   |   |   | 4 | 2 |

| | | | 1 | | | 8 | | 5 |
|---|---|---|---|---|---|---|---|---|
| | | 1 | 8 | 9 | | | | |
| 3 | | 5 | | 6 | 2 | | | |
| 9 | | | 5 | | | | | 7 |
| 8 | 5 | | | | | | 2 | 4 |
| 2 | | | | | 6 | | | 9 |
| | | | 2 | 5 | | 9 | | 8 |
| | | | | 7 | 9 | 3 | | |
| 1 | | 9 | | | 8 | | | |

| | 7 | | | | | 9 | | 1 |
|---|---|---|---|---|---|---|---|---|
| | | 3 | | | | 7 | 2 | |
| | | 5 | 7 | | 6 | | | |
| 6 | | | | | 7 | | | |
| | | 8 | 6 | | 5 | 2 | | |
| | | | 3 | | | | | 8 |
| | | | 4 | | 2 | 8 | | |
| | 6 | 7 | | | | 4 | | |
| 1 | | 4 | | | | | 9 | |

|   | 2 | 8 |   |   |   |   | 6 | 4 |
|---|---|---|---|---|---|---|---|---|
| 9 | 6 |   |   | 3 |   |   |   |   |
|   |   | 1 | 2 |   |   |   |   |   |
|   | 5 | 6 | 8 |   |   |   |   | 9 |
|   |   | 2 |   | 9 |   | 8 |   |   |
| 8 |   |   |   |   | 3 | 2 | 5 |   |
|   |   |   |   |   | 5 | 9 |   |   |
|   |   |   |   | 1 |   |   | 2 | 5 |
| 5 | 7 |   |   |   |   | 6 | 4 |   |

7/6

|   |   | 6 |   |   |   |   | 1 |   |
|---|---|---|---|---|---|---|---|---|
| 8 | 2 |   |   | 6 |   |   |   |   |
|   |   | 5 | 9 | 2 |   | 8 |   |   |
|   |   | 1 | 6 |   |   | 7 | 2 |   |
|   |   |   |   | 5 |   |   |   |   |
|   | 4 | 8 |   |   | 3 | 1 |   |   |
|   |   | 4 |   | 1 | 8 | 6 |   |   |
|   |   |   |   | 4 |   |   | 3 | 8 |
|   | 8 |   |   |   |   | 9 |   |   |

Puzzle 77:

|   |   |   |   |   |   |   | 8 |   |
|---|---|---|---|---|---|---|---|---|
| 2 | 8 |   | 9 |   |   | 1 |   |   |
| 7 |   |   |   | 2 |   |   |   |   |
| 5 |   |   |   |   | 2 |   | 3 |   |
| 8 |   | 4 | 5 |   | 6 | 2 |   | 7 |
|   | 1 |   | 4 |   |   |   |   | 8 |
|   |   |   |   | 9 |   |   |   | 5 |
|   |   | 6 |   |   | 7 |   | 4 | 3 |
|   | 5 |   |   |   |   |   |   |   |

Puzzle 78:

| 1 | 2 |   |   | 9 |   |   |   | 8 |
|---|---|---|---|---|---|---|---|---|
|   |   |   |   |   |   |   |   | 1 |
| 3 |   |   | 5 |   |   |   | 9 |   |
|   |   |   | 2 | 8 |   |   |   |   |
|   |   | 6 |   |   |   | 5 |   |   |
|   |   |   |   | 4 | 3 |   |   |   |
|   | 1 |   |   |   | 9 |   |   | 7 |
| 6 |   |   |   |   |   |   |   |   |
| 9 |   |   |   | 7 |   |   | 4 | 2 |

| | | | | 3 | 7 | | | |
|---|---|---|---|---|---|---|---|---|
| 6 | 4 | | | | | | | 7 |
| 5 | | 3 | | | | | | |
| | 8 | | | 7 | 4 | | | 9 |
| | 6 | | 1 | 2 | 9 | | 8 | |
| 1 | | | 3 | 6 | | | 5 | |
| | | | | | | 6 | | 2 |
| 9 | | | | | | | 3 | 8 |
| | | | 4 | 8 | | | | |

| | 8 | | | | | 1 | | |
|---|---|---|---|---|---|---|---|---|
| | | | | | 2 | | 9 | |
| | | 6 | | | 9 | | | 8 |
| 8 | | 1 | | | 3 | | | |
| | 9 | | | | | | 7 | |
| | | | 1 | | | 6 | | 4 |
| 9 | | | 4 | | | 7 | | |
| | 2 | | 6 | | | | | |
| | | 8 | | | | | 3 | |

| 7 |   | 9 |   |   | 5 | 8 |   | 4 |
|---|---|---|---|---|---|---|---|---|
| 2 |   |   | 6 |   |   |   | 9 |   |
|   |   | 5 |   |   |   |   |   |   |
| 9 |   | 3 |   |   |   |   | 5 |   |
| 5 |   |   | 1 |   | 9 |   |   | 7 |
|   | 2 |   |   |   |   | 9 |   | 8 |
|   |   |   |   |   |   | 2 |   |   |
|   | 1 |   |   |   | 7 |   |   | 3 |
| 8 |   | 2 | 3 |   |   | 6 |   | 9 |

| |   | 9 | 5 | 4 |   |   | 7 |   |
|---|---|---|---|---|---|---|---|---|
|   |   |   |   |   |   |   |   | 5 |
|   |   |   | 6 | 3 |   | 1 |   | 9 |
|   | 6 |   |   | 5 |   |   | 1 |   |
| 8 | 4 |   | 9 |   | 7 |   | 5 | 3 |
|   | 7 |   |   | 1 |   |   | 4 |   |
| 7 |   | 6 |   | 8 | 3 |   |   |   |
| 3 |   |   |   |   |   |   |   |   |
|   | 9 |   |   | 7 | 5 | 3 |   |   |

| 8 |   |   |   | 3 |   |   |   |   |
|---|---|---|---|---|---|---|---|---|
|   |   | 3 | 7 |   | 2 |   |   |   |
| 2 |   |   | 6 |   |   | 8 |   | 7 |
|   |   | 1 |   |   | 8 | 6 |   |   |
|   | 3 |   |   | 6 |   |   | 5 |   |
|   |   | 5 | 2 |   |   | 9 |   |   |
| 5 |   | 7 |   |   | 3 |   |   | 6 |
|   |   |   | 4 |   | 5 | 3 |   |   |
|   |   |   |   | 7 |   |   |   | 4 |

|   | 9 |   | 5 |   |   |   |   |   |
|---|---|---|---|---|---|---|---|---|
|   | 2 |   |   | 7 |   | 3 |   |   |
|   |   | 4 |   |   |   | 9 |   |   |
|   |   | 8 | 3 |   |   |   | 1 | 6 |
|   |   |   | 1 |   | 7 |   |   |   |
| 1 | 3 |   |   |   | 8 | 7 |   |   |
|   |   | 6 |   |   |   | 2 |   |   |
|   |   | 1 |   | 6 |   |   | 5 |   |
|   |   |   |   |   | 2 |   | 3 |   |

| | | 8 | 6 | | 7 | | 9 | 3 |
|---|---|---|---|---|---|---|---|---|
| | | | | 1 | | | 7 | |
| | | | | 8 | | | 6 | |
| | | | | 6 | 2 | 4 | | |
| | 6 | | | | | | 3 | |
| | 8 | 4 | 2 | | | | | |
| | 7 | | 4 | | | | | |
| | 9 | | 5 | | | | | |
| 8 | 1 | | 9 | | 3 | 5 | | |

| 9 | | 3 | | 4 | | | | 1 |
|---|---|---|---|---|---|---|---|---|
| | | | | | | | 6 | |
| | | | | | | 2 | 9 | 3 |
| | 3 | | | 6 | 4 | | 7 | |
| 1 | | | 8 | | 5 | | | 2 |
| | 4 | | 3 | 9 | | | 1 | |
| 4 | 7 | 8 | | | | | | |
| | 6 | | | | | | | |
| 2 | | | | 5 | | 4 | | 6 |

8 | 7

|   | 8 | 1 |   |   | 4 |   |   |   |
|---|---|---|---|---|---|---|---|---|
| 4 | 6 |   | 8 |   |   | 1 |   |   |
| 2 |   |   |   | 1 |   | 4 | 6 |   |
|   |   |   |   |   | 7 |   |   |   |
|   | 5 |   |   | 2 |   |   | 3 |   |
|   |   |   | 5 |   |   |   |   |   |
|   | 1 | 2 |   | 5 |   |   |   | 3 |
|   |   | 3 |   |   | 1 |   | 2 | 6 |
|   |   |   | 7 |   |   | 5 | 1 |   |

8 | 8

| 5 |   | 9 |   |   | 7 |   |   | 1 |
|---|---|---|---|---|---|---|---|---|
| 4 | 7 |   | 6 |   |   |   |   |   |
|   | 6 |   |   |   |   |   |   |   |
|   |   | 6 | 9 |   | 4 | 8 |   | 3 |
|   |   |   |   | 7 |   |   |   |   |
| 8 |   | 5 | 2 |   | 1 | 6 |   |   |
|   |   |   |   |   |   |   | 1 |   |
|   |   |   |   |   | 9 |   | 7 | 6 |
| 6 |   |   | 7 |   |   | 3 |   | 5 |

| | | | | 1 | | | 9 | 5 |
|---|---|---|---|---|---|---|---|---|
| | | | 3 | | | | | 7 |
| 7 | | | | 8 | | | 4 | |
| | | | 5 | 7 | | 1 | | |
| | 7 | 5 | | | | 6 | 3 | |
| | | 1 | | 4 | 8 | | | |
| | 4 | | | 2 | | | | 8 |
| 5 | | | | | 9 | | | |
| 9 | 2 | | | 5 | | | | |

| | 7 | | 6 | | | 1 | 8 | 5 |
|---|---|---|---|---|---|---|---|---|
| | | | | 7 | | | | |
| | | 1 | 2 | | | | | |
| 8 | 2 | | 3 | | | | 4 | |
| | 1 | | | | | | 3 | |
| | 3 | | | | 5 | | 7 | 8 |
| | | | | | 4 | 8 | | |
| | | | | 3 | | | | |
| 2 | 5 | 3 | | | 7 | | 6 | |

**Puzzle 9/1**

| 9 |   |   | 1 | 2 |   | 3 |   |   |
|---|---|---|---|---|---|---|---|---|
|   | 7 |   |   | 6 |   |   |   |   |
|   | 2 |   | 8 | 7 | 5 |   |   |   |
| 3 |   |   |   |   |   |   | 1 | 5 |
|   |   |   |   |   |   |   |   |   |
| 4 | 6 |   |   |   |   |   |   | 8 |
|   |   |   | 7 | 4 | 8 |   | 5 |   |
|   |   |   |   | 1 |   |   | 6 |   |
|   |   | 7 |   | 3 | 2 |   |   | 4 |

**Puzzle 9/2**

| 4 | 2 | 1 |   |   |   |   | 7 |   |
|---|---|---|---|---|---|---|---|---|
|   |   |   |   | 7 |   |   |   |   |
|   |   | 5 | 1 |   |   |   |   |   |
| 5 | 4 |   |   |   | 2 |   |   | 9 |
| 8 |   |   | 5 |   | 9 |   |   | 4 |
| 2 |   |   | 4 |   |   |   | 6 | 7 |
|   |   |   |   |   | 8 | 7 |   |   |
|   |   |   |   | 3 |   |   |   |   |
|   | 6 |   |   |   |   | 8 | 4 | 3 |

| 8 | 2 |   |   |   |   |   |   | 7 |
|---|---|---|---|---|---|---|---|---|
|   | 3 |   | 2 |   | 6 |   |   | 8 |
|   |   |   |   | 1 |   |   | 5 |   |
| 5 | 7 | 9 | 6 |   |   |   |   | 1 |
|   |   |   |   |   |   |   |   |   |
| 6 |   |   |   |   | 3 | 5 | 8 | 4 |
|   | 5 |   |   | 4 |   |   |   |   |
| 9 |   |   | 5 |   | 1 |   | 2 |   |
| 3 |   |   |   |   |   |   | 1 | 5 |

|   |   | 5 |   |   | 3 |   |   | 2 |
|---|---|---|---|---|---|---|---|---|
| 4 | 2 | 7 |   |   | 9 |   |   |   |
|   | 3 |   |   |   |   |   | 1 |   |
| 5 |   |   |   |   | 1 | 3 | 2 |   |
|   |   |   | 7 |   | 8 |   |   |   |
|   | 4 | 8 | 3 |   |   |   |   | 5 |
|   | 8 |   |   |   |   |   | 5 |   |
|   |   |   | 8 |   |   | 2 | 4 | 3 |
| 2 |   |   | 5 |   |   | 1 |   |   |

| | | | | 4 | | 1 | 9 | |
|---|---|---|---|---|---|---|---|---|
| | | | | | | 3 | | |
| | | | 1 | | 3 | | 7 | |
| 7 | | | | 1 | | | 3 | 2 |
| 1 | | 2 | | 3 | | 4 | | 5 |
| 5 | 8 | | | 6 | | | | 7 |
| | 1 | | 6 | | 2 | | | |
| | | 7 | | | | | | |
| | 6 | 9 | | 7 | | | | |

| | 9 | 5 | | | | | | 8 |
|---|---|---|---|---|---|---|---|---|
| | | | | | | | | |
| 8 | | | 4 | 5 | 7 | | | 3 |
| 1 | | 2 | | 3 | | 4 | | 5 |
| | 4 | | | 6 | | | 8 | |
| 5 | | 8 | | 2 | | 1 | | 6 |
| 3 | | | 1 | 9 | 8 | | | 4 |
| | | | | | | | | |
| 9 | | | | | | 5 | 3 | |

| 4 | 9 | 3 | 8 | 6 | 5 | 2 | 7 | 1 |
|---|---|---|---|---|---|---|---|---|
| 5 | 7 | 6 | 9 | 1 | 2 | 3 | 8 | 4 |
| 8 | 2 | 1 | 7 | 4 | 3 | 5 | 9 | 6 |
| 1 | 6 | 7 | 5 | 8 | 4 | 9 | 3 | 2 |
| 2 | 3 | 8 | 6 | 9 | 7 | 4 | 1 | 5 |
| 9 | 5 | 4 | 3 | 2 | 1 | 7 | 6 | 8 |
| 3 | 8 | 2 | 4 | 7 | 6 | 1 | 5 | 9 |
| 6 | 1 | 5 | 2 | 3 | 9 | 8 | 4 | 7 |
| 7 | 4 | 9 | 1 | 5 | 8 | 6 | 2 | 3 |

| 1 | 4 |   | 2 |   |   | 9 | 3 |   |
|---|---|---|---|---|---|---|---|---|
|   | 3 |   | 4 | 6 |   | 2 |   | 1 |
|   |   |   |   |   | 3 | 8 |   | 4 |
|   | 6 | 9 | 3 |   |   |   |   |   |
|   |   |   |   | 4 |   |   |   |   |
|   |   |   |   |   | 6 | 1 | 9 |   |
| 6 |   | 3 |   | 4 |   |   |   |   |
| 2 |   | 8 |   | 3 | 1 |   | 6 |   |
|   | 5 |   |   |   | 8 |   | 1 | 9 |

| 9 |   | 1 | 2 |   |   |   |   |   |
|---|---|---|---|---|---|---|---|---|
| 5 |   | 4 |   | 3 |   | 2 |   | 1 |
| 3 |   |   |   |   | 7 | 4 |   |   |
|   |   |   |   |   | 4 | 5 | 8 |   |
|   |   |   |   | 9 |   |   |   |   |
|   | 4 | 5 | 6 |   |   |   |   |   |
|   |   | 3 | 5 |   |   |   |   | 4 |
| 2 |   | 9 |   | 7 |   | 6 |   | 8 |
|   |   |   |   |   | 2 | 7 |   | 5 |

| 6 |   | 1 |   |   | 5 |   |   |   |
|---|---|---|---|---|---|---|---|---|
|   |   | 4 | 7 | 8 |   | 2 | 6 |   |
|   |   |   |   |   |   |   |   | 1 |
|   |   |   |   |   |   | 6 | 5 |   |
| 7 |   |   | 1 |   | 3 |   |   | 2 |
|   | 3 | 6 |   |   |   |   |   |   |
| 8 |   |   |   |   |   |   |   |   |
|   | 2 | 5 |   | 7 | 8 | 3 |   |   |
|   |   |   | 2 |   |   | 8 |   | 4 |

| 1 | 6 | 8 | 4 | 3 | 5 | 7 | 9 | 2 |
|---|---|---|---|---|---|---|---|---|
| 3 | 2 | 5 | 7 | 1 | 9 |   | 6 |   |
| 9 | 4 | 7 |   |   |   |   |   |   |
| 2 | 8 | 9 |   | 7 |   |   |   |   |
| 5 | 1 | 4 | 9 |   | 2 |   | 7 | 3 |
| 6 | 7 | 3 |   | 4 |   |   |   | 9 |
| 4 | 5 | 6 |   |   |   | 1 |   | 7 |
| 7 | 3 | 1 |   | 5 | 4 | 9 |   |   |
| 8 | 9 | 2 | 1 |   | 7 | 5 |   |   |

|   |   |   |   |   |   | 6 | 4 |   |
|---|---|---|---|---|---|---|---|---|
| 3 | 1 |   |   |   | 2 |   |   | 7 |
|   |   | 9 | 7 |   |   |   |   |   |
|   | 9 | 6 |   | 7 |   |   |   |   |
| 4 |   |   |   | 8 |   |   |   | 9 |
|   |   |   |   | 1 |   | 2 | 3 |   |
|   |   |   |   |   | 4 | 9 |   |   |
| 7 |   |   | 6 |   |   |   | 1 | 3 |
|   | 5 | 3 |   |   |   |   |   |   |

| 5 |   | 4 |   | 3 | 8 | 2 |   | 1 |
|---|---|---|---|---|---|---|---|---|
|   |   |   |   |   |   |   |   | 4 |
| 1 |   | 7 | 2 |   |   |   |   |   |
|   |   |   |   | 5 |   | 1 | 8 | 6 |
|   |   |   |   |   |   |   |   |   |
| 7 | 1 | 5 |   | 6 |   |   |   |   |
|   |   |   |   |   | 4 | 6 |   | 2 |
| 3 |   |   |   |   |   |   |   |   |
| 4 |   | 8 | 1 | 2 |   | 9 |   | 3 |

| 1 | 2 | 3 | 4 |   |   |   |   |   |
|---|---|---|---|---|---|---|---|---|
|   |   |   |   | 1 | 2 | 3 | 4 | 5 |
|   |   |   |   |   |   |   |   | 9 |
| 2 |   | 6 |   |   |   |   | 8 |   |
|   | 5 |   |   |   |   |   | 3 |   |
|   | 8 |   |   |   |   | 7 |   | 6 |
| 7 |   |   |   |   |   |   |   |   |
| 8 | 4 | 2 | 1 | 9 |   |   |   |   |
|   |   |   |   |   | 3 | 2 | 5 | 8 |

| 2 |   |   | 8 |   |   |   |   |   |
|---|---|---|---|---|---|---|---|---|
|   |   | 1 |   |   | 4 | 2 |   |   |
|   |   | 6 |   | 3 |   | 7 | 5 |   |
|   |   |   | 4 |   | 1 | 9 |   | 7 |
|   |   |   |   |   |   |   |   |   |
| 1 |   | 9 | 6 |   | 8 |   |   |   |
|   | 1 | 7 |   | 5 |   | 8 |   |   |
|   |   | 8 | 3 |   |   | 1 |   |   |
|   |   |   |   |   | 9 |   |   | 2 |

|   |   |   | 3 |   |   |   |   | 6 |
|---|---|---|---|---|---|---|---|---|
|   |   |   | 5 |   | 8 |   | 4 | 1 |
|   |   |   |   | 6 |   | 8 | 7 |   |
|   | 2 |   | 9 |   | 1 |   |   | 4 |
|   | 1 |   |   |   |   |   | 8 |   |
| 6 |   |   | 8 |   | 7 |   | 5 |   |
|   | 4 | 1 |   | 9 |   |   |   |   |
| 7 | 8 |   | 1 |   | 5 |   |   |   |
| 3 |   |   |   |   | 4 |   |   |   |

| 3 | 4 |   |   |   | 8 |   |   |   |
|---|---|---|---|---|---|---|---|---|
| 8 | 1 |   | 9 |   |   | 3 | 2 |   |
|   |   |   |   | 3 |   |   |   |   |
| 2 |   | 3 |   | 9 |   | 1 |   |   |
| 6 |   |   |   |   |   |   |   | 4 |
|   |   | 8 |   | 6 |   | 7 |   | 3 |
|   |   |   |   | 5 |   |   |   |   |
|   | 8 | 4 |   |   | 6 |   | 7 | 1 |
|   |   |   | 7 |   |   |   | 6 | 9 |

| 2 |   |   |   | 4 |   |   | 1 |   |
|---|---|---|---|---|---|---|---|---|
|   |   |   |   | 8 |   |   | 6 |   |
| 6 |   | 7 |   |   | 9 | 4 |   |   |
|   |   | 1 |   | 7 | 3 |   |   | 5 |
|   |   |   | 4 |   | 5 |   |   |   |
| 9 |   |   | 8 | 1 |   | 3 |   |   |
|   |   | 6 | 9 |   |   | 7 |   | 4 |
|   | 7 |   |   | 6 |   |   |   |   |
|   | 2 |   |   | 3 |   |   |   | 1 |

| | 1 | | 2 | | | 6 | 4 | |
|---|---|---|---|---|---|---|---|---|
| | 6 | | | 5 | | | | |
| 2 | | | | | 7 | | 9 | |
| 6 | 7 | | | | | | | |
| 5 | | | 8 | | 1 | | | 6 |
| | | | | | | | 3 | 5 |
| | 2 | | 4 | | | | | 3 |
| | | | | 7 | | | 6 | |
| | 3 | 9 | | | 6 | | 1 | |

| 7 | | | | | | 6 | 2 | |
|---|---|---|---|---|---|---|---|---|
| 4 | | | | 5 | 6 | 8 | | |
| 6 | 1 | | | 3 | | | | |
| | 6 | | | | 5 | | | 3 |
| | | 1 | 3 | | 2 | 9 | | |
| 3 | | | 9 | | | | 7 | |
| | | | | 9 | | | 1 | 7 |
| | | 7 | 6 | 2 | | | | 8 |
| | 9 | 8 | | | | | | 2 |

| | | | | | | | | |
|---|---|---|---|---|---|---|---|---|
|   | 8 | 7 | 4 |   |   |   | 6 |   |
|   | 6 | 9 | 8 |   |   |   |   |   |
|   |   |   | 9 |   |   | 7 | 1 |   |
|   |   | 3 | 7 |   |   |   | 5 |   |
| 5 |   |   |   | 1 |   |   |   | 2 |
|   | 7 |   |   |   | 8 | 3 |   |   |
|   | 1 | 5 |   |   | 9 |   |   |   |
|   |   |   |   |   | 7 | 9 | 3 |   |
|   | 3 |   |   |   | 4 | 1 | 8 |   |

| | | | | | | | | |
|---|---|---|---|---|---|---|---|---|
|   |   | 8 |   |   |   | 6 |   |   |
|   |   |   | 9 | 2 | 4 |   |   |   |
| 2 |   | 1 |   |   |   |   | 3 |   |
|   |   |   |   | 6 | 1 |   |   | 9 |
|   | 1 | 5 |   |   |   | 3 | 7 |   |
| 4 |   |   | 2 | 3 |   |   |   |   |
|   | 5 |   |   |   |   | 4 |   | 6 |
|   |   |   | 1 | 8 | 6 |   |   |   |
|   |   | 7 |   |   |   | 1 |   |   |

**1 1 3**

| 2 |   | 5 |   |   |   | 7 | 1 | 3 |
|---|---|---|---|---|---|---|---|---|
| 3 |   |   | 4 | 7 |   |   |   |   |
|   | 7 |   |   |   |   |   |   |   |
|   | 5 | 8 | 7 |   |   | 6 | 3 |   |
|   |   |   | 8 |   | 3 |   |   |   |
|   |   | 3 | 6 |   | 9 | 5 | 8 |   |
|   |   |   |   |   |   |   | 2 |   |
|   |   |   |   | 6 | 2 |   |   | 9 |
| 4 | 6 | 2 |   |   |   | 1 |   | 5 |

**1 1 4**

| 6 | 4 | 2 |   |   | 1 |   |   |   |
|---|---|---|---|---|---|---|---|---|
| 3 |   |   | 4 |   |   |   |   |   |
|   | 8 |   |   | 7 |   |   |   | 1 |
| 7 | 3 |   | 2 |   |   |   |   |   |
| 2 |   |   |   | 1 |   |   |   | 5 |
|   |   |   |   |   | 8 |   | 6 | 9 |
| 5 |   |   |   | 6 |   |   | 9 |   |
|   |   |   |   |   | 7 |   |   | 6 |
|   |   |   | 5 |   |   | 7 | 4 | 3 |

## 115

| | | | 5 | | | | | 1 |
|---|---|---|---|---|---|---|---|---|
| 7 | | 3 | | 9 | | | | |
| | | 5 | | | 6 | | 9 | 4 |
| | | 9 | | | | | 4 | 7 |
| | 3 | | | | | | 8 | |
| 8 | 6 | | | | | 1 | | |
| 2 | 7 | | 9 | | | 6 | | |
| | | | | 1 | | 9 | | 8 |
| 6 | | | | | 2 | | | |

## 116

| | | | | | | 4 | | |
|---|---|---|---|---|---|---|---|---|
| | | 6 | | 1 | | 8 | 9 | 3 |
| | | 7 | 3 | | 9 | | 6 | |
| | | 4 | | | | | | 8 |
| | | 2 | 4 | 6 | 1 | 3 | | |
| 1 | | | | | | 6 | | |
| | 5 | | 7 | | 2 | 9 | | |
| 4 | 7 | 8 | | 5 | | 1 | | |
| | | 9 | | | | | | |

| 7 |   |   | 3 |   |   | 8 | 1 |   |
|---|---|---|---|---|---|---|---|---|
| 5 |   |   |   |   |   |   |   |   |
| 6 | 1 |   |   | 9 | 7 |   |   |   |
|   |   |   |   | 3 | 1 |   |   |   |
| 1 | 8 |   | 5 |   | 9 |   | 4 | 7 |
|   |   |   | 7 | 8 |   |   |   |   |
|   |   |   | 2 | 4 |   |   | 6 | 8 |
|   |   |   |   |   |   |   |   | 2 |
|   | 5 | 3 |   |   | 8 |   |   | 9 |

|   |   |   |   |   | 6 | 1 |   |   |
|---|---|---|---|---|---|---|---|---|
| 7 |   | 4 |   | 8 |   |   | 9 | 5 |
| 6 |   |   |   |   |   |   | 2 |   |
| 8 |   | 1 | 7 |   |   | 4 |   |   |
|   | 3 |   |   | 1 |   |   | 7 |   |
|   |   | 7 |   |   | 9 | 5 |   | 1 |
|   | 9 |   |   |   |   |   |   | 2 |
| 1 | 8 |   |   | 9 |   | 7 |   | 4 |
|   |   | 5 | 8 |   |   |   |   |   |

Puzzle 119:

| 4 |   |   |   |   |   |   |   |   |
|---|---|---|---|---|---|---|---|---|
|   |   |   |   | 7 | 5 | 4 |   | 9 |
| 1 |   |   |   | 4 |   |   | 3 |   |
|   |   | 6 |   |   | 4 | 1 |   |   |
|   |   |   | 5 | 6 | 1 |   |   |   |
|   |   | 2 | 8 |   |   | 7 |   |   |
|   | 5 |   |   | 3 |   |   |   | 8 |
| 7 |   | 3 | 2 | 5 |   |   |   |   |
|   |   |   |   |   |   |   |   | 4 |

Puzzle 120:

|   |   |   |   | 1 |   |   |   | 6 |
|---|---|---|---|---|---|---|---|---|
| 1 |   |   | 4 | 9 |   | 5 |   | 8 |
| 6 |   | 9 | 2 | 8 |   |   |   |   |
|   | 1 | 3 |   |   |   |   | 6 |   |
| 7 |   |   |   |   |   |   |   | 9 |
|   | 6 |   |   |   |   | 1 | 7 |   |
|   |   |   | 4 | 7 | 2 |   |   | 3 |
| 3 |   | 7 |   | 2 | 9 |   |   | 1 |
| 4 |   |   |   | 3 |   |   |   |   |

| | | | 3 | | | 6 | | 9 |
|---|---|---|---|---|---|---|---|---|
| | | | | 7 | | 8 | 1 | 4 |
| 6 | | | | | 2 | | | |
| 4 | | | 9 | | | | | 5 |
| | | 8 | | 1 | | 7 | | |
| 5 | | | | | 6 | | | 1 |
| | | | 2 | | | | | 6 |
| 8 | 1 | 6 | | 4 | | | | |
| 9 | | 3 | | | 1 | | | |

| | 2 | | | 1 | | | | |
|---|---|---|---|---|---|---|---|---|
| | | | 8 | | | 2 | | |
| | | 1 | | 5 | | 8 | 7 | |
| | 7 | | | | 1 | 9 | 6 | |
| | | 8 | 7 | | 9 | 1 | | |
| | 1 | 4 | 6 | | | | 8 | |
| | 9 | 7 | | 2 | | 4 | | |
| | | 6 | | | 4 | | | |
| | | | | 7 | | | 1 | |

| | 8 | | | 6 | 1 | | | |
|---|---|---|---|---|---|---|---|---|
| 9 | 2 | | 8 | 3 | | | | |
| 3 | | | | | | | | 9 |
| | 9 | | | | 6 | | | 8 |
| | 1 | | | | | | 4 | |
| 5 | | | 3 | | | | 6 | |
| 2 | | | | | | | | 3 |
| | | | | 7 | 3 | | 1 | 6 |
| | | | 4 | 8 | | | 5 | |

| 1 | | | | 9 | | | 7 | 4 |
|---|---|---|---|---|---|---|---|---|
| | 2 | | 8 | | | 1 | | |
| 9 | | 3 | | | | | | |
| | | | 4 | | | | | 5 |
| 4 | | | 1 | 5 | 2 | | | 6 |
| 8 | | | | | 6 | | | |
| | | | | | | 7 | | 1 |
| | | 9 | | | 4 | | 8 | |
| 7 | 6 | | | 2 | | | | 9 |

1
2
5

| 9 | 2 |   |   | 6 |   |   |   | 8 |
|---|---|---|---|---|---|---|---|---|
|   | 8 |   |   |   |   |   | 7 | 5 |
|   |   | 7 | 8 |   |   |   |   |   |
|   | 4 |   | 6 |   | 7 |   |   |   |
|   |   | 3 |   | 5 |   | 4 |   |   |
|   |   |   | 9 |   | 4 |   | 8 |   |
|   |   |   |   |   | 6 | 3 |   |   |
| 3 | 6 |   |   |   |   |   | 2 |   |
| 2 |   |   |   | 8 |   |   | 5 | 1 |

1
2
6

| 8 |   |   |   |   | 3 |   | 1 |   |
|---|---|---|---|---|---|---|---|---|
|   | 5 | 6 | 8 |   |   |   |   |   |
| 3 | 4 |   |   |   |   |   | 9 |   |
|   |   | 5 | 7 |   | 6 |   |   |   |
| 2 |   | 1 |   |   |   | 7 |   | 9 |
|   |   |   | 1 |   | 5 | 6 |   |   |
|   | 1 |   |   |   |   |   | 3 | 7 |
|   |   |   |   |   | 8 | 5 | 6 |   |
|   | 7 |   | 5 |   |   |   |   | 8 |

127

| 2 |   |   |   | 8 |   |   |   | 9 |
|---|---|---|---|---|---|---|---|---|
|   |   | 6 |   | 4 |   |   |   | 8 |
|   | 8 |   |   |   |   |   |   |   |
| 9 |   | 8 | 7 |   |   | 5 |   |   |
|   |   | 2 |   |   |   | 3 |   |   |
|   |   | 1 |   |   | 9 | 4 |   | 7 |
|   |   |   |   |   |   |   | 1 |   |
| 3 |   |   |   | 2 |   | 6 |   |   |
| 1 |   |   |   | 6 |   |   |   | 5 |

128

|   |   |   |   |   | 2 | 9 | 7 |   |
|---|---|---|---|---|---|---|---|---|
| 8 |   |   |   | 4 |   |   |   | 3 |
|   |   | 9 |   | 5 |   |   |   |   |
|   | 3 | 2 |   |   |   |   | 1 | 4 |
| 4 |   |   |   |   |   |   |   | 5 |
| 7 | 1 |   |   |   |   | 8 | 6 |   |
|   |   |   |   | 9 |   | 3 |   |   |
| 1 |   |   |   | 8 |   |   |   | 2 |
|   | 2 | 7 | 4 |   |   |   |   |   |

**129**

| | 7 | | | | | | | |
|---|---|---|---|---|---|---|---|---|
| | | | 7 | 5 | | 4 | | |
| 5 | | 6 | | 2 | | | 3 | 8 |
| 4 | | 9 | | | 8 | | 1 | 5 |
| | | | | | | | | |
| 1 | 5 | | 6 | | | 2 | | 7 |
| 3 | 1 | | | 8 | | 9 | | 4 |
| | | 7 | | 9 | 1 | | | |
| | | | | | | | 7 | |

**130**

| | | 4 | | | 5 | | | |
|---|---|---|---|---|---|---|---|---|
| | 2 | 9 | 8 | | | | 4 | |
| | 5 | | | | 4 | | 8 | |
| 6 | 9 | | 7 | | | | | |
| | | 5 | | 8 | | 2 | | |
| | | | | | 3 | | 5 | 9 |
| | 3 | | 2 | | | | 7 | |
| | 8 | | | | 9 | 4 | 3 | |
| | | | 1 | | | 9 | | |

**1 3 1**

| 6 |   |   |   |   | 7 |   | 2 |   |
|---|---|---|---|---|---|---|---|---|
| 8 | 9 | 7 | 1 |   |   |   |   | 6 |
|   |   |   |   |   |   | 7 |   |   |
|   |   |   |   | 7 |   | 8 |   | 1 |
| 7 |   |   | 8 |   | 1 |   |   | 2 |
| 1 |   | 4 |   | 3 |   |   |   |   |
|   |   | 9 |   |   |   |   |   |   |
| 2 |   |   |   |   | 5 | 9 | 1 | 7 |
|   | 7 |   | 3 |   |   |   |   | 8 |

**1 3 2**

| 3 | 1 | 5 |   |   |   | 6 |   |   |
|---|---|---|---|---|---|---|---|---|
|   |   |   | 4 | 2 | 6 |   |   | 1 |
|   |   |   |   |   | 5 | 7 | 8 | 9 |
|   |   |   | 2 |   | 4 |   |   |   |
|   |   | 2 |   |   |   | 9 |   |   |
|   |   |   | 1 |   | 7 |   |   |   |
| 2 | 4 | 7 | 6 |   |   |   |   |   |
| 5 |   |   | 7 | 4 | 1 |   |   |   |
|   |   | 1 |   |   |   | 5 | 4 | 7 |

Puzzle 133

| | | | | | | | | |
|---|---|---|---|---|---|---|---|---|
| | | | | | | | | |
| 8 | | 3 | | 2 | | | 9 | |
| | | 5 | | 4 | 7 | | | |
| | 5 | 4 | 8 | | | | | 2 |
| 3 | | | 6 | | 2 | | | 5 |
| 6 | | | | | 4 | 8 | 3 | |
| | | | 4 | 9 | | 6 | | |
| | 7 | | | 8 | | 2 | | 9 |
| | | | | | | | | |

Puzzle 134

| | | | | | | | | |
|---|---|---|---|---|---|---|---|---|
| | 8 | 5 | | | 1 | | | |
| | 9 | | | 8 | | | | |
| | | 1 | | 2 | 6 | 5 | 7 | |
| | 7 | | | | 3 | 8 | | |
| | | 3 | | | | 9 | | |
| | | 8 | 2 | | | | 5 | |
| | 1 | 4 | 7 | 9 | | 3 | | |
| | | | | 4 | | | 8 | |
| | | | 1 | | | 7 | 9 | |

| | | | 3 | 4 | | | 2 | |
|---|---|---|---|---|---|---|---|---|
| | | | | | | | | |
| 6 | | 2 | 5 | | 1 | 4 | 9 | |
| | | 7 | | | 2 | 8 | | 3 |
| 9 | | | | | | | | 2 |
| 2 | | 8 | 4 | | | 9 | | |
| | 9 | 6 | 2 | | 7 | 3 | | 5 |
| | | | | | | | | |
| | 8 | | | 1 | 3 | | | |

| 5 | | 3 | | | 2 | | | 8 |
|---|---|---|---|---|---|---|---|---|
| | | | | | | | | |
| 1 | 2 | | 7 | | | | 5 | 9 |
| | | | | 4 | | 2 | 9 | |
| | 5 | | | | | | 4 | |
| | 7 | 6 | | 3 | | | | |
| 7 | 9 | | | | 5 | | 2 | 4 |
| | | | | | | | | |
| 6 | | | 9 | | | 1 | | 5 |

**137**

| 2 |   | 7 |   |   |   |   |   |   |
|---|---|---|---|---|---|---|---|---|
| 9 |   |   |   | 4 | 6 | 2 |   | 1 |
|   | 1 |   | 9 |   |   |   |   | 5 |
|   | 9 |   |   |   |   | 4 |   |   |
|   |   | 1 | 2 | 3 | 4 | 5 |   |   |
|   |   | 4 |   |   |   |   | 1 |   |
| 6 |   |   |   |   | 7 |   | 3 |   |
| 5 |   | 8 | 4 | 9 |   |   |   | 6 |
|   |   |   |   |   |   | 9 |   | 4 |

**138**

| 6 | 4 |   |   |   |   |   |   |   |
|---|---|---|---|---|---|---|---|---|
|   |   |   |   | 9 |   |   |   | 1 |
| 1 |   |   | 7 |   |   |   |   | 9 |
|   | 6 |   | 1 |   |   |   | 8 | 4 |
|   |   |   | 8 |   | 9 |   |   |   |
| 3 | 2 |   |   |   | 7 |   | 9 |   |
| 5 |   |   |   |   | 2 |   |   | 6 |
| 4 |   |   |   | 6 |   |   |   |   |
|   |   |   |   |   |   |   | 2 | 3 |

| | 3 | 2 | 5 | | | 6 | | |
|---|---|---|---|---|---|---|---|---|
| | 7 | | 4 | 8 | | | | |
| | | | | | 2 | | 1 | |
| | | 8 | 3 | | | | | 5 |
| | | 6 | | | | 1 | | |
| 5 | | | | | 8 | 3 | | |
| | 6 | | 8 | | | | | |
| | | | | 9 | 4 | | 8 | |
| | | 3 | | | 1 | 2 | 4 | |

| | 3 | 9 | 7 | 5 | 8 | 1 | 6 | |
|---|---|---|---|---|---|---|---|---|
| | | 8 | | | | | | |
| | | | | | | | | 7 |
| | 5 | | | 8 | | | 7 | |
| | | 1 | 5 | | 9 | 6 | | |
| | 8 | | | 2 | | | 3 | |
| 1 | | | | | | | | |
| | | | | | | 3 | | |
| | 2 | 7 | 1 | 6 | 3 | 8 | 5 | |

| 3 |   |   |   | 5 |   |   |   | 2 |
|---|---|---|---|---|---|---|---|---|
|   |   |   |   | 3 |   | 9 |   |   |
|   |   | 8 |   |   | 6 | 7 |   |   |
| 5 |   |   |   |   |   |   |   |   |
| 6 | 7 |   | 1 |   | 3 |   | 5 | 4 |
|   |   |   |   |   |   |   |   | 1 |
|   |   | 6 | 9 |   |   | 2 |   |   |
|   |   | 4 |   | 1 |   |   |   |   |
| 9 |   |   |   | 4 |   |   |   | 3 |

|   | 9 |   |   |   |   |   |   | 6 |
|---|---|---|---|---|---|---|---|---|
| 5 | 8 |   |   |   |   | 9 |   | 1 |
|   |   |   | 5 |   | 2 |   |   |   |
|   |   |   |   |   | 6 |   |   | 2 |
|   | 1 |   |   | 5 |   |   | 3 |   |
| 4 |   |   | 3 |   |   |   |   |   |
|   |   |   | 4 |   | 3 |   |   |   |
| 9 |   | 2 |   |   |   |   | 7 | 4 |
| 3 |   |   |   |   |   |   | 5 |   |

| | 1 | | | 9 | 3 | | | 5 |
|---|---|---|---|---|---|---|---|---|
| | | | 4 | | | | 1 | 3 |
| | | 8 | | 2 | | | | |
| | | | | | | 1 | 6 | |
| | | 4 | | | | 2 | | |
| | 8 | 9 | | | | | | |
| | | | | 7 | | 5 | | |
| 6 | 9 | | | | 8 | | | |
| 4 | | | 2 | 5 | | | 3 | |

| | | | | | | 4 | | |
|---|---|---|---|---|---|---|---|---|
| | 2 | | | 8 | | | 1 | 5 |
| 7 | | | 6 | | | 2 | | 9 |
| | 8 | 3 | 9 | 6 | | | | |
| | | 9 | | | | 5 | | |
| | | | | 3 | 4 | 8 | 9 | |
| 1 | | 2 | | | 8 | | | 6 |
| 3 | 6 | | | 7 | | | 2 | |
| | | 8 | | | | | | |

| | 3 | | | | | 7 | | |
|---|---|---|---|---|---|---|---|---|
| | 4 | | | 5 | 7 | | 8 | |
| | | | 9 | | | | 4 | |
| | | 5 | 6 | 4 | | | | 8 |
| | | 1 | 5 | | 3 | 4 | | |
| 4 | | | | 7 | 9 | 5 | | |
| | 6 | | | | 2 | | | |
| | 9 | | 1 | 8 | | | 7 | |
| | | 2 | | | | 6 | | |

| | 8 | 4 | | | | 5 | | |
|---|---|---|---|---|---|---|---|---|
| 9 | | | | 2 | | | 6 | |
| | | 6 | 7 | | | | 9 | 1 |
| | | | 4 | | 5 | 3 | | 9 |
| | | | | | | | | |
| 1 | | 5 | 3 | | 7 | | | |
| 4 | 1 | | | | 8 | 6 | | |
| | 3 | | | 7 | | | | 8 |
| | | 9 | | | | 1 | 3 | |

| | 4 | | | | | 8 | | |
|---|---|---|---|---|---|---|---|---|
| | | 2 | 4 | | 3 | | | |
| | | | | | 7 | 9 | | 4 |
| 7 | | | 8 | | | | | 1 |
| 1 | | 3 | | 5 | | 7 | | 9 |
| 2 | | | | | 4 | | | 8 |
| 4 | | 5 | 2 | | | | | |
| | | | 3 | | 1 | 4 | | |
| | | 9 | | | | | 2 | |

| | | 9 | | 1 | | | 7 | |
|---|---|---|---|---|---|---|---|---|
| | | 1 | | | | 8 | | |
| | | | 8 | 9 | | | 4 | 5 |
| 9 | | | 5 | | | | | 1 |
| | 2 | | 9 | | 1 | | 8 | |
| 1 | | | | | 8 | | | 3 |
| 3 | 5 | | | 7 | 6 | | | |
| | | 2 | | | | 5 | | |
| | 9 | | | 5 | | 2 | | |

**149**

| 9 |   | 5 | 7 |   |   |   |   |   |
|---|---|---|---|---|---|---|---|---|
|   | 8 |   | 2 |   |   |   |   | 3 |
|   |   | 7 |   |   | 1 |   |   | 8 |
|   |   | 4 | 6 |   |   |   |   | 5 |
| 7 | 1 |   |   | 5 |   |   | 6 | 2 |
| 5 |   |   |   |   | 4 | 9 |   |   |
| 2 |   |   | 1 |   |   | 3 |   |   |
| 1 |   |   |   |   | 8 |   | 2 |   |
|   |   |   |   |   | 7 | 6 |   | 1 |

**150**

|   |   |   |   |   |   |   | 3 |   |
|---|---|---|---|---|---|---|---|---|
|   |   |   | 4 | 7 |   |   |   | 1 |
|   | 6 |   | 3 | 2 | 1 |   | 8 |   |
|   |   | 3 |   |   |   | 4 |   | 9 |
|   |   | 2 |   | 1 |   | 5 |   |   |
| 4 |   | 1 |   |   |   | 6 |   |   |
|   | 3 |   | 9 | 8 | 7 |   | 5 |   |
| 7 |   |   |   | 4 | 3 |   |   |   |
|   | 1 |   |   |   |   |   |   |   |

151

| | | | | | | | | |
|---|---|---|---|---|---|---|---|---|
| | 5 | 4 | 6 | | | | 1 | |
| 6 | | 2 | 1 | 3 | | 8 | | |
| | | | | | 5 | | | |
| 1 | | 3 | | | 8 | | | |
| 7 | | | | | | | | 1 |
| | | | 3 | | | 4 | | 6 |
| | | | 7 | | | | | |
| | | 6 | | 2 | 1 | 3 | | 5 |
| | 2 | | | | 4 | 1 | 9 | |

152

| | | | | | | | | |
|---|---|---|---|---|---|---|---|---|
| 3 | | | | 2 | | | | |
| | | | | | 6 | | 8 | 2 |
| | | 8 | | | | | | 4 |
| | | | 5 | 9 | | 7 | 3 | |
| | | | | | | | | |
| | 5 | 4 | | 3 | 2 | | | |
| 8 | | | | | | 2 | | |
| 7 | 3 | | 4 | | | | | |
| | | | | 1 | | | | 6 |

| 9 |   |   | 4 | 1 |   |   | 5 |   |
|---|---|---|---|---|---|---|---|---|
| 1 |   |   |   |   |   | 3 | 6 |   |
|   |   | 7 |   |   |   |   |   | 1 |
|   | 5 |   | 9 |   |   |   | 8 |   |
|   |   | 2 |   |   |   | 4 |   |   |
|   | 9 |   |   |   | 6 |   | 2 |   |
| 6 |   |   |   |   |   | 5 |   |   |
|   | 8 | 5 |   |   |   |   |   | 6 |
|   | 7 |   |   | 5 | 9 |   |   | 3 |

|   |   |   | 1 |   |   |   |   |   |
|---|---|---|---|---|---|---|---|---|
| 6 |   |   | 7 |   | 2 | 1 |   | 9 |
|   | 1 |   |   | 8 |   | 7 |   |   |
| 2 | 3 |   | 8 |   |   |   | 5 |   |
|   |   |   |   |   |   |   |   |   |
|   | 8 |   |   |   | 9 |   | 1 | 3 |
|   |   | 4 |   | 3 |   |   | 9 |   |
| 7 |   | 3 | 6 |   | 8 |   |   | 4 |
|   |   |   |   |   | 7 |   |   |   |

Puzzle 155

| | | 6 | | | | | 5 | |
|---|---|---|---|---|---|---|---|---|
| 1 | | 3 | | | 4 | | | |
| | | | | 8 | | | 7 | |
| | | 8 | | | 3 | | | 2 |
| | | 2 | 9 | | 6 | 1 | | |
| 5 | | | 1 | | | 3 | | |
| | 5 | | | 1 | | | | |
| | | | 4 | | | 7 | | 6 |
| | 7 | | | | | 9 | | |

Puzzle 156

| | 3 | 9 | 5 | | | | 4 | |
|---|---|---|---|---|---|---|---|---|
| | 7 | | | 3 | | | 6 | |
| 5 | | | | | | 7 | | |
| | | 8 | 6 | | | 5 | | 3 |
| | | | 3 | | 9 | | | |
| 3 | | 2 | | | 8 | 1 | | |
| | | 3 | | | | | | 2 |
| | 9 | | | 6 | | | 1 | |
| | 2 | | | | 3 | 6 | 7 | |

82

**157**

| 8 |   |   |   |   |   | 7 |   | 9 |
|---|---|---|---|---|---|---|---|---|
|   |   |   | 8 |   |   |   |   | 6 |
|   | 3 | 7 |   |   | 9 | 2 |   | 5 |
|   |   |   |   | 2 | 3 |   |   |   |
| 3 | 9 |   | 6 |   | 8 |   | 2 | 4 |
|   |   |   | 9 | 4 |   |   |   |   |
| 6 |   | 1 | 2 |   |   | 3 | 9 |   |
| 2 |   |   |   |   | 6 |   |   |   |
| 5 |   | 3 |   |   |   |   |   | 2 |

**158**

|   |   | 7 | 2 |   |   |   |   | 9 |
|---|---|---|---|---|---|---|---|---|
| 2 |   | 1 |   |   | 4 |   |   |   |
|   | 3 |   |   | 6 |   |   | 5 |   |
|   |   | 2 | 4 | 1 | 3 | 9 |   |   |
|   |   |   |   |   |   |   |   |   |
|   |   | 4 | 6 | 7 | 5 | 2 |   |   |
|   | 4 |   |   | 5 |   |   | 2 |   |
|   |   |   | 3 |   |   | 5 |   | 1 |
| 7 |   |   |   |   | 1 | 4 |   |   |

159

| 6 | 4 |   |   | 7 |   |   | 1 |   |
|---|---|---|---|---|---|---|---|---|
| 2 |   |   |   |   |   | 6 |   |   |
|   |   | 1 | 9 |   |   |   | 7 |   |
| 9 |   |   | 5 |   |   | 1 | 8 | 7 |
|   |   |   | 2 |   | 9 |   |   |   |
| 8 | 5 | 6 |   |   | 1 |   |   | 2 |
|   | 9 |   |   |   | 4 | 7 |   |   |
|   |   | 2 |   |   |   |   |   | 1 |
|   | 7 |   |   | 9 |   |   | 6 | 8 |

160

| 4 | 9 |   |   | 2 |   |   |   | 8 |
|---|---|---|---|---|---|---|---|---|
| 6 |   |   | 1 |   |   |   | 9 |   |
| 5 |   |   |   |   |   | 4 | 3 |   |
|   |   |   |   | 7 |   |   | 2 |   |
|   |   |   | 5 | 9 | 2 |   |   |   |
|   | 1 |   |   | 6 |   |   |   |   |
|   | 2 | 4 |   |   |   |   |   | 9 |
|   | 3 |   |   |   | 7 |   |   | 6 |
| 7 |   |   |   | 4 |   |   | 8 | 3 |

**161**

| | | 1 | | 6 | | | | |
|---|---|---|---|---|---|---|---|---|
| | | 3 | 5 | | 2 | | 6 | |
| | | 5 | 9 | | | | | |
| | 6 | | 1 | 2 | | | | |
| | 3 | 2 | | | | 8 | 1 | |
| | | | | 4 | 7 | | 2 | |
| | | | | | 9 | 1 | | |
| | 8 | | 3 | | 1 | 9 | | |
| | | | | 7 | | 5 | | |

**162**

| | | 6 | | | | | | 9 |
|---|---|---|---|---|---|---|---|---|
| | | 9 | 5 | | | | 4 | |
| 8 | | 1 | 4 | | | | | 6 |
| 4 | | 8 | | 5 | | | 3 | |
| | | | | | | | | |
| | 5 | | | 1 | | 7 | | 2 |
| 9 | | | | | 1 | 8 | | 7 |
| | 8 | | | | 2 | 5 | | |
| 2 | | | | | | 6 | | |

| | | | 4 | | | 7 | 8 | |
|---|---|---|---|---|---|---|---|---|
| | | | 9 | | 8 | | | 1 |
| | | | | 2 | | | | 6 |
| 3 | | 2 | 8 | | 1 | | | |
| | 1 | 6 | | | | 5 | 7 | |
| | | | 7 | | 6 | 8 | | 2 |
| 5 | | | | 1 | | | | |
| 9 | | | 6 | | 4 | | | |
| | 4 | 1 | | | 7 | | | |

| | 5 | | 2 | | | | 8 | |
|---|---|---|---|---|---|---|---|---|
| | | | 7 | 5 | | 1 | | 9 |
| 8 | | | | 9 | | | | |
| | | 3 | | | | | | 2 |
| | | 4 | 5 | | 9 | 6 | | |
| 1 | | | | | | 5 | | |
| | | | | 1 | | | | 8 |
| 3 | | 5 | | 2 | 7 | | | |
| | 7 | | | | 3 | | 1 | |

| 7 | 5 |   |   |   | 9 | 8 |   | 1 |
|---|---|---|---|---|---|---|---|---|
|   |   |   |   |   |   |   | 9 |   |
|   |   |   | 6 | 3 |   |   |   | 5 |
|   |   | 8 |   | 4 |   | 6 |   |   |
|   |   |   | 3 |   | 5 |   |   |   |
|   |   | 5 |   | 8 |   | 9 |   |   |
| 3 |   |   |   | 1 | 8 |   |   |   |
|   | 2 |   |   |   |   |   |   |   |
| 8 |   | 1 | 2 |   |   |   | 4 | 7 |

|   |   |   | 6 |   | 4 |   |   |   |
|---|---|---|---|---|---|---|---|---|
| 1 |   |   | 9 |   |   |   |   |   |
| 6 |   |   |   |   |   | 9 | 5 | 7 |
|   |   | 7 |   | 9 |   |   | 8 |   |
| 8 |   | 1 |   | 7 |   | 2 |   | 6 |
|   | 9 |   |   | 4 |   | 7 |   |   |
| 7 | 3 | 8 |   |   |   |   |   | 5 |
|   |   |   |   |   | 2 |   |   | 1 |
|   |   |   | 5 |   | 3 |   |   |   |

Puzzle 167:

| | | 8 | | 1 | | 7 | 4 | 3 |
|---|---|---|---|---|---|---|---|---|
| 5 | | | | | 7 | | | 9 |
| | | | | | 3 | | | |
| 1 | | | | | | | 9 | 4 |
| | | 7 | | | | 5 | | |
| 9 | 3 | | | | | | | 6 |
| | | | 1 | | | | | |
| 7 | | | 9 | | | | | 5 |
| 6 | 8 | 5 | | 4 | | 9 | | |

Puzzle 168:

| | | | | | 6 | 9 | | |
|---|---|---|---|---|---|---|---|---|
| 7 | | | | | | | 4 | 8 |
| 6 | | | | | 4 | | 2 | |
| | 6 | | | | 9 | 1 | | |
| | 4 | | | 2 | | | 6 | |
| | | 1 | 8 | | | | 3 | |
| | 2 | | 6 | | | | | 7 |
| 4 | 3 | | | | | | | 1 |
| | | 8 | 3 | | | | | |

| | 1 | | 3 | | 8 | | | |
|---|---|---|---|---|---|---|---|---|
| | | 9 | | | | | | 5 |
| | | | | 7 | | 3 | 1 | |
| | | | 1 | 4 | | | 8 | |
| | | 5 | | | | 6 | | |
| | 7 | | | 6 | 3 | | | |
| | 9 | 4 | | 1 | | | | |
| 7 | | | | | | 5 | | |
| | | | 8 | | 6 | | 3 | |

| | 7 | | 8 | | | | | 3 |
|---|---|---|---|---|---|---|---|---|
| | 1 | 4 | | | | | | |
| | | 5 | | | 9 | | | |
| | 5 | 1 | | | | | | 6 |
| | | 6 | | 7 | | 2 | | |
| 2 | | | | | | 1 | 8 | |
| | | | 9 | | | 4 | | |
| | | | | | | 6 | 5 | |
| 3 | | | | | 4 | | 2 | |

| | | | | 8 | | 3 | 2 | |
|---|---|---|---|---|---|---|---|---|
| | | 8 | | | 9 | | | |
| 3 | | | | | 6 | | 7 | |
| | 2 | | | | | 6 | | |
| | | | 9 | 1 | 4 | | | |
| | | 9 | | | | | 4 | |
| | 6 | | 3 | | | | | 9 |
| | | | 2 | | | 1 | | |
| | 9 | 3 | | 5 | | | | |

| 2 | 1 | | | | 8 | 3 | | 5 |
|---|---|---|---|---|---|---|---|---|
| 9 | | | | | | | | |
| | | 5 | | | | 6 | 8 | |
| 6 | | | 3 | 7 | | | 9 | |
| | | | | | | | | |
| | 9 | | | 4 | 1 | | | 8 |
| | 6 | 2 | | | | 5 | | |
| | | | | | | | | 4 |
| 1 | | 7 | 2 | | | | 6 | 3 |

**173**

| | 3 | 6 | | | 9 | | | 2 |
|---|---|---|---|---|---|---|---|---|
| | 7 | 8 | 3 | | | | | |
| | | | | 5 | | | 8 | |
| | | | | 3 | | 4 | | |
| | | 9 | 1 | 6 | 8 | 2 | | |
| | | 5 | | 9 | | | | |
| | 9 | | | 4 | | | | |
| | | | | | 6 | 5 | 4 | |
| 2 | | | 9 | | | 3 | 7 | |

**174**

| | | | 8 | | | 3 | 9 | |
|---|---|---|---|---|---|---|---|---|
| 7 | | 1 | | | | | 2 | |
| | 5 | | | 1 | | | | 8 |
| | | | | | | | 5 | |
| | | | 2 | 7 | 4 | | | |
| | 3 | | | | | | | |
| 3 | | | | 6 | | | 7 | |
| | 1 | | | | | 8 | | 9 |
| | 2 | 6 | | | 1 | | | |

| 3 |   |   |   | 5 |   | 2 |   |   |
|---|---|---|---|---|---|---|---|---|
| 4 |   |   |   | 1 | 9 |   |   | 5 |
|   | 5 |   |   |   |   | 1 | 6 | 7 |
| 8 | 2 |   |   |   |   |   | 1 |   |
|   |   | 5 |   |   |   | 7 |   |   |
|   | 4 |   |   |   |   |   | 5 | 3 |
| 1 | 6 | 7 |   |   |   |   | 3 |   |
| 9 |   |   | 6 | 2 |   |   |   | 1 |
|   |   | 2 |   | 3 |   |   |   | 6 |

| 4 |   |   | 2 |   | 5 |   | 3 |   |
|---|---|---|---|---|---|---|---|---|
|   |   | 6 |   |   | 1 | 2 |   |   |
|   | 5 |   |   |   | 7 |   | 1 |   |
| 1 | 9 |   |   |   |   |   |   | 5 |
|   |   | 5 |   |   |   | 7 |   |   |
| 6 |   |   |   |   |   |   | 8 | 3 |
|   | 4 |   | 1 |   |   |   | 7 |   |
|   |   | 1 | 7 |   |   | 3 |   |   |
|   | 2 |   | 4 |   | 3 |   |   | 9 |

| 5 |   | 3 |   |   | 1 |   |   |   |
|---|---|---|---|---|---|---|---|---|
| 4 |   |   |   | 3 | 8 |   | 1 |   |
|   |   |   |   |   |   | 5 |   |   |
|   |   | 4 |   |   |   |   | 2 |   |
| 8 | 6 |   | 7 |   | 2 |   | 3 | 1 |
|   | 7 |   |   |   |   | 6 |   |   |
|   |   | 9 |   |   |   |   |   |   |
|   | 2 |   | 9 | 8 |   |   |   | 5 |
|   |   |   | 4 |   |   | 1 |   | 2 |

|   |   |   | 9 | 4 | 6 |   |   |   |
|---|---|---|---|---|---|---|---|---|
| 9 |   | 5 |   |   |   | 8 | 4 |   |
| 1 |   |   |   |   |   | 3 |   |   |
| 3 | 6 |   |   |   |   |   | 8 |   |
|   | 1 |   | 4 | 2 | 3 |   | 6 |   |
|   | 5 |   |   |   |   |   | 1 | 3 |
|   |   | 1 |   |   |   |   |   | 5 |
|   | 9 | 3 |   |   |   | 1 |   | 4 |
|   |   |   | 3 | 1 | 2 |   |   |   |

| 7 | 1 |   | 5 |   |   |   | 9 |   |
|---|---|---|---|---|---|---|---|---|
|   |   | 6 |   |   |   |   | 4 | 2 |
|   | 9 | 3 | 2 |   |   |   |   |   |
|   |   |   |   | 5 |   | 6 |   | 1 |
|   |   |   |   | 3 |   |   |   |   |
| 1 |   | 7 |   | 6 |   |   |   |   |
|   |   |   |   |   | 5 | 3 | 6 |   |
| 6 | 8 |   |   |   |   | 5 |   |   |
|   | 3 |   |   |   | 9 |   | 7 | 4 |

|   | 8 |   |   |   | 7 |   |   | 6 |
|---|---|---|---|---|---|---|---|---|
|   |   | 3 |   |   |   |   |   |   |
|   |   | 7 | 2 |   | 6 |   |   |   |
|   |   |   |   |   | 8 |   |   | 3 |
| 4 | 5 |   |   | 3 |   |   | 2 | 9 |
| 1 |   |   | 9 |   |   |   |   |   |
|   |   |   | 4 |   | 2 | 5 |   |   |
|   |   |   |   |   |   | 1 |   |   |
| 9 |   |   | 7 |   |   |   | 8 |   |

| | 2 | | 9 | | | 8 | 3 | |
|---|---|---|---|---|---|---|---|---|
| | 6 | | | | 8 | 7 | | |
| 3 | | | | | | | | |
| | 7 | | 8 | | | | | |
| | | 8 | | 6 | | 5 | | |
| | | | | | 5 | | 1 | |
| | | | | | | | | 6 |
| | | 6 | 7 | | | | 9 | |
| | 3 | 1 | | | 9 | | 2 | |

| 2 | | | | | | | | |
|---|---|---|---|---|---|---|---|---|
| | 3 | | 5 | 9 | 6 | | | 8 |
| | | 5 | | 7 | | 9 | 4 | |
| | | 6 | | | 9 | | | |
| 8 | | | | 2 | | | | 6 |
| | | | 6 | | | 4 | | |
| | 5 | 1 | | 6 | | 8 | | |
| 3 | | | 7 | 4 | 2 | | 1 | |
| | | | | | | | | 9 |

**183**

| | 9 | | 1 | | | | 2 | |
|---|---|---|---|---|---|---|---|---|
| | | | | 7 | | | | 6 |
| | 1 | 4 | | | 5 | | | 9 |
| | | | | | 2 | | | |
| 7 | | 1 | | | | 9 | | 4 |
| | | | 3 | | | | | |
| 2 | | | 9 | | | 3 | 7 | |
| 1 | | | | 6 | | | | |
| | 3 | | | | 4 | | 1 | |

**184**

| | | 8 | | | | | 5 | |
|---|---|---|---|---|---|---|---|---|
| | | 9 | | | 7 | | 4 | 6 |
| | | 6 | 9 | | 1 | | | |
| | | 7 | | | | | | 2 |
| | | | | 2 | | | | |
| 8 | | | | | | 9 | | |
| | | | 2 | | 9 | 5 | | |
| 7 | 4 | | 1 | | | 2 | | |
| | 5 | | | | | 3 | | |

| | | 2 | 7 | | | | | |
|---|---|---|---|---|---|---|---|---|
| | 7 | | | | 4 | | | |
| | 3 | | | 6 | | | 8 | 1 |
| | | | 3 | | 6 | 4 | | |
| 9 | 5 | | | | | | 6 | 8 |
| | | 6 | 4 | | 9 | | | |
| 1 | 2 | | | 9 | | | 3 | |
| | | | 6 | | | | 1 | |
| | | | | | 1 | 2 | | |

| | 4 | | | | 6 | | | |
|---|---|---|---|---|---|---|---|---|
| | | 6 | 4 | | | 3 | | |
| | | 7 | 8 | | | | 6 | 1 |
| 3 | | | 2 | 7 | | 6 | | |
| | | | | | | | | |
| | | 2 | | 9 | 3 | | | 4 |
| 5 | 6 | | | | | 2 | 9 | |
| | | 4 | | | | 7 | 8 | |
| | | | 6 | | | | 5 | |

**187**

| | 3 | | | | 9 | | | |
|---|---|---|---|---|---|---|---|---|
| | | 9 | 3 | | | | 7 | |
| | | | 2 | 4 | | 5 | | |
| | 5 | | 4 | | | | | 1 |
| 2 | 1 | | | | | | 4 | 9 |
| 6 | | | | | 2 | | 8 | |
| | | 1 | | 3 | 6 | | | |
| | 8 | | | | | 1 | 3 | |
| | | | 5 | | | | 1 | |

**188**

| 1 | 3 | | | | 4 | | | 7 |
|---|---|---|---|---|---|---|---|---|
| | | | | 8 | | | | |
| | 9 | | | | | | 2 | 4 |
| 3 | | 6 | 9 | | 8 | | | |
| | | | 2 | | 5 | | | |
| | | | 4 | | 3 | 7 | | 2 |
| 2 | 7 | | | | | | 8 | |
| | | | | 9 | | | | |
| 8 | | | 3 | | | | 1 | 9 |

| | 3 | | | | 2 | | | |
|---|---|---|---|---|---|---|---|---|
| 5 | | 1 | | | 8 | | | |
| | | | 9 | 6 | | 2 | | |
| | 4 | 9 | | | | | | |
| 8 | | | | 3 | | | | 4 |
| | | | | | | 5 | 2 | |
| | | 4 | | 9 | 6 | | | |
| | | | 4 | | | 1 | | 6 |
| | | | 2 | | | | 5 | |

| 9 | | | 6 | | | | 8 | 7 |
|---|---|---|---|---|---|---|---|---|
| | | | | 3 | 4 | | | |
| 4 | | 6 | | 1 | | | | |
| | 8 | | | | 6 | 2 | | 4 |
| | 9 | | | | | | 5 | |
| 6 | | 2 | 4 | | | | 1 | |
| | | | | 8 | | 1 | | 3 |
| | | | 1 | 6 | | | | |
| 5 | 1 | | | | 9 | | | 6 |

| | | 2 | 9 | | | 7 | | |
|---|---|---|---|---|---|---|---|---|
| | 1 | | 2 | | 4 | | | 8 |
| | 9 | | | | | | 1 | 3 |
| | | | | | | | | 5 |
| | 4 | 6 | | 5 | | 1 | 7 | |
| 8 | | | | | | | | |
| 4 | 3 | | | | | | 8 | |
| 7 | | | 1 | | 5 | | 4 | |
| | | 1 | | | 8 | 6 | | |

| 3 | | | | | | | 4 | 2 |
|---|---|---|---|---|---|---|---|---|
| | | | | | 7 | 8 | | |
| | | | 5 | 6 | | | 3 | |
| 9 | 1 | | | 2 | 6 | | | |
| | | 8 | | 1 | | 4 | | |
| | | | 8 | 7 | | | 1 | 6 |
| | 3 | | | 5 | 8 | | | |
| | | 1 | 2 | | | | | |
| 8 | 4 | | | | | | | 7 |

## 193

| | 7 | | 8 | | | 9 | | |
|---|---|---|---|---|---|---|---|---|
| | | | | | 4 | 6 | | 3 |
| | | 8 | | 1 | | | | |
| 9 | | | 5 | | | | | |
| 8 | | | 4 | | 9 | | | 2 |
| | | | 7 | | | | | 1 |
| | | | 6 | | 3 | | | |
| 1 | | 3 | 5 | | | | | |
| | | 4 | | | 3 | | 2 | |

## 194

| | | 3 | | | | | | |
|---|---|---|---|---|---|---|---|---|
| | | 9 | 4 | | | | 8 | |
| | 5 | 6 | 1 | | | | | 2 |
| | | 2 | 8 | | 6 | | | 7 |
| 9 | | | 7 | | 5 | | | 6 |
| 7 | | | 3 | | 1 | 5 | | |
| 3 | | | | | 8 | 7 | 9 | |
| | 2 | | | | 7 | 8 | | |
| | | | | | 2 | | | |

**195**

| | | 3 | | 7 | | 9 | | |
|---|---|---|---|---|---|---|---|---|
| | | | | 4 | | 3 | 2 | |
| 5 | | | 6 | | 2 | | | |
| 8 | | 5 | | | | | 1 | |
| | 6 | | | | | | 8 | |
| | 1 | | | | | 2 | | 3 |
| | | | 1 | | 9 | | | 2 |
| | 4 | 2 | | 5 | | | | |
| | | 6 | | 8 | | 7 | | |

**196**

| | 7 | | 6 | | | 3 | | 8 |
|---|---|---|---|---|---|---|---|---|
| 9 | 4 | | | | | 7 | | |
| | | 3 | | | | | 2 | |
| | | | | | 4 | | 9 | 2 |
| | | | 8 | | 5 | | | |
| 4 | 8 | | 9 | | | | | |
| | 3 | | | | | 9 | | |
| | | 1 | | | | | 6 | 3 |
| 6 | | 5 | | | 3 | | 4 | |

| 9 |   |   |   | 3 |   | 2 |   |   |
|---|---|---|---|---|---|---|---|---|
| 5 | 3 |   | 4 |   | 7 |   |   |   |
|   |   |   |   | 2 |   |   | 5 |   |
|   | 8 |   |   |   | 2 |   | 6 |   |
|   |   | 6 |   |   |   | 8 |   |   |
|   | 1 |   | 7 |   |   |   | 9 |   |
|   | 2 |   |   | 6 |   |   |   |   |
|   |   |   | 2 |   | 5 |   | 4 | 9 |
|   |   | 4 |   | 7 |   |   |   | 2 |

| 9 |   |   |   | 8 | 1 |   |   |   |
|---|---|---|---|---|---|---|---|---|
|   | 8 |   |   |   | 9 | 2 | 6 |   |
| 1 |   |   | 3 |   |   |   | 5 |   |
|   |   | 8 | 9 |   |   |   | 1 |   |
|   |   |   |   |   |   |   |   |   |
|   | 3 |   |   |   | 2 | 6 |   |   |
|   | 4 |   |   |   | 3 |   |   | 6 |
|   | 9 | 5 | 8 |   |   |   | 4 |   |
|   |   |   | 7 | 5 |   |   |   | 9 |

**199**

| 7 |   | 2 |   | 8 |   |   |   |   |
|---|---|---|---|---|---|---|---|---|
|   |   |   |   |   | 7 |   |   |   |
|   |   | 4 |   |   |   | 9 | 1 |   |
| 2 |   |   | 5 |   |   | 4 |   |   |
| 3 |   | 5 | 7 |   | 9 | 2 |   | 6 |
|   |   | 7 |   |   | 6 |   |   | 3 |
|   | 9 | 1 |   |   |   | 5 |   |   |
|   |   |   | 6 |   |   |   |   |   |
|   |   |   |   | 5 |   | 7 |   | 4 |

**200**

|   |   | 9 | 3 |   |   |   |   | 5 |
|---|---|---|---|---|---|---|---|---|
|   |   | 6 |   |   |   | 7 | 3 |   |
|   | 7 |   |   |   | 5 | 1 |   |   |
|   |   |   | 2 | 1 |   |   | 4 |   |
|   | 6 |   |   |   |   |   | 2 |   |
|   | 4 |   |   | 5 | 9 |   |   |   |
|   |   | 4 | 8 |   |   |   | 7 |   |
|   | 2 | 8 |   |   |   | 3 |   |   |
| 7 |   |   |   |   | 6 | 9 |   |   |

**201**

| | | | | | | | 6 | 9 |
|---|---|---|---|---|---|---|---|---|
| | | | | 6 | | 5 | | |
| | 4 | | | 8 | | | | 3 |
| 5 | | | 2 | | | | 4 | 1 |
| 8 | | | 5 | 3 | 1 | | | 6 |
| 7 | 3 | | | | 6 | | | 5 |
| 6 | | | | 4 | | | 8 | |
| | | 8 | | 5 | | | | |
| 4 | 9 | | | | | | | |

**202**

| | 5 | | 6 | 7 | | | | |
|---|---|---|---|---|---|---|---|---|
| | | 8 | 3 | | | | | |
| | 4 | | | | 8 | 6 | 3 | 2 |
| | | | | | | 1 | 9 | |
| 9 | | 6 | | | | 4 | | 7 |
| | 1 | 4 | | | | | | |
| 4 | 9 | 2 | 8 | | | | 5 | |
| | | | | | 2 | 8 | | |
| | | | | 4 | 3 | | 6 | |

| | | | | | 6 | | | |
|---|---|---|---|---|---|---|---|---|
| 6 | | | 4 | | | 2 | 5 | |
| | | | 2 | | | 1 | | 9 |
| 1 | | | | | | 9 | 7 | |
| | 7 | | 5 | | 3 | | 4 | |
| | 6 | 9 | | | | | | 8 |
| 7 | | 1 | | | 9 | | | |
| | 3 | 4 | | | 1 | | | 5 |
| | | | 7 | | | | | |

| 5 | 7 | 6 | 4 | 3 | | | | |
|---|---|---|---|---|---|---|---|---|
| 4 | | 3 | 1 | | | | 5 | |
| | 1 | | | | | 4 | | |
| | | | | 4 | 7 | | 3 | 2 |
| | | | | | | | | |
| 6 | 3 | | 5 | 8 | | | | |
| | | 5 | | | | | 9 | |
| | 2 | | | | 4 | 7 | | 1 |
| | | | | 1 | 2 | 3 | 4 | 5 |

205

| | | | | | 4 | 3 | | 8 |
| | | 9 | 5 | 3 | | 1 | | |
| | | 4 | | | 8 | | | 7 |
| 5 | | | 3 | | | | | |
| | 8 | 7 | | | | 4 | 9 | |
| | | | | | 9 | | | 2 |
| 1 | | | 4 | | | 2 | | |
| | | 5 | | 2 | 1 | 8 | | |
| 9 | | 8 | 6 | | | | | |

206

| 8 | | | | | | | 4 | |
| 3 | | | | 1 | 2 | | 5 | |
| | | | | | 4 | | | 9 |
| | | 1 | | | | | 2 | |
| 2 | | 4 | | 3 | | 5 | | 8 |
| | 3 | | | | | 7 | | |
| 4 | | | 6 | | | | | |
| | 6 | | 2 | 8 | | | | 7 |
| | 7 | | | | | | | 5 |

|   | 3 |   |   | 4 |   |   |   |   |
|---|---|---|---|---|---|---|---|---|
| 9 |   |   |   | 1 |   |   |   | 7 |
|   | 5 | 4 |   |   | 2 | 3 |   |   |
| 6 |   |   |   |   |   | 1 |   |   |
|   |   |   | 7 |   | 4 |   |   |   |
|   |   | 9 |   |   |   |   |   | 8 |
|   |   | 5 | 1 |   |   | 8 | 6 |   |
| 1 |   |   |   | 8 |   |   |   | 4 |
|   |   |   |   | 3 |   |   | 2 |   |

| 1 |   |   |   |   | 8 | 5 | 6 |   |
|---|---|---|---|---|---|---|---|---|
|   |   |   |   | 5 |   |   | 2 | 9 |
|   |   |   | 4 |   |   | 1 |   |   |
|   |   | 7 | 5 | 6 |   |   | 4 |   |
|   | 6 |   |   |   |   |   | 5 |   |
|   | 1 |   |   | 3 | 4 | 2 |   |   |
|   |   | 3 |   |   | 2 |   |   |   |
| 5 | 7 |   |   | 4 |   |   |   |   |
|   | 2 | 8 | 7 |   |   |   |   | 3 |

| | | | 4 | | | | | |
|---|---|---|---|---|---|---|---|---|
| 9 | | 7 | | | | 5 | | 8 |
| | | | 5 | | | | 7 | 1 |
| | 5 | | 8 | | 9 | | 3 | |
| | 8 | 9 | | | | 7 | 6 | |
| | 2 | | 3 | | 7 | | 5 | |
| 2 | 6 | | | | 5 | | | |
| 5 | | 4 | | | | 2 | | 7 |
| | | | | | 2 | | | |

| | | | | | | | | |
|---|---|---|---|---|---|---|---|---|
| | 4 | 5 | | 8 | | | | 1 |
| | | | 2 | 6 | 3 | | | 9 |
| | | 1 | | | 2 | 3 | 8 | |
| | 9 | | | | | | 1 | |
| | 7 | 3 | 4 | | | 6 | | |
| 5 | | | 1 | 4 | 6 | | | |
| 9 | | | | 3 | | 1 | 6 | |
| | | | | | | | | |

| 4 | 6 |   | 3 |   |   |   |   | 7 |
|---|---|---|---|---|---|---|---|---|
| 3 |   |   | 6 |   |   |   |   |   |
|   |   | 5 |   |   | 7 |   |   |   |
|   | 3 |   |   | 7 |   | 6 |   | 2 |
|   | 5 |   |   | 8 |   |   | 3 |   |
| 9 |   | 4 |   | 3 |   |   | 8 |   |
|   |   |   | 1 |   |   | 2 |   |   |
|   |   |   |   |   | 3 |   |   | 8 |
| 8 |   |   |   |   | 9 |   | 7 | 4 |

|   |   |   |   | 7 | 2 |   |   |   |
|---|---|---|---|---|---|---|---|---|
| 5 |   |   | 6 |   |   |   | 9 | 7 |
|   | 4 | 3 |   |   |   |   |   |   |
| 4 |   |   |   | 8 |   | 5 | 7 |   |
|   |   |   |   |   |   |   |   |   |
|   | 2 | 7 |   | 9 |   |   |   | 1 |
|   |   |   |   |   |   | 9 | 5 |   |
| 9 | 3 |   |   |   | 1 |   |   | 4 |
|   |   |   | 2 | 6 |   |   |   |   |

213

| | | | | 5 | | | 8 | |
|---|---|---|---|---|---|---|---|---|
| | | | | 1 | | | | 4 |
| | | | 8 | 2 | | 7 | 3 | 1 |
| 2 | | | | | 6 | | 1 | 3 |
| | | 6 | | | | 5 | | |
| 1 | 9 | | 5 | | | | | 6 |
| 3 | 4 | 8 | | 6 | 2 | | | |
| 6 | | | | 4 | | | | |
| | 5 | | | 8 | | | | |

214

| 7 | | | 6 | 5 | | 9 | | |
|---|---|---|---|---|---|---|---|---|
| 6 | | | | | 1 | 8 | | |
| | | | | | 3 | | | 4 |
| | | 3 | | | | 1 | | 7 |
| 5 | 7 | | | | | | 3 | 8 |
| 8 | | 1 | | | | 2 | | |
| 3 | | | 1 | | | | | |
| | | 7 | 4 | | | | | 9 |
| | | 9 | | 6 | 8 | | | 5 |

| | | 7 | | | | | 2 | |
|---|---|---|---|---|---|---|---|---|
| | | | | | 5 | | | 6 |
| | 1 | 2 | 8 | | | | | |
| | 7 | 8 | 5 | | | 2 | | |
| | | | 2 | | 4 | | | |
| | | 4 | | | 1 | 7 | 5 | |
| | | | | | 8 | 5 | 7 | |
| 3 | | | 4 | | | | | |
| | 6 | | | | | 9 | | |

| | 3 | | 6 | | | | 9 | |
|---|---|---|---|---|---|---|---|---|
| 5 | | | | 3 | 8 | | | |
| | | 9 | | | | 4 | | |
| 4 | 5 | 3 | | 6 | | | | 7 |
| 2 | | | | 5 | | | | 4 |
| 8 | | | | 4 | | 3 | 5 | 6 |
| | | 5 | | | | 6 | | |
| | | | 5 | 2 | | | | 8 |
| | 2 | | | | 3 | | 7 | |

**217**

| | | | 6 | | | 1 | 4 | |
|---|---|---|---|---|---|---|---|---|
| 1 | | | | | 7 | | 3 | 6 |
| | | 2 | | 1 | | 9 | | |
| | | 4 | | 6 | | | | |
| 6 | | | | | | | | 9 |
| | | | | 3 | | 5 | | |
| | | 5 | | 2 | | 3 | | |
| 8 | 2 | | 3 | | | | | 4 |
| | 9 | 7 | | | 1 | | | |

**218**

| | | 7 | 6 | | | 2 | | |
|---|---|---|---|---|---|---|---|---|
| 9 | 6 | | | 4 | 3 | | 1 | |
| 3 | | | | | | | 7 | |
| 1 | | | | | 5 | | | 2 |
| | | 8 | | | | 9 | | |
| 4 | | | 3 | | | | | 1 |
| | 2 | | | | | | | 9 |
| | 1 | | 2 | 7 | | | 4 | 8 |
| | | 4 | | | 6 | 3 | | |

| | | | 1 | 6 | 5 | | | |
|---|---|---|---|---|---|---|---|---|
| 7 | 5 | 1 | | | 2 | | | |
| 8 | | | | | | | | 5 |
| | | 3 | 5 | 1 | | 9 | 8 | |
| 5 | | | | 9 | | | | 1 |
| 1 | 9 | | | 3 | 4 | 6 | 5 | |
| 2 | | 5 | | | | | | 9 |
| | | | 4 | | | 5 | | 7 |
| | | | | 8 | 5 | | | |

| | | 1 | | 7 | | | 8 | |
|---|---|---|---|---|---|---|---|---|
| 6 | | 3 | | | | | | 4 |
| 8 | 4 | | 2 | | | | | |
| | 6 | | 8 | | 1 | | | |
| | | 9 | | 5 | | 3 | | |
| | | | 4 | | 3 | | 6 | |
| | | | | | 6 | | 1 | 2 |
| 5 | | | | | | 7 | | 8 |
| | 1 | | | 8 | | 4 | | |

| 7 | 1 | 6 | 9 |   |   |   | 4 |   |
|---|---|---|---|---|---|---|---|---|
|   |   |   |   | 1 |   |   |   | 2 |
| 4 |   |   |   | 6 |   |   | 3 |   |
|   |   |   | 1 |   |   | 3 | 6 |   |
|   |   |   | 4 |   | 6 |   |   |   |
|   | 9 | 1 |   |   | 2 |   |   |   |
|   | 4 |   |   | 7 |   |   |   | 3 |
| 1 |   |   |   | 5 |   |   |   |   |
|   | 6 |   |   |   | 8 | 9 | 5 | 1 |

| 9 |   |   |   | 8 | 3 |   |   | 7 |
|---|---|---|---|---|---|---|---|---|
|   | 4 |   |   | 7 |   |   |   |   |
|   |   | 8 |   |   |   | 1 |   | 9 |
|   |   | 2 |   |   | 4 |   | 7 |   |
| 3 |   |   |   | 6 |   |   |   | 2 |
|   | 1 |   | 2 |   |   | 3 |   |   |
| 8 |   | 1 |   |   |   | 5 |   |   |
|   |   |   |   | 3 |   |   | 6 |   |
| 7 |   |   | 6 | 9 |   |   |   | 1 |

2 2 3

| 7 |   |   |   |   |   |   |   | 9 |
|---|---|---|---|---|---|---|---|---|
|   | 5 |   | 9 |   | 3 |   | 4 |   |
|   |   |   | 6 |   | 7 | 1 |   |   |
|   |   | 3 |   |   |   |   | 1 |   |
|   |   | 4 | 5 |   | 6 | 7 |   |   |
|   | 2 |   |   |   |   | 9 |   |   |
|   |   | 9 | 3 |   | 8 |   |   |   |
|   | 1 |   | 4 |   | 9 |   | 3 |   |
| 2 |   |   |   |   |   |   |   | 8 |

2 2 4

|   |   | 9 | 5 |   |   |   |   |   |
|---|---|---|---|---|---|---|---|---|
| 2 |   | 1 | 8 |   |   |   | 7 |   |
|   | 5 |   | 7 | 9 |   | 4 |   |   |
|   | 7 |   |   |   | 3 |   |   |   |
|   | 6 |   |   |   |   |   | 9 |   |
|   |   |   | 1 |   |   |   | 4 |   |
|   |   | 3 |   | 1 | 7 |   | 8 |   |
|   | 2 |   |   |   | 8 | 7 |   | 9 |
|   |   |   |   |   | 5 | 3 |   |   |

| | | | | | 4 | 5 | 7 | |
|---|---|---|---|---|---|---|---|---|
| 4 | | 1 | | | | | 3 | 9 |
| | | | 3 | | 6 | 4 | | |
| | 8 | | | 3 | 5 | | | 6 |
| | | | | | | | | |
| 9 | | | 4 | 6 | | | 8 | |
| | | 4 | 6 | | 9 | | | |
| 6 | 5 | | | | | 2 | | 1 |
| | 9 | 2 | 1 | | | | | |

| | | 6 | | | | 2 | | |
|---|---|---|---|---|---|---|---|---|
| | | | | 7 | 1 | | | |
| | | | 8 | | | 7 | 6 | |
| | 2 | | | 9 | | 3 | 8 | |
| | 9 | | 5 | | 8 | | 2 | |
| | 4 | 1 | | 3 | | | 5 | |
| | 1 | 8 | | | 2 | | | |
| | | | 3 | 6 | | | | |
| | | 4 | | | | 5 | | |

| | | | | | | | 7 | |
|---|---|---|---|---|---|---|---|---|
| | 5 | 2 | | | | | 9 | |
| | | 9 | | 7 | 3 | | | 5 |
| | | | 7 | 5 | | 8 | 4 | |
| | | | 3 | | 9 | | | |
| | 2 | 7 | | 1 | 4 | | | |
| 8 | | | 1 | 3 | | 9 | | |
| | 4 | | | | | 5 | 6 | |
| | 6 | | | | | | | |

| 6 | | | | | | | | |
|---|---|---|---|---|---|---|---|---|
| | | | 9 | 8 | 3 | | | |
| | 7 | | 3 | | | | | 2 |
| | 6 | | | 4 | | 2 | 9 | |
| 2 | 1 | | | 7 | | | 6 | 3 |
| | 3 | 5 | | 2 | | | 7 | |
| 4 | | | | | 2 | | 3 | |
| | | 8 | 7 | 6 | | | | |
| | | | | | | | | 9 |

| | | | 9 | | | | 1 | |
|---|---|---|---|---|---|---|---|---|
| | | | 6 | 5 | | | | 8 |
| 1 | | | | 8 | | 5 | | |
| 7 | | 2 | 5 | | 8 | | 4 | |
| | | 4 | | | | 2 | | |
| | 1 | | 4 | | 3 | 6 | | 7 |
| | | 7 | | 6 | | | | 2 |
| 8 | | | | 1 | 5 | | | |
| | 9 | | | | 7 | | | |

| 6 | | | | | 1 | | | |
|---|---|---|---|---|---|---|---|---|
| | | | 6 | 2 | | 4 | | |
| | | 9 | | 8 | | | 2 | |
| | 3 | | | 1 | | | | 7 |
| 1 | 4 | 7 | | | | 8 | 5 | 6 |
| 9 | | | | 7 | | | 3 | |
| | 1 | | | 6 | | 7 | | |
| | | 3 | | 4 | 2 | | | |
| | | | 8 | | | | | 4 |

2
3
3

| 8 |   |   |   | 7 |   |   |   | 6 |
|---|---|---|---|---|---|---|---|---|
|   | 4 | 7 |   | 2 |   | 5 |   |   |
|   |   |   | 4 |   |   | 7 |   |   |
|   |   |   |   |   |   | 9 |   | 7 |
| 6 | 1 |   |   |   |   |   | 4 | 2 |
| 4 |   | 5 |   |   |   |   |   |   |
|   |   | 2 |   |   | 8 |   |   |   |
|   |   | 8 |   | 5 |   | 2 | 7 |   |
| 5 |   |   |   | 6 |   |   |   | 1 |

2
3
4

|   |   |   |   |   | 1 | 3 | 7 |   |
|---|---|---|---|---|---|---|---|---|
| 4 |   |   | 5 |   |   |   |   |   |
| 6 | 5 |   |   |   | 7 |   | 4 |   |
|   |   |   | 1 |   | 8 | 5 |   |   |
| 8 |   |   |   |   |   |   |   | 7 |
|   |   | 5 | 6 |   | 2 |   |   |   |
|   | 4 |   | 3 |   |   |   | 6 | 9 |
|   |   |   |   | 9 |   |   |   | 2 |
|   | 9 | 1 | 2 |   |   |   |   |   |

Puzzle 1:

| 9 |   | 8 |   |   | 7 |   |   |   |
|---|---|---|---|---|---|---|---|---|
| 6 | 4 |   |   |   |   |   |   |   |
|   |   |   |   | 5 |   |   | 1 |   |
|   | 2 |   |   |   | 8 | 7 |   | 4 |
|   |   |   |   |   |   |   |   |   |
| 1 |   | 3 | 4 |   |   |   | 9 |   |
|   | 5 |   |   | 2 |   |   |   |   |
|   |   |   |   |   |   |   | 3 | 5 |
|   |   |   | 8 |   |   | 9 |   | 2 |

Puzzle 2:

|   |   |   |   |   |   | 3 | 7 |   |
|---|---|---|---|---|---|---|---|---|
|   |   | 1 |   | 6 |   |   |   |   |
|   |   |   | 5 |   |   |   |   | 9 |
| 4 |   |   |   |   |   | 9 |   | 5 |
|   | 5 |   | 1 |   | 7 |   | 6 |   |
| 3 |   | 8 |   |   |   |   |   | 4 |
| 8 |   |   |   |   | 9 |   |   |   |
|   |   |   |   | 8 |   | 1 |   |   |
|   | 4 | 2 |   |   |   |   |   |   |

| | | | 7 | | 4 | | | |
|---|---|---|---|---|---|---|---|---|
| | 7 | 5 | | | | | | 6 |
| | | 1 | | | | | 9 | |
| | | | | 5 | | 1 | 4 | |
| 2 | | | | 9 | | | | 3 |
| | 8 | 9 | | 7 | | | | |
| | 2 | | | | | 7 | | |
| 9 | | | | | | 6 | 8 | |
| | | | 6 | | 5 | | | |

| | | | 9 | 7 | | 8 | | |
|---|---|---|---|---|---|---|---|---|
| | | | | | 4 | | | 7 |
| | 1 | | | | | 9 | | |
| | 5 | 4 | | | | | | 6 |
| | 6 | | | 5 | | | 7 | |
| 3 | | | | | | 4 | 2 | |
| | | 7 | | | | | 3 | |
| 8 | | | 1 | | | | | |
| | | 3 | | 2 | 8 | | | |

| 1 | 4 | 6 |   |   |   |   |   |   |
|---|---|---|---|---|---|---|---|---|
| 2 | 5 |   |   | 6 |   |   |   |   |
| 3 | 8 |   | 7 |   |   |   |   |   |
|   | 6 |   | 4 |   |   |   | 9 |   |
| 9 |   | 4 |   | 5 |   | 1 |   | 3 |
|   | 1 |   |   |   | 7 |   | 2 |   |
|   |   |   |   |   | 3 |   | 4 | 5 |
|   |   |   |   | 1 |   |   | 7 | 6 |
|   |   |   |   |   |   | 8 | 3 | 1 |

|   | 6 |   | 3 | 2 |   |   |   |   |
|---|---|---|---|---|---|---|---|---|
| 2 | 9 |   |   |   |   | 3 |   |   |
|   |   |   |   | 4 |   |   |   |   |
| 3 |   | 6 |   |   | 5 |   | 9 |   |
|   |   | 1 | 2 | 3 | 4 | 5 |   |   |
|   | 5 |   | 8 |   |   | 1 |   | 3 |
|   |   |   |   | 5 |   |   |   |   |
|   |   | 8 |   |   |   |   | 7 | 9 |
|   |   |   |   | 9 | 3 |   | 4 |   |

**241**

| | | | | | | 2 | 8 | |
|---|---|---|---|---|---|---|---|---|
| | 3 | 9 | 8 | | | 1 | | |
| | | | 7 | 1 | 2 | | | |
| | 6 | | | 2 | | | 9 | 4 |
| | | | | 3 | | | | |
| 1 | 8 | | | 4 | | | 5 | |
| | | | 9 | 5 | 4 | | | |
| | | 8 | | | 1 | 4 | 2 | |
| | 1 | 3 | | | | | | |

**242**

| | 3 | | 2 | | 1 | | | 8 |
|---|---|---|---|---|---|---|---|---|
| 4 | | 2 | | 3 | | 5 | | |
| | | | | | | | | |
| 1 | | 9 | 7 | | | | 3 | |
| | 8 | | 5 | 4 | 6 | | 7 | |
| | 6 | | | | 3 | 8 | | 5 |
| | | | | | | | | |
| | | 8 | | 6 | | 2 | | 4 |
| 6 | | | 3 | | 2 | | 8 | |

| | 8 | 9 | | 6 | | | 7 | 5 |
|---|---|---|---|---|---|---|---|---|
| | | | 3 | 5 | 1 | 6 | | |
| | | | | | | | | |
| | | | 7 | 6 | | | 5 | |
| | | 7 | | | | 9 | | |
| | 6 | | 4 | 8 | | | | |
| | | | | | | | | |
| | 9 | 4 | 8 | 2 | | | | |
| 7 | 5 | | | 9 | | 6 | 4 | |

| | | | | | | | | |
|---|---|---|---|---|---|---|---|---|
| | | | 6 | 3 | 4 | 8 | 7 | |
| | | 1 | | 5 | | 4 | | 3 |
| 5 | | | 3 | | | | | 4 |
| | 2 | | | | | | 9 | |
| 3 | | | | | 7 | | | 6 |
| 4 | | 5 | | 9 | | 7 | | |
| | 6 | 2 | 4 | 1 | 5 | | | |
| | | | | | | | | |

2
4
5

| | | | 6 | | | 5 | 9 | 1 |
|---|---|---|---|---|---|---|---|---|
| | | | | 5 | | | | |
| | | 2 | | 9 | 1 | | 8 | |
| 6 | 9 | | | | | | | 3 |
| | | | 5 | | 2 | | | |
| 7 | | | | | | | 1 | 5 |
| | 4 | | 2 | 8 | | 3 | | |
| | | | | 6 | | | | |
| 3 | 6 | 9 | | | 4 | | | |

2
4
6

| | | 7 | | 8 | 4 | 2 | | |
|---|---|---|---|---|---|---|---|---|
| | | 3 | | | | | | |
| | | | 3 | | 7 | 4 | | |
| | 1 | | | 5 | | 9 | 4 | |
| | 5 | | 4 | | 9 | | 6 | |
| | 4 | 6 | | 7 | | | 2 | |
| | | 5 | 1 | | 3 | | | |
| | | | | | | 1 | | |
| | | 1 | 2 | 4 | | 3 | | |

| | | | | | 8 | | 2 | 6 |
|---|---|---|---|---|---|---|---|---|
| | 8 | | 3 | | | | | |
| | | 4 | | | 7 | | | |
| 1 | 4 | | 5 | 3 | | 9 | | |
| 5 | | 9 | | | | 3 | | 2 |
| | | 2 | | 9 | 4 | | 6 | 1 |
| | | | 2 | | | 6 | | |
| | | | | | 6 | | 1 | |
| 6 | 1 | | 8 | | | | | |

| | | | | | | 6 | 4 | 1 |
|---|---|---|---|---|---|---|---|---|
| | | | 9 | 1 | 4 | | | |
| 5 | 4 | 1 | | | | 8 | | 9 |
| | 3 | | 4 | | | | | 2 |
| | | 4 | | | | 7 | | |
| 2 | | | | | 5 | | 8 | |
| 8 | | 5 | | | | 2 | 1 | 3 |
| | | | 3 | 2 | 1 | | | |
| 1 | 2 | 3 | | | | | | |

**249**

| | | | | | 2 | 5 | 7 | 1 |
|---|---|---|---|---|---|---|---|---|
| | | 5 | | | 1 | | 3 | |
| | 8 | | | | | | | |
| | | 2 | 4 | 8 | | 6 | | |
| 4 | | | | 6 | | | | 5 |
| | | 3 | | 2 | 9 | 7 | | |
| | | | | | | | 6 | |
| | 5 | | 7 | | | 3 | | |
| 7 | 6 | 9 | 2 | | | | | |

**250**

| | | | | 4 | | | | |
|---|---|---|---|---|---|---|---|---|
| 7 | | | | 6 | 1 | | 2 | 4 |
| | | 3 | | | 5 | | 1 | |
| | | 7 | | | 8 | | 3 | |
| 6 | | 2 | 9 | | 3 | 7 | | 8 |
| | 8 | | 2 | | | 9 | | |
| | 3 | | 5 | | | 4 | | |
| 8 | 5 | | 1 | 3 | | | | 7 |
| | | | | 8 | | | | |

**2 5 1**

| | 4 | | | | 8 | | 5 | 6 |
|---|---|---|---|---|---|---|---|---|
| | | | 5 | | | 2 | | |
| | 1 | | 6 | | 2 | 4 | | |
| | | | | | 5 | 8 | | 1 |
| | 7 | | | | | | 3 | |
| 6 | | 9 | 1 | | | | | |
| | | 1 | 8 | | 9 | | 2 | |
| | | 4 | | | 1 | | | |
| 2 | 9 | | 3 | | | | 7 | |

**2 5 2**

| | 8 | | 7 | | 3 | 5 | | |
|---|---|---|---|---|---|---|---|---|
| 1 | | | 2 | | 4 | | | |
| | | 3 | | | | 4 | | |
| | 7 | | | | 6 | | | 3 |
| | | 1 | | | | 7 | | |
| 2 | | | 3 | | | | 9 | |
| | | 7 | | | | 8 | | |
| | | | 8 | | 1 | | | 9 |
| | | 9 | 6 | | 5 | | 1 | |

Puzzle 253

| | | | | 2 | 8 | | | |
|---|---|---|---|---|---|---|---|---|
| | | 9 | 4 | | | | 6 | |
| 1 | 8 | | | | | | | |
| | 3 | 7 | 8 | | 5 | | | 4 |
| 6 | 5 | | | | | | 9 | 7 |
| 9 | | | 6 | | 2 | 5 | 8 | |
| | | | | | | | 7 | 5 |
| | 4 | | | | 7 | 1 | | |
| | | | 1 | 5 | | | | |

Puzzle 254

| | | | | | | 1 | | |
|---|---|---|---|---|---|---|---|---|
| | | 4 | | 8 | | | | 5 |
| 1 | | 8 | 9 | | | | | |
| | | 5 | | 7 | 4 | | 3 | |
| 7 | 6 | | | 2 | | | 5 | 4 |
| | 4 | | 6 | 3 | | 2 | | |
| | | | | | 2 | 7 | | 8 |
| 5 | | | | 6 | | 9 | | |
| | | 6 | | | | | | |

**255**

| 1 |   | 2 | 9 | 3 |   | 4 |   | 5 |
|---|---|---|---|---|---|---|---|---|
|   |   | 4 | 1 | 2 |   |   |   |   |
|   |   | 9 |   |   | 4 |   |   | 1 |
|   | 6 |   |   | 4 |   | 2 |   |   |
|   |   |   |   |   |   |   |   |   |
|   |   | 3 |   | 9 |   |   | 7 |   |
| 8 |   |   | 4 |   |   | 5 |   |   |
|   |   |   |   | 7 | 2 | 8 |   |   |
| 4 |   | 5 |   | 6 | 9 | 3 |   | 7 |

**256**

|   | 9 |   |   |   | 5 |   | 1 |   |
|---|---|---|---|---|---|---|---|---|
|   |   |   |   | 6 |   | 4 |   |   |
| 8 |   | 1 |   |   |   |   | 6 |   |
| 2 |   |   | 6 |   |   |   | 7 |   |
| 6 |   |   |   | 1 |   |   |   | 2 |
|   | 7 |   |   |   | 4 |   |   | 8 |
|   | 3 |   |   |   |   | 9 |   | 1 |
|   |   | 7 |   | 8 |   |   |   |   |
|   | 6 |   | 4 |   |   |   | 2 |   |

**257**

| 5 |   | 4 |   | 3 |   | 2 |   | 1 |
|---|---|---|---|---|---|---|---|---|
|   |   | 7 |   |   | 4 |   | 9 |   |
| 9 |   | 8 |   |   |   |   | 5 |   |
|   |   |   |   |   |   |   |   | 4 |
|   |   | 6 | 8 |   | 7 | 5 |   |   |
| 4 |   |   |   |   |   |   |   |   |
|   | 7 |   |   |   |   | 9 |   | 2 |
|   | 4 |   | 3 |   |   | 1 |   |   |
| 3 |   | 5 |   | 1 |   | 8 |   | 7 |

**258**

| 6 |   |   |   | 3 |   | 1 | 7 |   |
|---|---|---|---|---|---|---|---|---|
|   |   |   |   |   | 6 | 2 |   |   |
| 9 | 3 |   |   |   |   |   |   |   |
|   |   |   | 9 |   |   |   |   | 4 |
| 2 | 4 |   |   | 5 |   |   | 6 | 7 |
| 5 |   |   |   |   | 7 |   |   |   |
|   |   |   |   |   |   |   | 4 | 2 |
|   |   | 7 | 4 |   |   |   |   |   |
|   | 5 | 9 |   | 2 |   |   |   | 1 |

| | | 4 | | 3 | | | 7 | 6 |
|---|---|---|---|---|---|---|---|---|
| | 9 | | | | | | | |
| 1 | 7 | | 8 | | | 2 | | |
| | | | 9 | 2 | | | | |
| 9 | | | 7 | | 1 | | | 5 |
| | | | | 6 | 8 | | | |
| | | 2 | | | 3 | | 4 | 8 |
| | | | | | | | 9 | |
| 6 | 4 | | | 8 | | 3 | | |

| 1 | | | | 5 | 9 | | 4 | 6 |
|---|---|---|---|---|---|---|---|---|
| 5 | | | | 8 | | | | |
| | | | | | | | 9 | |
| 9 | 6 | | 8 | | | | | 5 |
| 2 | | 5 | | | | 6 | | 4 |
| 8 | | | | | 5 | | 7 | 9 |
| | 4 | | | | | | | |
| | | | | 9 | | | | 8 |
| 3 | 9 | | 4 | 7 | | | | 1 |

**261**

| | 7 | | | 6 | | | | 4 |
|---|---|---|---|---|---|---|---|---|
| | | | 9 | | | 5 | | 3 |
| 8 | | | 7 | | | | | |
| | | | | 5 | 1 | | 6 | |
| | 8 | 2 | 6 | | | 4 | 7 | 9 |
| | 4 | | 8 | 9 | | | | |
| | | | | | 6 | | | 7 |
| 9 | | 6 | | | 2 | | | |
| 4 | | | | 8 | | | 3 | |

**262**

| | 1 | | | | 7 | 3 | | |
|---|---|---|---|---|---|---|---|---|
| | | 4 | | | | 9 | | 8 |
| | 8 | | 9 | 3 | | | | |
| | | | | 2 | | 1 | | 9 |
| | | | | | | | | |
| 2 | | 5 | | 4 | | | | |
| | | | | 6 | 2 | | 5 | |
| 3 | | 6 | | | | 8 | | |
| | | 1 | 3 | | | | 7 | |

| | | 3 | | | 2 | | 8 | 5 |
|---|---|---|---|---|---|---|---|---|
| 8 | | | | | | | | |
| | 2 | | | 6 | | 1 | | |
| 3 | | | | 4 | | | | |
| 7 | | 1 | | | | 3 | | 9 |
| | | | | 8 | | | | 2 |
| | | 6 | | 2 | | | 3 | |
| | | | | | | | | 7 |
| 4 | 7 | | 3 | | | 5 | | |

| | 2 | 9 | | 8 | | | | 5 |
|---|---|---|---|---|---|---|---|---|
| 6 | | 7 | | | 3 | | 2 | |
| | | | | | | | 7 | |
| | | 3 | 8 | | 4 | 7 | | |
| | | | | | | | | |
| | | 1 | 9 | | 6 | 4 | | |
| | 4 | | | | | | | |
| | 8 | | 1 | | | 3 | | 6 |
| 7 | | | | 6 | | 8 | 4 | |

| | | | | 8 | | 3 | | |
|---|---|---|---|---|---|---|---|---|
| | | | | | 7 | | 2 | 6 |
| 2 | | | | | 3 | 1 | 8 | 4 |
| | | 9 | | | | | | 3 |
| 3 | 7 | | | 9 | | | 4 | 8 |
| 6 | | | | | | 2 | | |
| 7 | 6 | 3 | 5 | | | | | 2 |
| 8 | 4 | | 7 | | | | | |
| | | 5 | | 6 | | | | |

| | 2 | | | | | 7 | | 6 |
|---|---|---|---|---|---|---|---|---|
| | 4 | | | | 7 | | 1 | |
| | | | 6 | | | 4 | | 9 |
| | | | 1 | | | 2 | | 3 |
| | 6 | | | | | | 5 | |
| 3 | | 7 | | | 6 | | | |
| 6 | | 4 | | | 8 | | | |
| | 8 | | 7 | | | | 2 | |
| 9 | | 2 | | | | | 4 | |

| 9 |   |   | 6 |   |   | 8 |   |   |
|---|---|---|---|---|---|---|---|---|
| 7 |   |   |   |   |   |   | 5 | 6 |
|   |   |   |   | 9 |   | 7 | 2 | 3 |
|   | 2 |   |   | 5 | 8 |   |   |   |
|   |   |   | 2 | 7 | 6 |   |   |   |
|   |   |   | 9 | 1 |   |   | 8 |   |
| 2 | 5 | 1 |   | 3 |   |   |   |   |
| 3 | 8 |   |   |   |   |   |   | 2 |
|   |   | 9 |   |   | 2 |   |   | 5 |

|   | 1 |   | 5 |   |   | 3 |   |   |
|---|---|---|---|---|---|---|---|---|
|   |   | 7 |   |   |   |   |   | 8 |
|   |   |   |   | 4 | 1 |   | 7 |   |
|   |   |   | 6 |   | 5 |   |   | 1 |
| 2 | 6 |   |   |   |   |   | 9 | 3 |
| 8 |   |   | 2 |   | 4 |   |   |   |
|   | 8 |   | 7 | 2 |   |   |   |   |
| 7 |   |   |   |   |   | 6 |   |   |
|   |   | 9 |   |   | 3 |   | 1 |   |

| | | | | | 5 | | | |
|---|---|---|---|---|---|---|---|---|
| | 5 | 9 | | 6 | | | | |
| 8 | | | 9 | 1 | | 4 | | |
| | | 4 | 3 | | | | | 2 |
| | 2 | 6 | | | | 8 | 9 | |
| 9 | | | | | 1 | 5 | | |
| | | 7 | | 3 | 4 | | | 8 |
| | | | | 8 | | 7 | 6 | |
| | | | 2 | | | | | |

| | | | | 1 | | 6 | | |
|---|---|---|---|---|---|---|---|---|
| 9 | | | | | 3 | | | |
| 7 | 8 | | | 2 | 9 | 4 | | |
| 2 | | 6 | | 8 | | 3 | | |
| | | | | | | | | |
| | | 9 | | 4 | | 7 | | 6 |
| | | 5 | 7 | 6 | | | 2 | 1 |
| | | | 4 | | | | | 7 |
| | | 7 | | 5 | | | | |

**271**

| | 1 | | | | | 8 | | 3 |
|---|---|---|---|---|---|---|---|---|
| | 7 | | | 1 | 3 | | | |
| | | | 6 | | | | 9 | |
| | | | | | 4 | 9 | 6 | |
| 1 | | 4 | 8 | | 6 | 5 | | 2 |
| | 6 | 9 | 1 | | | | | |
| | 9 | | | | 5 | | | |
| | | | 7 | 4 | | | 8 | |
| 8 | | 7 | | | | | 3 | |

**272**

| | 1 | | 3 | | | 7 | 5 | 9 |
|---|---|---|---|---|---|---|---|---|
| | 6 | | | | | | | |
| 3 | | 5 | 7 | | | | | 1 |
| | | 3 | | | | | 6 | |
| 7 | | | 6 | | 3 | | | 8 |
| | 8 | | | | | 4 | | |
| 8 | | | | | 9 | 1 | | 4 |
| | | | | | | | 2 | |
| 1 | 7 | 9 | | | 4 | | 8 | |

| 3 |   |   | 6 | 7 |   |   | 5 |   |
|---|---|---|---|---|---|---|---|---|
|   |   |   | 1 |   |   | 9 |   |   |
| 5 |   |   |   |   |   | 6 |   |   |
|   |   |   | 9 |   | 2 | 7 |   | 8 |
|   |   | 1 |   | 6 |   | 5 |   |   |
| 7 |   | 9 | 3 |   | 1 |   |   |   |
|   |   | 3 |   |   |   |   |   | 5 |
|   |   | 7 |   |   | 4 |   |   |   |
|   | 2 |   |   | 1 | 3 |   |   | 4 |

|   |   |   |   | 4 |   | 1 |   |   |
|---|---|---|---|---|---|---|---|---|
|   |   |   |   |   | 8 | 2 |   |   |
|   | 8 | 5 |   | 3 |   |   |   | 9 |
|   |   |   |   |   | 2 |   | 8 | 7 |
|   |   |   |   |   |   |   |   |   |
| 6 | 1 |   | 4 |   |   |   |   |   |
| 1 |   |   |   | 5 |   | 4 | 2 |   |
|   |   | 3 | 8 |   |   |   |   |   |
|   |   | 7 |   | 6 |   |   |   |   |

**275**

| | | | 8 | | | | 5 | 4 |
|---|---|---|---|---|---|---|---|---|
| | | 8 | | | | | | |
| 6 | | | 4 | | | 1 | | 8 |
| | | 9 | 3 | | | 5 | | |
| | 4 | | 2 | | 5 | | 9 | |
| | | 7 | | | 1 | 4 | | |
| 7 | | 3 | | | 6 | | | 1 |
| | | | | | | 6 | | |
| 1 | 5 | | | | 2 | | | |

**276**

| 7 | 6 | | | | | 2 | | 3 |
|---|---|---|---|---|---|---|---|---|
| 5 | | | | 7 | 8 | 1 | 9 | |
| | | | 2 | | | | | |
| | | | 7 | 9 | | | | 2 |
| 1 | | | | | | | | 4 |
| 2 | | | | 4 | 3 | | | |
| | | | | | 7 | | | |
| | 5 | 1 | 9 | 3 | | | | 7 |
| 9 | | 8 | | | | | 6 | 1 |

| | | | | 2 | | 5 | 3 | |
|---|---|---|---|---|---|---|---|---|
| | | | | | | | | 8 |
| | 6 | | 1 | 8 | | | 2 | 9 |
| | | | | 9 | | 8 | | 5 |
| | | 5 | 7 | | 8 | 3 | | |
| 8 | | 2 | | 4 | | | | |
| 4 | 8 | | | 5 | 1 | | 9 | |
| 7 | | | | | | | | |
| | 1 | 9 | | 6 | | | | |

| | | | | | 2 | | | |
|---|---|---|---|---|---|---|---|---|
| 9 | | | 1 | | | | 3 | |
| 7 | | | | | | 5 | 2 | |
| | 4 | | | | | | | 6 |
| | | | 9 | 4 | 7 | | | |
| 8 | | | | | | | 5 | |
| | 2 | 5 | | | | | | 4 |
| | 6 | | | | 3 | | | 8 |
| | | | 6 | | | | | |

| 9 | 5 |   | 3 |   |   |   |   |   |
|---|---|---|---|---|---|---|---|---|
| 2 |   | 1 |   |   | 4 | 3 |   |   |
|   | 4 |   | 5 |   |   | 2 |   |   |
| 4 |   |   | 7 |   |   | 9 |   |   |
|   | 9 |   |   |   |   |   | 7 |   |
|   |   | 2 |   |   | 6 |   |   | 8 |
|   |   | 9 |   |   | 8 |   | 5 |   |
|   |   | 4 | 1 |   |   | 8 |   | 3 |
|   |   |   |   |   | 7 |   | 9 | 4 |

|   | 5 |   |   |   |   |   |   |   |
|---|---|---|---|---|---|---|---|---|
|   | 2 | 3 | 6 | 4 |   |   |   |   |
|   |   | 6 |   | 8 |   | 3 |   | 1 |
| 3 |   |   |   |   | 1 |   | 9 |   |
|   | 8 |   |   |   |   |   | 4 |   |
|   | 1 |   | 4 |   |   |   |   | 6 |
| 2 |   | 9 |   | 5 |   | 7 |   |   |
|   |   |   |   | 7 | 4 | 5 | 3 |   |
|   |   |   |   |   |   |   | 1 |   |

**2 8 1**

| | 5 | | | | | | | |
|---|---|---|---|---|---|---|---|---|
| 8 | | 7 | | 2 | | | | |
| 2 | | | | | 5 | 1 | 8 | |
| 1 | 3 | 4 | | | | | | |
| 7 | 8 | | 4 | | 9 | | 3 | 6 |
| | | | | | | 5 | 4 | 1 |
| | 7 | 9 | 6 | | | | | 4 |
| | | | | 3 | | 7 | | 8 |
| | | | | | | | 1 | |

**2 8 2**

| | | 8 | | 3 | 9 | | 2 | |
|---|---|---|---|---|---|---|---|---|
| | 2 | | 4 | | | 7 | | |
| 1 | | | | 2 | | | | |
| 4 | | | 8 | 9 | | 1 | | |
| | | 9 | | | | 3 | | |
| | | 3 | | 6 | 7 | | | 5 |
| | | | | 5 | | | | 3 |
| | | 2 | | | 6 | | 4 | |
| | 8 | | 3 | 7 | | 2 | | |

**283**

| | | | 3 | | | | 4 | |
|---|---|---|---|---|---|---|---|---|
| 5 | | | 7 | | | 9 | | |
| | | | | | | 1 | 8 | |
| | 4 | | | | 8 | | 3 | |
| | | 7 | 9 | | 4 | 5 | | |
| | 8 | | 5 | | | | 2 | |
| | 2 | 3 | | | | | | |
| | | 8 | | | 1 | | | 4 |
| | 6 | | | | 3 | | | |

**284**

| | | | | 7 | | 3 | 5 | |
|---|---|---|---|---|---|---|---|---|
| | | 2 | | | | | 9 | |
| | 1 | | | | 3 | | | 8 |
| | | | 3 | | | | | 5 |
| | 3 | 6 | 1 | | 5 | 8 | 4 | |
| 5 | | | | | 8 | | | |
| 4 | | | 2 | | | | 1 | |
| | 5 | | | | | 6 | | |
| | 7 | 1 | | 3 | | | | |

Puzzle 285:

| | | | | | 3 | | 9 | 2 |
|---|---|---|---|---|---|---|---|---|
| | | 3 | | | 2 | | | |
| 6 | | | | | | 4 | | 1 |
| | 7 | 4 | 1 | 6 | | | 2 | |
| | 5 | | | 7 | | | 4 | |
| | 6 | | | 2 | 4 | 5 | 1 | |
| 5 | | 6 | | | | | | 4 |
| | | | 4 | | | 1 | | |
| 8 | 4 | | 9 | | | | | |

Puzzle 286:

| 5 | | | 9 | | | | | |
|---|---|---|---|---|---|---|---|---|
| | 2 | 4 | | 7 | | | | |
| | | 3 | 4 | | | 8 | 1 | |
| | 4 | | | 9 | 3 | | | 7 |
| | | | | | | | | |
| 7 | | | 2 | 5 | | | 9 | |
| | 5 | 7 | | | 6 | 1 | | |
| | | | | 1 | | 2 | 7 | |
| | | | | | 7 | | | 3 |

| | 8 | | 7 | | | 4 | | 5 |
|---|---|---|---|---|---|---|---|---|
| | | | | 4 | 5 | | 9 | |
| | | | | | 6 | 3 | | 1 |
| | | | 4 | 1 | | | 3 | |
| 9 | | | | | | | | 4 |
| | 7 | | | 5 | 9 | | | |
| 8 | | 6 | 3 | | | | | |
| | 9 | | 5 | 2 | | | | |
| 3 | | 5 | | | 7 | | 4 | |

| | 9 | | | 7 | 1 | | | |
|---|---|---|---|---|---|---|---|---|
| | | 6 | | | | | | 3 |
| | | | | 9 | | | | 7 |
| | | 4 | 9 | | | | 8 | |
| | 8 | 3 | 4 | | 2 | 6 | 7 | |
| | 2 | | | | 6 | 5 | | |
| 7 | | | | 1 | | | | |
| 6 | | | | | | 1 | | |
| | | | 5 | 6 | | | 2 | |

| | 3 | | | 9 | | | | 8 |
|---|---|---|---|---|---|---|---|---|
| | | | 5 | | | | | 4 |
| 6 | | | | | 8 | 2 | 3 | |
| | 6 | 8 | | | 1 | | | |
| 1 | | | 4 | 7 | 9 | | | 2 |
| | | | 8 | | | 3 | 1 | |
| | 9 | 5 | 2 | | | | | 1 |
| 8 | | | | | 7 | | | |
| 4 | | | | 5 | | | 2 | |

| | 5 | | 3 | 8 | | | | |
|---|---|---|---|---|---|---|---|---|
| | | | | 4 | | | 5 | 3 |
| | 3 | 7 | | | 9 | 8 | | |
| | | 3 | 4 | | | | | 9 |
| 5 | | | | | | | | 6 |
| 8 | | | | | 6 | 5 | | |
| | | 2 | 9 | | | 4 | 1 | |
| 3 | 1 | | | 7 | | | | |
| | | | | 6 | 1 | | 9 | |

| | 8 | 2 | 5 | | 4 | | | |
|---|---|---|---|---|---|---|---|---|
| | | | 1 | | | | | |
| 3 | 9 | | 6 | 7 | | | | |
| | | 8 | | | | 4 | 7 | |
| | | 3 | | 8 | | 9 | | |
| | 5 | 9 | | | | 2 | | |
| | | | | 1 | 5 | | 2 | 9 |
| | | | | | 3 | | | |
| | | | 7 | | 2 | 1 | 5 | |

| | | | 7 | 6 | | 1 | 5 | 8 |
|---|---|---|---|---|---|---|---|---|
| | | | | 4 | | 3 | | |
| | | | 1 | | | | 7 | 6 |
| 4 | | | | | | 6 | | |
| | 9 | | | 7 | | | 8 | |
| | | 3 | | | | | | 4 |
| 7 | 3 | | | | 9 | | | |
| | | 9 | | 2 | | | | |
| 5 | 1 | 6 | | 3 | 7 | | | |

| 9 | 1 |   | 6 |   |   |   |   |   |
|---|---|---|---|---|---|---|---|---|
|   |   | 5 | 1 |   |   |   | 8 |   |
| 6 |   |   |   |   | 5 | 2 |   | 3 |
| 8 |   | 2 |   |   |   | 4 |   | 1 |
|   |   |   |   |   |   |   |   |   |
| 4 |   | 9 |   |   |   | 5 |   | 2 |
| 7 |   | 4 | 8 |   |   |   |   | 6 |
|   | 8 |   |   |   |   | 9 | 3 |   |
|   |   |   |   |   | 6 |   | 5 | 4 |

| 1 |   |   |   |   |   | 5 |   |   |
|---|---|---|---|---|---|---|---|---|
|   |   | 8 |   |   |   |   |   |   |
|   |   |   | 4 |   | 8 |   | 7 | 1 |
| 3 |   |   |   | 6 | 4 | 9 |   |   |
|   |   | 2 | 9 |   | 7 | 1 |   |   |
|   |   | 9 | 3 | 1 |   |   |   | 2 |
| 7 | 4 |   | 5 |   | 9 |   |   |   |
|   |   |   |   |   |   | 4 |   |   |
|   |   | 3 |   |   |   |   |   | 6 |

| 9 |   |   |   | 7 |   | 6 | 5 |   |
|---|---|---|---|---|---|---|---|---|
|   |   |   |   |   | 9 |   | 2 | 1 |
|   | 1 |   |   |   |   | 3 |   |   |
|   |   |   |   | 3 | 5 |   |   | 4 |
| 5 |   |   | 7 |   | 6 |   |   | 3 |
| 3 |   |   | 9 | 1 |   |   |   |   |
|   |   | 9 |   |   |   |   | 8 |   |
| 6 | 3 |   | 1 |   |   |   |   |   |
|   | 4 | 8 |   | 6 |   |   |   | 5 |

| 1 |   | 5 |   |   |   |   | 4 |   |
|---|---|---|---|---|---|---|---|---|
|   | 9 |   |   |   |   |   |   | 5 |
| 2 |   |   | 9 | 1 |   |   | 3 |   |
|   |   | 2 |   | 9 | 7 |   |   |   |
|   | 1 |   |   |   |   |   | 8 |   |
|   |   |   | 3 | 4 |   | 9 |   |   |
|   | 4 |   |   | 7 | 2 |   |   | 6 |
| 7 |   |   |   |   |   |   | 9 |   |
|   | 3 |   |   |   |   | 7 |   | 4 |

| | 3 | | 2 | | | 1 | | 8 |
|---|---|---|---|---|---|---|---|---|
| 9 | 2 | | | | | | | |
| | | | | 7 | 3 | | | |
| | 8 | | 9 | | | 3 | 4 | |
| | | | 5 | | 4 | | | |
| | 4 | 2 | | | 8 | | 9 | |
| | | | 8 | 5 | | | | |
| | | | | | | | 7 | 1 |
| 1 | | 4 | | | 6 | | 8 | |

| | | | 7 | | | | 1 | |
|---|---|---|---|---|---|---|---|---|
| | | | | | 4 | 6 | 2 | 8 |
| 2 | | | | | 6 | | | 4 |
| 5 | | | | 3 | | 8 | 6 | |
| | | | | 5 | | | | |
| | 4 | 7 | | 6 | | | | 3 |
| 4 | | | 1 | | | | | 6 |
| 6 | 3 | 9 | 8 | | | | | |
| | 2 | | | | 5 | | | |

| | | 9 | 1 | | | | | 4 |
|---|---|---|---|---|---|---|---|---|
| | | | | | | 2 | | |
| | | 1 | 8 | 4 | 6 | | | 9 |
| 7 | 8 | | | | | | | 2 |
| | | | | 7 | | | | |
| 1 | | | | | | | 7 | 6 |
| 5 | | | 9 | 8 | 1 | 3 | | |
| | | 3 | | | | | | |
| 6 | | | | | 2 | 5 | | |

| | | | 2 | 1 | | | | 6 |
|---|---|---|---|---|---|---|---|---|
| | 3 | | | | | | 2 | |
| | | 4 | | | | 1 | | |
| | 7 | 6 | | 9 | | 3 | | 5 |
| | | | | | | | | |
| 4 | | 5 | | 2 | | 7 | 1 | |
| | | 1 | | | | 4 | | |
| | 8 | | | | | | 6 | |
| 9 | | | | 3 | 7 | | | |

**1**

| 5 | 4 | 7 | 6 | 3 | 2 | 8 | 9 | 1 |
|---|---|---|---|---|---|---|---|---|
| 9 | 1 | 6 | 7 | 4 | 8 | 5 | 3 | 2 |
| 3 | 8 | 2 | 9 | 1 | 5 | 4 | 6 | 7 |
| 6 | 5 | 1 | 8 | 2 | 4 | 9 | 7 | 3 |
| 7 | 3 | 4 | 5 | 9 | 1 | 6 | 2 | 8 |
| 2 | 9 | 8 | 3 | 6 | 7 | 1 | 4 | 5 |
| 8 | 6 | 5 | 2 | 7 | 9 | 3 | 1 | 4 |
| 4 | 7 | 9 | 1 | 8 | 3 | 2 | 5 | 6 |
| 1 | 2 | 3 | 4 | 5 | 6 | 7 | 8 | 9 |

**2**

| 9 | 5 | 7 | 4 | 6 | 3 | 2 | 8 | 1 |
|---|---|---|---|---|---|---|---|---|
| 3 | 2 | 6 | 7 | 8 | 1 | 4 | 5 | 9 |
| 4 | 1 | 8 | 2 | 5 | 9 | 6 | 7 | 3 |
| 1 | 9 | 2 | 6 | 3 | 5 | 8 | 4 | 7 |
| 7 | 8 | 3 | 9 | 4 | 2 | 5 | 1 | 6 |
| 5 | 6 | 4 | 1 | 7 | 8 | 9 | 3 | 2 |
| 2 | 3 | 5 | 8 | 9 | 7 | 1 | 6 | 4 |
| 8 | 4 | 9 | 3 | 1 | 6 | 7 | 2 | 5 |
| 6 | 7 | 1 | 5 | 2 | 4 | 3 | 9 | 8 |

**3**

| 6 | 5 | 9 | 8 | 7 | 1 | 4 | 2 | 3 |
|---|---|---|---|---|---|---|---|---|
| 8 | 7 | 2 | 9 | 4 | 3 | 1 | 6 | 5 |
| 3 | 1 | 4 | 2 | 5 | 6 | 7 | 8 | 9 |
| 7 | 3 | 8 | 4 | 2 | 5 | 6 | 9 | 1 |
| 2 | 6 | 5 | 1 | 9 | 8 | 3 | 4 | 7 |
| 4 | 9 | 1 | 6 | 3 | 7 | 2 | 5 | 8 |
| 5 | 8 | 6 | 3 | 1 | 2 | 9 | 7 | 4 |
| 9 | 2 | 3 | 7 | 8 | 4 | 5 | 1 | 6 |
| 1 | 4 | 7 | 5 | 6 | 9 | 8 | 3 | 2 |

**4**

| 6 | 7 | 8 | 2 | 5 | 4 | 9 | 3 | 1 |
|---|---|---|---|---|---|---|---|---|
| 2 | 1 | 4 | 9 | 8 | 3 | 7 | 6 | 5 |
| 5 | 3 | 9 | 7 | 6 | 1 | 8 | 4 | 2 |
| 8 | 4 | 1 | 6 | 9 | 2 | 3 | 5 | 7 |
| 3 | 5 | 6 | 4 | 7 | 8 | 1 | 2 | 9 |
| 7 | 9 | 2 | 3 | 1 | 5 | 6 | 8 | 4 |
| 4 | 2 | 7 | 1 | 3 | 6 | 5 | 9 | 8 |
| 1 | 6 | 5 | 8 | 2 | 9 | 4 | 7 | 3 |
| 9 | 8 | 3 | 5 | 4 | 7 | 2 | 1 | 6 |

**5**

| 5 | 9 | 3 | 2 | 7 | 4 | 1 | 6 | 8 |
|---|---|---|---|---|---|---|---|---|
| 1 | 8 | 7 | 6 | 3 | 9 | 4 | 5 | 2 |
| 6 | 2 | 4 | 5 | 1 | 8 | 7 | 9 | 3 |
| 2 | 1 | 6 | 9 | 5 | 3 | 8 | 7 | 4 |
| 7 | 5 | 8 | 1 | 4 | 2 | 6 | 3 | 9 |
| 3 | 4 | 9 | 7 | 8 | 6 | 2 | 1 | 5 |
| 9 | 6 | 1 | 8 | 2 | 5 | 3 | 4 | 7 |
| 8 | 3 | 5 | 4 | 6 | 7 | 9 | 2 | 1 |
| 4 | 7 | 2 | 3 | 9 | 1 | 5 | 8 | 6 |

**6**

| 4 | 3 | 5 | 2 | 1 | 6 | 7 | 8 | 9 |
|---|---|---|---|---|---|---|---|---|
| 2 | 8 | 6 | 9 | 5 | 7 | 1 | 3 | 4 |
| 1 | 9 | 7 | 4 | 3 | 8 | 2 | 6 | 5 |
| 3 | 1 | 2 | 6 | 8 | 9 | 4 | 5 | 7 |
| 7 | 4 | 8 | 3 | 2 | 5 | 6 | 9 | 1 |
| 5 | 6 | 9 | 1 | 7 | 4 | 3 | 2 | 8 |
| 9 | 2 | 1 | 8 | 4 | 3 | 5 | 7 | 6 |
| 8 | 5 | 4 | 7 | 6 | 2 | 9 | 1 | 3 |
| 6 | 7 | 3 | 5 | 9 | 1 | 8 | 4 | 2 |

**7**

| 1 | 9 | 5 | 2 | 6 | 7 | 8 | 3 | 4 |
|---|---|---|---|---|---|---|---|---|
| 6 | 7 | 4 | 9 | 8 | 3 | 2 | 1 | 5 |
| 3 | 8 | 2 | 4 | 5 | 1 | 7 | 9 | 6 |
| 2 | 1 | 6 | 3 | 9 | 8 | 4 | 5 | 7 |
| 7 | 4 | 9 | 6 | 1 | 5 | 3 | 2 | 8 |
| 8 | 5 | 3 | 7 | 2 | 4 | 9 | 6 | 1 |
| 5 | 3 | 8 | 1 | 4 | 9 | 6 | 7 | 2 |
| 9 | 2 | 1 | 8 | 7 | 6 | 5 | 4 | 3 |
| 4 | 6 | 7 | 5 | 3 | 2 | 1 | 8 | 9 |

**8**

| 4 | 6 | 8 | 9 | 2 | 7 | 1 | 3 | 5 |
|---|---|---|---|---|---|---|---|---|
| 9 | 7 | 1 | 6 | 3 | 5 | 8 | 4 | 2 |
| 5 | 2 | 3 | 1 | 4 | 8 | 9 | 7 | 6 |
| 8 | 9 | 5 | 4 | 6 | 1 | 3 | 2 | 7 |
| 6 | 1 | 7 | 2 | 8 | 3 | 4 | 5 | 9 |
| 3 | 4 | 2 | 5 | 7 | 9 | 6 | 1 | 8 |
| 1 | 3 | 6 | 7 | 9 | 2 | 5 | 8 | 4 |
| 2 | 5 | 4 | 8 | 1 | 6 | 7 | 9 | 3 |
| 7 | 8 | 9 | 3 | 5 | 4 | 2 | 6 | 1 |

**9**

| 6 | 8 | 5 | 4 | 9 | 1 | 7 | 3 | 2 |
|---|---|---|---|---|---|---|---|---|
| 3 | 7 | 9 | 5 | 8 | 2 | 1 | 6 | 4 |
| 2 | 1 | 4 | 6 | 3 | 7 | 9 | 8 | 5 |
| 7 | 3 | 8 | 1 | 6 | 5 | 4 | 2 | 9 |
| 4 | 5 | 2 | 9 | 7 | 3 | 6 | 1 | 8 |
| 1 | 9 | 6 | 2 | 4 | 8 | 5 | 7 | 3 |
| 8 | 4 | 3 | 7 | 5 | 6 | 2 | 9 | 1 |
| 5 | 6 | 1 | 8 | 2 | 9 | 3 | 4 | 7 |
| 9 | 2 | 7 | 3 | 1 | 4 | 8 | 5 | 6 |

**10**

| 7 | 6 | 8 | 4 | 9 | 1 | 5 | 2 | 3 |
|---|---|---|---|---|---|---|---|---|
| 3 | 5 | 1 | 8 | 2 | 7 | 6 | 9 | 4 |
| 2 | 9 | 4 | 5 | 6 | 3 | 7 | 8 | 1 |
| 5 | 7 | 6 | 1 | 4 | 8 | 2 | 3 | 9 |
| 9 | 4 | 2 | 3 | 7 | 6 | 8 | 1 | 5 |
| 8 | 1 | 3 | 2 | 5 | 9 | 4 | 7 | 6 |
| 1 | 2 | 5 | 9 | 8 | 4 | 3 | 6 | 7 |
| 4 | 3 | 7 | 6 | 1 | 2 | 9 | 5 | 8 |
| 6 | 8 | 9 | 7 | 3 | 5 | 1 | 4 | 2 |

**11**

| 7 | 3 | 9 | 2 | 6 | 5 | 4 | 8 | 1 |
|---|---|---|---|---|---|---|---|---|
| 6 | 4 | 8 | 9 | 3 | 1 | 2 | 5 | 7 |
| 5 | 2 | 1 | 8 | 7 | 4 | 9 | 6 | 3 |
| 9 | 7 | 3 | 5 | 4 | 2 | 6 | 1 | 8 |
| 2 | 1 | 6 | 7 | 9 | 8 | 3 | 4 | 5 |
| 8 | 5 | 4 | 3 | 1 | 6 | 7 | 9 | 2 |
| 4 | 8 | 2 | 6 | 5 | 3 | 1 | 7 | 9 |
| 3 | 6 | 7 | 1 | 8 | 9 | 5 | 2 | 4 |
| 1 | 9 | 5 | 4 | 2 | 7 | 8 | 3 | 6 |

**12**

| 9 | 6 | 4 | 7 | 8 | 1 | 3 | 2 | 5 |
|---|---|---|---|---|---|---|---|---|
| 5 | 8 | 3 | 2 | 9 | 4 | 1 | 7 | 6 |
| 1 | 2 | 7 | 3 | 5 | 6 | 4 | 8 | 9 |
| 6 | 9 | 8 | 5 | 1 | 2 | 7 | 3 | 4 |
| 7 | 1 | 5 | 8 | 4 | 3 | 9 | 6 | 2 |
| 3 | 4 | 2 | 6 | 7 | 9 | 8 | 5 | 1 |
| 2 | 3 | 1 | 4 | 6 | 7 | 5 | 9 | 8 |
| 4 | 5 | 6 | 9 | 3 | 8 | 2 | 1 | 7 |
| 8 | 7 | 9 | 1 | 2 | 5 | 6 | 4 | 3 |

**13**

| 9 | 5 | 7 | 4 | 1 | 3 | 8 | 2 | 6 |
|---|---|---|---|---|---|---|---|---|
| 3 | 4 | 2 | 6 | 5 | 8 | 9 | 7 | 1 |
| 1 | 6 | 8 | 7 | 9 | 2 | 5 | 3 | 4 |
| 8 | 2 | 5 | 1 | 7 | 9 | 6 | 4 | 3 |
| 4 | 3 | 1 | 8 | 2 | 6 | 7 | 5 | 9 |
| 6 | 7 | 9 | 5 | 3 | 4 | 1 | 8 | 2 |
| 2 | 9 | 6 | 3 | 8 | 5 | 4 | 1 | 7 |
| 5 | 1 | 4 | 2 | 6 | 7 | 3 | 9 | 8 |
| 7 | 8 | 3 | 9 | 4 | 1 | 2 | 6 | 5 |

**14**

| 7 | 9 | 6 | 1 | 4 | 2 | 3 | 8 | 5 |
|---|---|---|---|---|---|---|---|---|
| 4 | 1 | 3 | 9 | 8 | 5 | 7 | 2 | 6 |
| 8 | 2 | 5 | 7 | 6 | 3 | 4 | 9 | 1 |
| 9 | 8 | 1 | 5 | 2 | 4 | 6 | 7 | 3 |
| 2 | 5 | 4 | 3 | 7 | 6 | 9 | 1 | 8 |
| 6 | 3 | 7 | 8 | 9 | 1 | 2 | 5 | 4 |
| 3 | 7 | 2 | 6 | 5 | 8 | 1 | 4 | 9 |
| 5 | 6 | 9 | 4 | 1 | 7 | 8 | 3 | 2 |
| 1 | 4 | 8 | 2 | 3 | 9 | 5 | 6 | 7 |

**15**

| 3 | 7 | 2 | 8 | 1 | 5 | 6 | 9 | 4 |
|---|---|---|---|---|---|---|---|---|
| 9 | 8 | 4 | 7 | 6 | 2 | 5 | 1 | 3 |
| 1 | 6 | 5 | 9 | 3 | 4 | 2 | 8 | 7 |
| 2 | 4 | 7 | 5 | 8 | 9 | 1 | 3 | 6 |
| 5 | 1 | 8 | 6 | 7 | 3 | 4 | 2 | 9 |
| 6 | 3 | 9 | 2 | 4 | 1 | 7 | 5 | 8 |
| 7 | 9 | 6 | 1 | 5 | 8 | 3 | 4 | 2 |
| 8 | 5 | 3 | 4 | 2 | 6 | 9 | 7 | 1 |
| 4 | 2 | 1 | 3 | 9 | 7 | 8 | 6 | 5 |

**16**

| 4 | 8 | 5 | 6 | 3 | 2 | 7 | 9 | 1 |
|---|---|---|---|---|---|---|---|---|
| 6 | 1 | 2 | 4 | 9 | 7 | 8 | 3 | 5 |
| 3 | 9 | 7 | 1 | 5 | 8 | 6 | 4 | 2 |
| 5 | 4 | 1 | 9 | 2 | 6 | 3 | 8 | 7 |
| 9 | 6 | 8 | 5 | 7 | 3 | 2 | 1 | 4 |
| 7 | 2 | 3 | 8 | 1 | 4 | 9 | 5 | 6 |
| 8 | 3 | 4 | 7 | 6 | 1 | 5 | 2 | 9 |
| 1 | 7 | 9 | 2 | 8 | 5 | 4 | 6 | 3 |
| 2 | 5 | 6 | 3 | 4 | 9 | 1 | 7 | 8 |

**17**

| 5 | 1 | 8 | 3 | 6 | 2 | 7 | 4 | 9 |
|---|---|---|---|---|---|---|---|---|
| 3 | 2 | 4 | 1 | 7 | 9 | 8 | 5 | 6 |
| 7 | 6 | 9 | 4 | 8 | 5 | 2 | 3 | 1 |
| 4 | 8 | 7 | 9 | 5 | 6 | 1 | 2 | 3 |
| 1 | 3 | 6 | 2 | 4 | 7 | 5 | 9 | 8 |
| 2 | 9 | 5 | 8 | 3 | 1 | 6 | 7 | 4 |
| 6 | 5 | 3 | 7 | 9 | 8 | 4 | 1 | 2 |
| 9 | 7 | 2 | 6 | 1 | 4 | 3 | 8 | 5 |
| 8 | 4 | 1 | 5 | 2 | 3 | 9 | 6 | 7 |

**18**

| 1 | 5 | 4 | 2 | 6 | 7 | 9 | 3 | 8 |
|---|---|---|---|---|---|---|---|---|
| 3 | 7 | 9 | 4 | 5 | 8 | 6 | 2 | 1 |
| 2 | 8 | 6 | 1 | 3 | 9 | 7 | 5 | 4 |
| 8 | 2 | 3 | 7 | 9 | 6 | 1 | 4 | 5 |
| 7 | 9 | 5 | 8 | 4 | 1 | 3 | 6 | 2 |
| 6 | 4 | 1 | 5 | 2 | 3 | 8 | 9 | 7 |
| 9 | 1 | 2 | 3 | 8 | 5 | 4 | 7 | 6 |
| 5 | 6 | 8 | 9 | 7 | 4 | 2 | 1 | 3 |
| 4 | 3 | 7 | 6 | 1 | 2 | 5 | 8 | 9 |

**19**

| 3 | 9 | 2 | 5 | 7 | 1 | 4 | 8 | 6 |
|---|---|---|---|---|---|---|---|---|
| 1 | 6 | 5 | 2 | 8 | 4 | 9 | 3 | 7 |
| 8 | 4 | 7 | 3 | 6 | 9 | 5 | 2 | 1 |
| 2 | 3 | 1 | 8 | 4 | 6 | 7 | 5 | 9 |
| 7 | 5 | 6 | 9 | 2 | 3 | 8 | 1 | 4 |
| 9 | 8 | 4 | 7 | 1 | 5 | 3 | 6 | 2 |
| 6 | 1 | 3 | 4 | 9 | 8 | 2 | 7 | 5 |
| 4 | 2 | 8 | 1 | 5 | 7 | 6 | 9 | 3 |
| 5 | 7 | 9 | 6 | 3 | 2 | 1 | 4 | 8 |

**20**

| 2 | 3 | 6 | 7 | 5 | 9 | 1 | 4 | 8 |
|---|---|---|---|---|---|---|---|---|
| 5 | 8 | 7 | 2 | 4 | 1 | 6 | 3 | 9 |
| 9 | 1 | 4 | 3 | 8 | 6 | 2 | 7 | 5 |
| 8 | 4 | 1 | 9 | 6 | 3 | 5 | 2 | 7 |
| 6 | 2 | 5 | 8 | 7 | 4 | 9 | 1 | 3 |
| 7 | 9 | 3 | 5 | 1 | 2 | 8 | 6 | 4 |
| 4 | 5 | 2 | 1 | 3 | 8 | 7 | 9 | 6 |
| 1 | 6 | 8 | 4 | 9 | 7 | 3 | 5 | 2 |
| 3 | 7 | 9 | 6 | 2 | 5 | 4 | 8 | 1 |

**21**

| 5 | 6 | 9 | 2 | 4 | 3 | 7 | 1 | 8 |
|---|---|---|---|---|---|---|---|---|
| 8 | 1 | 3 | 6 | 5 | 7 | 4 | 2 | 9 |
| 4 | 7 | 2 | 1 | 8 | 9 | 5 | 6 | 3 |
| 3 | 2 | 4 | 9 | 6 | 1 | 8 | 5 | 7 |
| 9 | 5 | 7 | 4 | 2 | 8 | 6 | 3 | 1 |
| 1 | 8 | 6 | 7 | 3 | 5 | 9 | 4 | 2 |
| 6 | 3 | 1 | 8 | 7 | 4 | 2 | 9 | 5 |
| 7 | 4 | 5 | 3 | 9 | 2 | 1 | 8 | 6 |
| 2 | 9 | 8 | 5 | 1 | 6 | 3 | 7 | 4 |

**22**

| 7 | 5 | 3 | 4 | 8 | 6 | 1 | 2 | 9 |
|---|---|---|---|---|---|---|---|---|
| 9 | 4 | 1 | 3 | 7 | 2 | 5 | 8 | 6 |
| 6 | 8 | 2 | 9 | 5 | 1 | 4 | 3 | 7 |
| 1 | 9 | 8 | 2 | 6 | 5 | 7 | 4 | 3 |
| 5 | 7 | 6 | 8 | 4 | 3 | 2 | 9 | 1 |
| 2 | 3 | 4 | 1 | 9 | 7 | 6 | 5 | 8 |
| 8 | 6 | 7 | 5 | 3 | 4 | 9 | 1 | 2 |
| 3 | 2 | 5 | 6 | 1 | 9 | 8 | 7 | 4 |
| 4 | 1 | 9 | 7 | 2 | 8 | 3 | 6 | 5 |

**23**

| 6 | 9 | 8 | 3 | 1 | 5 | 2 | 4 | 7 |
|---|---|---|---|---|---|---|---|---|
| 4 | 1 | 7 | 6 | 8 | 2 | 9 | 3 | 5 |
| 5 | 3 | 2 | 7 | 9 | 4 | 8 | 6 | 1 |
| 1 | 2 | 3 | 8 | 6 | 7 | 4 | 5 | 9 |
| 7 | 5 | 9 | 2 | 4 | 1 | 6 | 8 | 3 |
| 8 | 6 | 4 | 5 | 3 | 9 | 1 | 7 | 2 |
| 3 | 8 | 1 | 9 | 7 | 6 | 5 | 2 | 4 |
| 9 | 7 | 5 | 4 | 2 | 8 | 3 | 1 | 6 |
| 2 | 4 | 6 | 1 | 5 | 3 | 7 | 9 | 8 |

**24**

| 6 | 2 | 8 | 4 | 3 | 1 | 7 | 5 | 9 |
|---|---|---|---|---|---|---|---|---|
| 9 | 7 | 5 | 2 | 6 | 8 | 1 | 4 | 3 |
| 4 | 3 | 1 | 7 | 5 | 9 | 2 | 8 | 6 |
| 7 | 4 | 2 | 3 | 1 | 5 | 6 | 9 | 8 |
| 5 | 8 | 9 | 6 | 7 | 2 | 3 | 1 | 4 |
| 3 | 1 | 6 | 8 | 9 | 4 | 5 | 7 | 2 |
| 1 | 5 | 3 | 9 | 8 | 6 | 4 | 2 | 7 |
| 2 | 9 | 7 | 5 | 4 | 3 | 8 | 6 | 1 |
| 8 | 6 | 4 | 1 | 2 | 7 | 9 | 3 | 5 |

**25**

| 8 | 1 | 6 | 3 | 9 | 4 | 5 | 2 | 7 |
|---|---|---|---|---|---|---|---|---|
| 5 | 9 | 4 | 6 | 7 | 2 | 8 | 1 | 3 |
| 7 | 2 | 3 | 1 | 5 | 8 | 6 | 4 | 9 |
| 4 | 7 | 9 | 2 | 6 | 1 | 3 | 5 | 8 |
| 3 | 5 | 8 | 7 | 4 | 9 | 2 | 6 | 1 |
| 1 | 6 | 2 | 5 | 8 | 3 | 7 | 9 | 4 |
| 6 | 3 | 7 | 4 | 1 | 5 | 9 | 8 | 2 |
| 9 | 4 | 5 | 8 | 2 | 7 | 1 | 3 | 6 |
| 2 | 8 | 1 | 9 | 3 | 6 | 4 | 7 | 5 |

**26**

| 2 | 6 | 4 | 7 | 8 | 5 | 1 | 3 | 9 |
|---|---|---|---|---|---|---|---|---|
| 5 | 1 | 7 | 4 | 3 | 9 | 2 | 8 | 6 |
| 9 | 3 | 8 | 1 | 2 | 6 | 4 | 5 | 7 |
| 8 | 7 | 9 | 2 | 4 | 3 | 6 | 1 | 5 |
| 4 | 2 | 6 | 8 | 5 | 1 | 9 | 7 | 3 |
| 1 | 5 | 3 | 9 | 6 | 7 | 8 | 4 | 2 |
| 7 | 4 | 1 | 3 | 9 | 2 | 5 | 6 | 8 |
| 3 | 9 | 5 | 6 | 1 | 8 | 7 | 2 | 4 |
| 6 | 8 | 2 | 5 | 7 | 4 | 3 | 9 | 1 |

**27**

| 7 | 4 | 6 | 5 | 3 | 9 | 8 | 1 | 2 |
|---|---|---|---|---|---|---|---|---|
| 1 | 9 | 3 | 8 | 2 | 6 | 4 | 5 | 7 |
| 2 | 5 | 8 | 1 | 7 | 4 | 3 | 9 | 6 |
| 3 | 2 | 5 | 4 | 8 | 7 | 1 | 6 | 9 |
| 8 | 7 | 1 | 9 | 6 | 2 | 5 | 4 | 3 |
| 4 | 6 | 9 | 3 | 1 | 5 | 7 | 2 | 8 |
| 6 | 3 | 2 | 7 | 5 | 1 | 9 | 8 | 4 |
| 5 | 8 | 4 | 2 | 9 | 3 | 6 | 7 | 1 |
| 9 | 1 | 7 | 6 | 4 | 8 | 2 | 3 | 5 |

**28**

| 7 | 5 | 2 | 3 | 8 | 9 | 4 | 6 | 1 |
|---|---|---|---|---|---|---|---|---|
| 4 | 3 | 9 | 7 | 1 | 6 | 8 | 5 | 2 |
| 6 | 1 | 8 | 5 | 4 | 2 | 9 | 3 | 7 |
| 5 | 8 | 1 | 4 | 9 | 3 | 7 | 2 | 6 |
| 3 | 2 | 7 | 8 | 6 | 1 | 5 | 9 | 4 |
| 9 | 6 | 4 | 2 | 5 | 7 | 1 | 8 | 3 |
| 8 | 9 | 6 | 1 | 2 | 4 | 3 | 7 | 5 |
| 1 | 7 | 5 | 6 | 3 | 8 | 2 | 4 | 9 |
| 2 | 4 | 3 | 9 | 7 | 5 | 6 | 1 | 8 |

**29**

| 3 | 5 | 7 | 6 | 1 | 9 | 8 | 4 | 2 |
|---|---|---|---|---|---|---|---|---|
| 4 | 1 | 8 | 5 | 3 | 2 | 7 | 6 | 9 |
| 6 | 9 | 2 | 8 | 7 | 4 | 1 | 5 | 3 |
| 8 | 4 | 9 | 1 | 5 | 6 | 3 | 2 | 7 |
| 7 | 3 | 6 | 9 | 2 | 8 | 4 | 1 | 5 |
| 5 | 2 | 1 | 7 | 4 | 3 | 9 | 8 | 6 |
| 2 | 6 | 4 | 3 | 9 | 1 | 5 | 7 | 8 |
| 9 | 8 | 5 | 4 | 6 | 7 | 2 | 3 | 1 |
| 1 | 7 | 3 | 2 | 8 | 5 | 6 | 9 | 4 |

**30**

| 4 | 7 | 9 | 5 | 6 | 2 | 1 | 8 | 3 |
|---|---|---|---|---|---|---|---|---|
| 1 | 6 | 2 | 7 | 3 | 8 | 5 | 9 | 4 |
| 5 | 3 | 8 | 1 | 4 | 9 | 6 | 2 | 7 |
| 7 | 8 | 3 | 4 | 9 | 1 | 2 | 5 | 6 |
| 6 | 2 | 4 | 8 | 7 | 5 | 9 | 3 | 1 |
| 9 | 1 | 5 | 6 | 2 | 3 | 7 | 4 | 8 |
| 8 | 5 | 7 | 9 | 1 | 4 | 3 | 6 | 2 |
| 2 | 9 | 6 | 3 | 8 | 7 | 4 | 1 | 5 |
| 3 | 4 | 1 | 2 | 5 | 6 | 8 | 7 | 9 |

**31**

| 9 | 8 | 2 | 3 | 7 | 6 | 5 | 1 | 4 |
|---|---|---|---|---|---|---|---|---|
| 1 | 4 | 3 | 5 | 9 | 2 | 8 | 6 | 7 |
| 6 | 5 | 7 | 4 | 8 | 1 | 3 | 2 | 9 |
| 8 | 7 | 9 | 1 | 6 | 3 | 4 | 5 | 2 |
| 2 | 1 | 5 | 8 | 4 | 7 | 9 | 3 | 6 |
| 4 | 3 | 6 | 2 | 5 | 9 | 7 | 8 | 1 |
| 7 | 2 | 1 | 9 | 3 | 8 | 6 | 4 | 5 |
| 5 | 9 | 8 | 6 | 2 | 4 | 1 | 7 | 3 |
| 3 | 6 | 4 | 7 | 1 | 5 | 2 | 9 | 8 |

**32**

| 6 | 9 | 7 | 2 | 1 | 8 | 3 | 4 | 5 |
|---|---|---|---|---|---|---|---|---|
| 2 | 5 | 8 | 9 | 3 | 4 | 6 | 7 | 1 |
| 3 | 1 | 4 | 7 | 5 | 6 | 8 | 9 | 2 |
| 7 | 4 | 5 | 8 | 9 | 3 | 1 | 2 | 6 |
| 9 | 8 | 6 | 5 | 2 | 1 | 7 | 3 | 4 |
| 1 | 3 | 2 | 6 | 4 | 7 | 5 | 8 | 9 |
| 5 | 2 | 3 | 1 | 8 | 9 | 4 | 6 | 7 |
| 4 | 7 | 9 | 3 | 6 | 5 | 2 | 1 | 8 |
| 8 | 6 | 1 | 4 | 7 | 2 | 9 | 5 | 3 |

**33**

| 5 | 1 | 6 | 3 | 8 | 2 | 4 | 7 | 9 |
|---|---|---|---|---|---|---|---|---|
| 8 | 4 | 7 | 9 | 5 | 6 | 3 | 2 | 1 |
| 2 | 3 | 9 | 1 | 7 | 4 | 6 | 8 | 5 |
| 1 | 5 | 8 | 2 | 9 | 3 | 7 | 4 | 6 |
| 7 | 9 | 2 | 6 | 4 | 8 | 1 | 5 | 3 |
| 4 | 6 | 3 | 7 | 1 | 5 | 2 | 9 | 8 |
| 9 | 8 | 1 | 4 | 6 | 7 | 5 | 3 | 2 |
| 3 | 7 | 5 | 8 | 2 | 1 | 9 | 6 | 4 |
| 6 | 2 | 4 | 5 | 3 | 9 | 8 | 1 | 7 |

**34**

| 3 | 4 | 8 | 2 | 5 | 6 | 1 | 9 | 7 |
|---|---|---|---|---|---|---|---|---|
| 5 | 2 | 6 | 9 | 7 | 1 | 4 | 8 | 3 |
| 1 | 9 | 7 | 4 | 8 | 3 | 6 | 5 | 2 |
| 8 | 1 | 4 | 7 | 2 | 5 | 9 | 3 | 6 |
| 6 | 7 | 5 | 3 | 9 | 8 | 2 | 4 | 1 |
| 2 | 3 | 9 | 6 | 1 | 4 | 5 | 7 | 8 |
| 9 | 5 | 2 | 8 | 6 | 7 | 3 | 1 | 4 |
| 4 | 8 | 1 | 5 | 3 | 2 | 7 | 6 | 9 |
| 7 | 6 | 3 | 1 | 4 | 9 | 8 | 2 | 5 |

**35**

| 8 | 1 | 3 | 4 | 5 | 7 | 2 | 9 | 6 |
|---|---|---|---|---|---|---|---|---|
| 9 | 6 | 5 | 1 | 8 | 2 | 7 | 4 | 3 |
| 4 | 2 | 7 | 9 | 3 | 6 | 8 | 5 | 1 |
| 5 | 7 | 8 | 6 | 9 | 3 | 1 | 2 | 4 |
| 2 | 9 | 6 | 7 | 1 | 4 | 3 | 8 | 5 |
| 3 | 4 | 1 | 8 | 2 | 5 | 9 | 6 | 7 |
| 6 | 8 | 2 | 5 | 7 | 1 | 4 | 3 | 9 |
| 7 | 3 | 4 | 2 | 6 | 9 | 5 | 1 | 8 |
| 1 | 5 | 9 | 3 | 4 | 8 | 6 | 7 | 2 |

**36**

| 6 | 9 | 1 | 5 | 8 | 3 | 2 | 4 | 7 |
|---|---|---|---|---|---|---|---|---|
| 2 | 4 | 8 | 6 | 1 | 7 | 9 | 3 | 5 |
| 7 | 5 | 3 | 2 | 9 | 4 | 6 | 1 | 8 |
| 4 | 3 | 9 | 7 | 5 | 6 | 1 | 8 | 2 |
| 1 | 6 | 7 | 4 | 2 | 8 | 5 | 9 | 3 |
| 8 | 2 | 5 | 9 | 3 | 1 | 7 | 6 | 4 |
| 5 | 7 | 4 | 3 | 6 | 9 | 8 | 2 | 1 |
| 9 | 8 | 2 | 1 | 4 | 5 | 3 | 7 | 6 |
| 3 | 1 | 6 | 8 | 7 | 2 | 4 | 5 | 9 |

**37**

| 8 | 6 | 3 | 1 | 9 | 4 | 2 | 7 | 5 |
|---|---|---|---|---|---|---|---|---|
| 4 | 2 | 1 | 6 | 7 | 5 | 3 | 9 | 8 |
| 5 | 9 | 7 | 8 | 3 | 2 | 6 | 4 | 1 |
| 6 | 7 | 5 | 3 | 1 | 8 | 4 | 2 | 9 |
| 1 | 3 | 4 | 7 | 2 | 9 | 5 | 8 | 6 |
| 9 | 8 | 2 | 5 | 4 | 6 | 1 | 3 | 7 |
| 2 | 5 | 8 | 9 | 6 | 3 | 7 | 1 | 4 |
| 7 | 4 | 6 | 2 | 8 | 1 | 9 | 5 | 3 |
| 3 | 1 | 9 | 4 | 5 | 7 | 8 | 6 | 2 |

**38**

| 6 | 2 | 8 | 3 | 5 | 1 | 7 | 9 | 4 |
|---|---|---|---|---|---|---|---|---|
| 1 | 5 | 7 | 2 | 9 | 4 | 6 | 3 | 8 |
| 4 | 9 | 3 | 6 | 7 | 8 | 5 | 2 | 1 |
| 2 | 7 | 5 | 4 | 3 | 6 | 8 | 1 | 9 |
| 8 | 1 | 6 | 7 | 2 | 9 | 3 | 4 | 5 |
| 9 | 3 | 4 | 8 | 1 | 5 | 2 | 6 | 7 |
| 7 | 6 | 9 | 1 | 8 | 2 | 4 | 5 | 3 |
| 3 | 4 | 1 | 5 | 6 | 7 | 9 | 8 | 2 |
| 5 | 8 | 2 | 9 | 4 | 3 | 1 | 7 | 6 |

**39**

| 5 | 7 | 3 | 9 | 8 | 2 | 6 | 1 | 4 |
|---|---|---|---|---|---|---|---|---|
| 4 | 8 | 9 | 5 | 1 | 6 | 2 | 3 | 7 |
| 6 | 1 | 2 | 7 | 3 | 4 | 5 | 8 | 9 |
| 7 | 6 | 4 | 3 | 5 | 8 | 1 | 9 | 2 |
| 9 | 2 | 8 | 1 | 4 | 7 | 3 | 5 | 6 |
| 1 | 3 | 5 | 6 | 2 | 9 | 7 | 4 | 8 |
| 8 | 5 | 7 | 2 | 9 | 3 | 4 | 6 | 1 |
| 2 | 4 | 1 | 8 | 6 | 5 | 9 | 7 | 3 |
| 3 | 9 | 6 | 4 | 7 | 1 | 8 | 2 | 5 |

**40**

| 5 | 4 | 6 | 7 | 9 | 1 | 8 | 2 | 3 |
|---|---|---|---|---|---|---|---|---|
| 7 | 9 | 1 | 8 | 3 | 2 | 4 | 6 | 5 |
| 3 | 2 | 8 | 4 | 5 | 6 | 1 | 7 | 9 |
| 9 | 6 | 3 | 2 | 4 | 7 | 5 | 8 | 1 |
| 8 | 7 | 4 | 5 | 1 | 3 | 6 | 9 | 2 |
| 2 | 1 | 5 | 6 | 8 | 9 | 7 | 3 | 4 |
| 6 | 3 | 7 | 1 | 2 | 4 | 9 | 5 | 8 |
| 1 | 8 | 9 | 3 | 7 | 5 | 2 | 4 | 6 |
| 4 | 5 | 2 | 9 | 6 | 8 | 3 | 1 | 7 |

**4/1**

| | | | | | | | | |
|---|---|---|---|---|---|---|---|---|
| 3 | 4 | 1 | 6 | 8 | 2 | 7 | 5 | 9 |
| 5 | 9 | 2 | 1 | 7 | 3 | 4 | 6 | 8 |
| 7 | 8 | 6 | 5 | 9 | 4 | 1 | 2 | 3 |
| 1 | 6 | 7 | 9 | 3 | 8 | 2 | 4 | 5 |
| 4 | 3 | 9 | 7 | 2 | 5 | 6 | 8 | 1 |
| 8 | 2 | 5 | 4 | 6 | 1 | 3 | 9 | 7 |
| 6 | 5 | 8 | 3 | 4 | 7 | 9 | 1 | 2 |
| 9 | 1 | 3 | 2 | 5 | 6 | 8 | 7 | 4 |
| 2 | 7 | 4 | 8 | 1 | 9 | 5 | 3 | 6 |

**4/2**

| | | | | | | | | |
|---|---|---|---|---|---|---|---|---|
| 5 | 9 | 8 | 3 | 7 | 2 | 1 | 4 | 6 |
| 1 | 7 | 3 | 9 | 4 | 6 | 2 | 8 | 5 |
| 6 | 2 | 4 | 8 | 1 | 5 | 3 | 7 | 9 |
| 3 | 6 | 9 | 7 | 8 | 1 | 4 | 5 | 2 |
| 8 | 1 | 2 | 5 | 3 | 4 | 9 | 6 | 7 |
| 7 | 4 | 5 | 6 | 2 | 9 | 8 | 1 | 3 |
| 2 | 5 | 6 | 4 | 9 | 8 | 7 | 3 | 1 |
| 4 | 3 | 1 | 2 | 5 | 7 | 6 | 9 | 8 |
| 9 | 8 | 7 | 1 | 6 | 3 | 5 | 2 | 4 |

**4/3**

| | | | | | | | | |
|---|---|---|---|---|---|---|---|---|
| 6 | 7 | 1 | 3 | 8 | 5 | 4 | 9 | 2 |
| 5 | 9 | 3 | 6 | 2 | 4 | 1 | 8 | 7 |
| 4 | 8 | 2 | 1 | 7 | 9 | 5 | 3 | 6 |
| 2 | 3 | 4 | 8 | 9 | 7 | 6 | 5 | 1 |
| 1 | 6 | 7 | 2 | 5 | 3 | 8 | 4 | 9 |
| 8 | 5 | 9 | 4 | 1 | 6 | 2 | 7 | 3 |
| 3 | 2 | 8 | 9 | 4 | 1 | 7 | 6 | 5 |
| 7 | 4 | 6 | 5 | 3 | 2 | 9 | 1 | 8 |
| 9 | 1 | 5 | 7 | 6 | 8 | 3 | 2 | 4 |

**4/4**

| | | | | | | | | |
|---|---|---|---|---|---|---|---|---|
| 9 | 4 | 6 | 7 | 1 | 8 | 2 | 5 | 3 |
| 1 | 8 | 5 | 9 | 2 | 3 | 4 | 7 | 6 |
| 3 | 7 | 2 | 4 | 5 | 6 | 1 | 8 | 9 |
| 4 | 5 | 3 | 6 | 8 | 2 | 7 | 9 | 1 |
| 7 | 6 | 9 | 1 | 4 | 5 | 3 | 2 | 8 |
| 2 | 1 | 8 | 3 | 7 | 9 | 6 | 4 | 5 |
| 6 | 3 | 7 | 5 | 9 | 4 | 8 | 1 | 2 |
| 8 | 9 | 4 | 2 | 6 | 1 | 5 | 3 | 7 |
| 5 | 2 | 1 | 8 | 3 | 7 | 9 | 6 | 4 |

**4/5**

| | | | | | | | | |
|---|---|---|---|---|---|---|---|---|
| 2 | 4 | 1 | 7 | 8 | 3 | 5 | 6 | 9 |
| 9 | 8 | 3 | 1 | 5 | 6 | 2 | 4 | 7 |
| 5 | 7 | 6 | 9 | 4 | 2 | 1 | 3 | 8 |
| 3 | 2 | 7 | 5 | 6 | 8 | 9 | 1 | 4 |
| 4 | 5 | 9 | 3 | 7 | 1 | 6 | 8 | 2 |
| 6 | 1 | 8 | 4 | 2 | 9 | 7 | 5 | 3 |
| 1 | 6 | 2 | 8 | 3 | 7 | 4 | 9 | 5 |
| 7 | 3 | 5 | 6 | 9 | 4 | 8 | 2 | 1 |
| 8 | 9 | 4 | 2 | 1 | 5 | 3 | 7 | 6 |

**4/6**

| | | | | | | | | |
|---|---|---|---|---|---|---|---|---|
| 2 | 1 | 7 | 3 | 4 | 5 | 9 | 6 | 8 |
| 9 | 8 | 4 | 2 | 7 | 6 | 3 | 5 | 1 |
| 5 | 3 | 6 | 8 | 9 | 1 | 4 | 2 | 7 |
| 6 | 2 | 9 | 1 | 5 | 8 | 7 | 3 | 4 |
| 8 | 4 | 3 | 9 | 6 | 7 | 5 | 1 | 2 |
| 1 | 7 | 5 | 4 | 3 | 2 | 6 | 8 | 9 |
| 4 | 5 | 2 | 7 | 1 | 3 | 8 | 9 | 6 |
| 7 | 6 | 1 | 5 | 8 | 9 | 2 | 4 | 3 |
| 3 | 9 | 8 | 6 | 2 | 4 | 1 | 7 | 5 |

**4/7**

| | | | | | | | | |
|---|---|---|---|---|---|---|---|---|
| 6 | 9 | 2 | 5 | 3 | 7 | 4 | 8 | 1 |
| 3 | 8 | 1 | 4 | 9 | 6 | 5 | 7 | 2 |
| 4 | 7 | 5 | 8 | 1 | 2 | 9 | 3 | 6 |
| 2 | 3 | 7 | 9 | 8 | 5 | 1 | 6 | 4 |
| 9 | 6 | 4 | 1 | 7 | 3 | 2 | 5 | 8 |
| 1 | 5 | 8 | 6 | 2 | 4 | 7 | 9 | 3 |
| 5 | 4 | 9 | 2 | 6 | 8 | 3 | 1 | 7 |
| 8 | 2 | 3 | 7 | 5 | 1 | 6 | 4 | 9 |
| 7 | 1 | 6 | 3 | 4 | 9 | 8 | 2 | 5 |

**4/8**

| | | | | | | | | |
|---|---|---|---|---|---|---|---|---|
| 2 | 3 | 8 | 4 | 1 | 7 | 5 | 6 | 9 |
| 9 | 7 | 5 | 3 | 8 | 6 | 4 | 2 | 1 |
| 6 | 1 | 4 | 5 | 9 | 2 | 7 | 3 | 8 |
| 8 | 6 | 7 | 9 | 5 | 3 | 2 | 1 | 4 |
| 3 | 9 | 2 | 1 | 6 | 4 | 8 | 5 | 7 |
| 4 | 5 | 1 | 2 | 7 | 8 | 6 | 9 | 3 |
| 1 | 4 | 3 | 7 | 2 | 5 | 9 | 8 | 6 |
| 7 | 2 | 6 | 8 | 3 | 9 | 1 | 4 | 5 |
| 5 | 8 | 9 | 6 | 4 | 1 | 3 | 7 | 2 |

**49**

| 1 | 4 | 9 | 7 | 6 | 2 | 3 | 8 | 5 |
|---|---|---|---|---|---|---|---|---|
| 7 | 3 | 8 | 5 | 9 | 1 | 4 | 6 | 2 |
| 5 | 6 | 2 | 3 | 8 | 4 | 1 | 7 | 9 |
| 9 | 2 | 7 | 4 | 3 | 8 | 6 | 5 | 1 |
| 3 | 1 | 6 | 9 | 2 | 5 | 8 | 4 | 7 |
| 4 | 8 | 5 | 6 | 1 | 7 | 9 | 2 | 3 |
| 6 | 9 | 4 | 2 | 5 | 3 | 7 | 1 | 8 |
| 8 | 5 | 3 | 1 | 7 | 6 | 2 | 9 | 4 |
| 2 | 7 | 1 | 8 | 4 | 9 | 5 | 3 | 6 |

**50**

| 3 | 5 | 6 | 2 | 9 | 7 | 1 | 8 | 4 |
|---|---|---|---|---|---|---|---|---|
| 9 | 8 | 7 | 6 | 1 | 4 | 2 | 5 | 3 |
| 4 | 1 | 2 | 5 | 8 | 3 | 6 | 7 | 9 |
| 5 | 9 | 4 | 8 | 6 | 1 | 7 | 3 | 2 |
| 8 | 2 | 3 | 9 | 7 | 5 | 4 | 6 | 1 |
| 7 | 6 | 1 | 3 | 4 | 2 | 5 | 9 | 8 |
| 6 | 4 | 9 | 1 | 5 | 8 | 3 | 2 | 7 |
| 2 | 7 | 8 | 4 | 3 | 6 | 9 | 1 | 5 |
| 1 | 3 | 5 | 7 | 2 | 9 | 8 | 4 | 6 |

**51**

| 4 | 8 | 7 | 5 | 2 | 6 | 3 | 9 | 1 |
|---|---|---|---|---|---|---|---|---|
| 5 | 2 | 9 | 1 | 3 | 4 | 7 | 6 | 8 |
| 3 | 1 | 6 | 9 | 7 | 8 | 4 | 5 | 2 |
| 7 | 6 | 8 | 3 | 5 | 2 | 1 | 4 | 9 |
| 2 | 4 | 5 | 8 | 9 | 1 | 6 | 3 | 7 |
| 1 | 9 | 3 | 6 | 4 | 7 | 8 | 2 | 5 |
| 6 | 3 | 2 | 7 | 1 | 9 | 5 | 8 | 4 |
| 9 | 5 | 1 | 4 | 8 | 3 | 2 | 7 | 6 |
| 8 | 7 | 4 | 2 | 6 | 5 | 9 | 1 | 3 |

**52**

| 6 | 5 | 2 | 1 | 3 | 4 | 8 | 9 | 7 |
|---|---|---|---|---|---|---|---|---|
| 8 | 3 | 1 | 5 | 9 | 7 | 4 | 6 | 2 |
| 9 | 7 | 4 | 6 | 2 | 8 | 1 | 5 | 3 |
| 1 | 9 | 7 | 8 | 4 | 2 | 5 | 3 | 6 |
| 3 | 8 | 5 | 7 | 6 | 9 | 2 | 1 | 4 |
| 2 | 4 | 6 | 3 | 1 | 5 | 7 | 8 | 9 |
| 5 | 6 | 9 | 2 | 7 | 1 | 3 | 4 | 8 |
| 4 | 2 | 8 | 9 | 5 | 3 | 6 | 7 | 1 |
| 7 | 1 | 3 | 4 | 8 | 6 | 9 | 2 | 5 |

**53**

| 4 | 7 | 2 | 9 | 8 | 1 | 5 | 6 | 3 |
|---|---|---|---|---|---|---|---|---|
| 6 | 8 | 3 | 5 | 4 | 7 | 2 | 1 | 9 |
| 9 | 5 | 1 | 6 | 3 | 2 | 8 | 7 | 4 |
| 8 | 9 | 4 | 2 | 6 | 3 | 7 | 5 | 1 |
| 5 | 2 | 6 | 1 | 7 | 4 | 9 | 3 | 8 |
| 1 | 3 | 7 | 8 | 5 | 9 | 6 | 4 | 2 |
| 3 | 1 | 9 | 7 | 2 | 6 | 4 | 8 | 5 |
| 2 | 6 | 8 | 4 | 1 | 5 | 3 | 9 | 7 |
| 7 | 4 | 5 | 3 | 9 | 8 | 1 | 2 | 6 |

**54**

| 1 | 3 | 8 | 2 | 9 | 4 | 6 | 5 | 7 |
|---|---|---|---|---|---|---|---|---|
| 6 | 9 | 5 | 3 | 7 | 8 | 1 | 2 | 4 |
| 4 | 2 | 7 | 5 | 1 | 6 | 3 | 9 | 8 |
| 7 | 1 | 6 | 9 | 8 | 3 | 2 | 4 | 5 |
| 8 | 5 | 2 | 4 | 6 | 7 | 9 | 3 | 1 |
| 3 | 4 | 9 | 1 | 2 | 5 | 8 | 7 | 6 |
| 5 | 6 | 4 | 8 | 3 | 2 | 7 | 1 | 9 |
| 9 | 7 | 3 | 6 | 5 | 1 | 4 | 8 | 2 |
| 2 | 8 | 1 | 7 | 4 | 9 | 5 | 6 | 3 |

**55**

| 1 | 6 | 4 | 7 | 2 | 3 | 9 | 8 | 5 |
|---|---|---|---|---|---|---|---|---|
| 2 | 8 | 3 | 5 | 4 | 9 | 1 | 7 | 6 |
| 7 | 9 | 5 | 6 | 1 | 8 | 3 | 2 | 4 |
| 9 | 2 | 1 | 8 | 3 | 5 | 4 | 6 | 7 |
| 8 | 5 | 6 | 4 | 9 | 7 | 2 | 1 | 3 |
| 4 | 3 | 7 | 1 | 6 | 2 | 5 | 9 | 8 |
| 6 | 7 | 2 | 9 | 5 | 4 | 8 | 3 | 1 |
| 3 | 4 | 8 | 2 | 7 | 1 | 6 | 5 | 9 |
| 5 | 1 | 9 | 3 | 8 | 6 | 7 | 4 | 2 |

**56**

| 3 | 7 | 4 | 5 | 9 | 8 | 1 | 2 | 6 |
|---|---|---|---|---|---|---|---|---|
| 8 | 9 | 2 | 3 | 6 | 1 | 4 | 5 | 7 |
| 1 | 6 | 5 | 2 | 4 | 7 | 9 | 8 | 3 |
| 6 | 5 | 3 | 9 | 8 | 4 | 2 | 7 | 1 |
| 9 | 1 | 8 | 6 | 7 | 2 | 3 | 4 | 5 |
| 2 | 4 | 7 | 1 | 5 | 3 | 8 | 6 | 9 |
| 4 | 8 | 9 | 7 | 3 | 5 | 6 | 1 | 2 |
| 5 | 3 | 1 | 8 | 2 | 6 | 7 | 9 | 4 |
| 7 | 2 | 6 | 4 | 1 | 9 | 5 | 3 | 8 |

## 5/7

| 8 | 3 | 2 | 6 | 9 | 4 | 1 | 7 | 5 |
|---|---|---|---|---|---|---|---|---|
| 1 | 4 | 7 | 5 | 2 | 8 | 6 | 9 | 3 |
| 6 | 5 | 9 | 7 | 3 | 1 | 4 | 8 | 2 |
| 7 | 2 | 3 | 9 | 6 | 5 | 8 | 1 | 4 |
| 9 | 1 | 6 | 4 | 8 | 3 | 2 | 5 | 7 |
| 4 | 8 | 5 | 2 | 1 | 7 | 3 | 6 | 9 |
| 5 | 7 | 1 | 8 | 4 | 2 | 9 | 3 | 6 |
| 3 | 9 | 4 | 1 | 7 | 6 | 5 | 2 | 8 |
| 2 | 6 | 8 | 3 | 5 | 9 | 7 | 4 | 1 |

## 5/8

| 9 | 8 | 2 | 5 | 7 | 4 | 1 | 3 | 6 |
|---|---|---|---|---|---|---|---|---|
| 1 | 7 | 6 | 8 | 3 | 9 | 4 | 2 | 5 |
| 5 | 4 | 3 | 6 | 2 | 1 | 9 | 8 | 7 |
| 3 | 9 | 7 | 2 | 1 | 5 | 8 | 6 | 4 |
| 2 | 6 | 5 | 4 | 8 | 3 | 7 | 9 | 1 |
| 8 | 1 | 4 | 9 | 6 | 7 | 3 | 5 | 2 |
| 4 | 3 | 9 | 7 | 5 | 6 | 2 | 1 | 8 |
| 7 | 5 | 8 | 1 | 9 | 2 | 6 | 4 | 3 |
| 6 | 2 | 1 | 3 | 4 | 8 | 5 | 7 | 9 |

## 5/9

| 8 | 7 | 4 | 3 | 1 | 6 | 2 | 9 | 5 |
|---|---|---|---|---|---|---|---|---|
| 9 | 2 | 1 | 5 | 7 | 4 | 3 | 8 | 6 |
| 6 | 5 | 3 | 9 | 2 | 8 | 4 | 1 | 7 |
| 1 | 4 | 2 | 6 | 3 | 7 | 8 | 5 | 9 |
| 5 | 3 | 9 | 1 | 8 | 2 | 7 | 6 | 4 |
| 7 | 6 | 8 | 4 | 5 | 9 | 1 | 3 | 2 |
| 2 | 1 | 6 | 8 | 4 | 5 | 9 | 7 | 3 |
| 3 | 9 | 7 | 2 | 6 | 1 | 5 | 4 | 8 |
| 4 | 8 | 5 | 7 | 9 | 3 | 6 | 2 | 1 |

## 6/0

| 4 | 2 | 9 | 3 | 5 | 8 | 6 | 1 | 7 |
|---|---|---|---|---|---|---|---|---|
| 6 | 3 | 5 | 9 | 1 | 7 | 2 | 4 | 8 |
| 1 | 8 | 7 | 2 | 6 | 4 | 5 | 3 | 9 |
| 3 | 7 | 6 | 1 | 2 | 9 | 4 | 8 | 5 |
| 9 | 5 | 8 | 7 | 4 | 3 | 1 | 2 | 6 |
| 2 | 4 | 1 | 5 | 8 | 6 | 7 | 9 | 3 |
| 7 | 9 | 4 | 6 | 3 | 2 | 8 | 5 | 1 |
| 8 | 1 | 3 | 4 | 7 | 5 | 9 | 6 | 2 |
| 5 | 6 | 2 | 8 | 9 | 1 | 3 | 7 | 4 |

## 6/1

| 8 | 2 | 7 | 5 | 9 | 3 | 4 | 6 | 1 |
|---|---|---|---|---|---|---|---|---|
| 1 | 9 | 4 | 6 | 2 | 7 | 5 | 3 | 8 |
| 6 | 5 | 3 | 8 | 1 | 4 | 7 | 2 | 9 |
| 3 | 6 | 5 | 1 | 7 | 8 | 9 | 4 | 2 |
| 7 | 8 | 9 | 2 | 4 | 5 | 3 | 1 | 6 |
| 2 | 4 | 1 | 9 | 3 | 6 | 8 | 7 | 5 |
| 5 | 3 | 2 | 4 | 6 | 9 | 1 | 8 | 7 |
| 9 | 7 | 6 | 3 | 8 | 1 | 2 | 5 | 4 |
| 4 | 1 | 8 | 7 | 5 | 2 | 6 | 9 | 3 |

## 6/2

| 3 | 6 | 1 | 9 | 5 | 2 | 8 | 7 | 4 |
|---|---|---|---|---|---|---|---|---|
| 5 | 2 | 9 | 4 | 7 | 8 | 1 | 3 | 6 |
| 4 | 7 | 8 | 6 | 1 | 3 | 5 | 2 | 9 |
| 1 | 5 | 4 | 7 | 6 | 9 | 2 | 8 | 3 |
| 8 | 9 | 7 | 3 | 2 | 4 | 6 | 1 | 5 |
| 2 | 3 | 6 | 5 | 8 | 1 | 9 | 4 | 7 |
| 7 | 8 | 3 | 1 | 9 | 6 | 4 | 5 | 2 |
| 6 | 4 | 2 | 8 | 3 | 5 | 7 | 9 | 1 |
| 9 | 1 | 5 | 2 | 4 | 7 | 3 | 6 | 8 |

## 6/3

| 5 | 1 | 7 | 2 | 8 | 3 | 6 | 9 | 4 |
|---|---|---|---|---|---|---|---|---|
| 4 | 6 | 8 | 7 | 1 | 9 | 3 | 5 | 2 |
| 9 | 2 | 3 | 4 | 5 | 6 | 1 | 8 | 7 |
| 7 | 3 | 5 | 6 | 9 | 8 | 2 | 4 | 1 |
| 6 | 4 | 9 | 1 | 2 | 7 | 5 | 3 | 8 |
| 2 | 8 | 1 | 3 | 4 | 5 | 9 | 7 | 6 |
| 3 | 7 | 4 | 9 | 6 | 1 | 8 | 2 | 5 |
| 1 | 5 | 2 | 8 | 3 | 4 | 7 | 6 | 9 |
| 8 | 9 | 6 | 5 | 7 | 2 | 4 | 1 | 3 |

## 6/4

| 3 | 2 | 1 | 9 | 7 | 5 | 6 | 4 | 8 |
|---|---|---|---|---|---|---|---|---|
| 5 | 4 | 8 | 2 | 1 | 6 | 9 | 3 | 7 |
| 9 | 7 | 6 | 8 | 4 | 3 | 1 | 2 | 5 |
| 4 | 9 | 5 | 6 | 8 | 2 | 7 | 1 | 3 |
| 1 | 3 | 7 | 5 | 9 | 4 | 2 | 8 | 6 |
| 8 | 6 | 2 | 1 | 3 | 7 | 4 | 5 | 9 |
| 2 | 1 | 9 | 3 | 6 | 8 | 5 | 7 | 4 |
| 6 | 8 | 4 | 7 | 5 | 1 | 3 | 9 | 2 |
| 7 | 5 | 3 | 4 | 2 | 9 | 8 | 6 | 1 |

## 6/5

| 5 | 4 | 9 | 8 | 1 | 6 | 2 | 7 | 3 |
|---|---|---|---|---|---|---|---|---|
| 6 | 7 | 8 | 9 | 3 | 2 | 1 | 4 | 5 |
| 1 | 3 | 2 | 7 | 5 | 4 | 8 | 9 | 6 |
| 3 | 9 | 5 | 1 | 4 | 8 | 6 | 2 | 7 |
| 8 | 2 | 7 | 6 | 9 | 5 | 4 | 3 | 1 |
| 4 | 6 | 1 | 2 | 7 | 3 | 9 | 5 | 8 |
| 9 | 8 | 6 | 5 | 2 | 7 | 3 | 1 | 4 |
| 7 | 1 | 3 | 4 | 6 | 9 | 5 | 8 | 2 |
| 2 | 5 | 4 | 3 | 8 | 1 | 7 | 6 | 9 |

## 6/6

| 2 | 4 | 3 | 5 | 8 | 1 | 6 | 7 | 9 |
|---|---|---|---|---|---|---|---|---|
| 1 | 8 | 9 | 2 | 7 | 6 | 3 | 5 | 4 |
| 6 | 5 | 7 | 9 | 4 | 3 | 1 | 2 | 8 |
| 7 | 9 | 4 | 8 | 6 | 5 | 2 | 3 | 1 |
| 3 | 2 | 1 | 4 | 9 | 7 | 8 | 6 | 5 |
| 8 | 6 | 5 | 1 | 3 | 2 | 4 | 9 | 7 |
| 9 | 3 | 8 | 6 | 5 | 4 | 7 | 1 | 2 |
| 5 | 7 | 2 | 3 | 1 | 8 | 9 | 4 | 6 |
| 4 | 1 | 6 | 7 | 2 | 9 | 5 | 8 | 3 |

## 6/7

| 6 | 1 | 7 | 3 | 8 | 5 | 4 | 9 | 2 |
|---|---|---|---|---|---|---|---|---|
| 3 | 4 | 5 | 2 | 6 | 9 | 1 | 7 | 8 |
| 8 | 9 | 2 | 7 | 1 | 4 | 3 | 6 | 5 |
| 5 | 2 | 9 | 6 | 7 | 3 | 8 | 1 | 4 |
| 1 | 6 | 3 | 8 | 4 | 2 | 9 | 5 | 7 |
| 4 | 7 | 8 | 5 | 9 | 1 | 2 | 3 | 6 |
| 2 | 5 | 4 | 1 | 3 | 6 | 7 | 8 | 9 |
| 9 | 8 | 1 | 4 | 5 | 7 | 6 | 2 | 3 |
| 7 | 3 | 6 | 9 | 2 | 8 | 5 | 4 | 1 |

## 6/8

| 3 | 8 | 9 | 1 | 2 | 5 | 4 | 6 | 7 |
|---|---|---|---|---|---|---|---|---|
| 7 | 6 | 1 | 8 | 3 | 4 | 9 | 5 | 2 |
| 5 | 4 | 2 | 7 | 9 | 6 | 1 | 8 | 3 |
| 2 | 7 | 8 | 5 | 6 | 1 | 3 | 9 | 4 |
| 1 | 3 | 5 | 2 | 4 | 9 | 6 | 7 | 8 |
| 4 | 9 | 6 | 3 | 8 | 7 | 5 | 2 | 1 |
| 9 | 5 | 7 | 4 | 1 | 8 | 2 | 3 | 6 |
| 8 | 1 | 3 | 6 | 5 | 2 | 7 | 4 | 9 |
| 6 | 2 | 4 | 9 | 7 | 3 | 8 | 1 | 5 |

## 6/9

| 7 | 1 | 3 | 5 | 6 | 4 | 9 | 8 | 2 |
|---|---|---|---|---|---|---|---|---|
| 9 | 8 | 2 | 1 | 7 | 3 | 4 | 6 | 5 |
| 4 | 6 | 5 | 8 | 2 | 9 | 3 | 7 | 1 |
| 2 | 3 | 8 | 4 | 5 | 1 | 7 | 9 | 6 |
| 6 | 9 | 4 | 7 | 8 | 2 | 1 | 5 | 3 |
| 5 | 7 | 1 | 3 | 9 | 6 | 2 | 4 | 8 |
| 3 | 5 | 9 | 2 | 4 | 8 | 6 | 1 | 7 |
| 8 | 2 | 6 | 9 | 1 | 7 | 5 | 3 | 4 |
| 1 | 4 | 7 | 6 | 3 | 5 | 8 | 2 | 9 |

## 7/0

| 1 | 9 | 8 | 7 | 5 | 2 | 3 | 6 | 4 |
|---|---|---|---|---|---|---|---|---|
| 5 | 3 | 6 | 8 | 9 | 4 | 1 | 2 | 7 |
| 2 | 7 | 4 | 6 | 1 | 3 | 8 | 9 | 5 |
| 7 | 6 | 3 | 5 | 8 | 1 | 2 | 4 | 9 |
| 4 | 1 | 9 | 3 | 2 | 6 | 7 | 5 | 8 |
| 8 | 5 | 2 | 9 | 4 | 7 | 6 | 3 | 1 |
| 6 | 2 | 5 | 4 | 7 | 8 | 9 | 1 | 3 |
| 9 | 8 | 1 | 2 | 3 | 5 | 4 | 7 | 6 |
| 3 | 4 | 7 | 1 | 6 | 9 | 5 | 8 | 2 |

## 7/1

| 5 | 3 | 9 | 7 | 4 | 2 | 1 | 8 | 6 |
|---|---|---|---|---|---|---|---|---|
| 2 | 6 | 1 | 3 | 5 | 8 | 9 | 7 | 4 |
| 8 | 4 | 7 | 6 | 9 | 1 | 2 | 3 | 5 |
| 7 | 9 | 6 | 4 | 8 | 5 | 3 | 1 | 2 |
| 4 | 1 | 5 | 9 | 2 | 3 | 8 | 6 | 7 |
| 3 | 2 | 8 | 1 | 7 | 6 | 4 | 5 | 9 |
| 1 | 5 | 4 | 8 | 6 | 9 | 7 | 2 | 3 |
| 6 | 7 | 3 | 2 | 1 | 4 | 5 | 9 | 8 |
| 9 | 8 | 2 | 5 | 3 | 7 | 6 | 4 | 1 |

## 7/2

| 8 | 5 | 7 | 1 | 4 | 3 | 2 | 9 | 6 |
|---|---|---|---|---|---|---|---|---|
| 1 | 2 | 4 | 5 | 9 | 6 | 3 | 8 | 7 |
| 6 | 3 | 9 | 7 | 8 | 2 | 5 | 1 | 4 |
| 4 | 9 | 2 | 6 | 3 | 7 | 8 | 5 | 1 |
| 3 | 1 | 6 | 8 | 2 | 5 | 4 | 7 | 9 |
| 7 | 8 | 5 | 4 | 1 | 9 | 6 | 2 | 3 |
| 2 | 7 | 3 | 9 | 5 | 4 | 1 | 6 | 8 |
| 9 | 4 | 8 | 2 | 6 | 1 | 7 | 3 | 5 |
| 5 | 6 | 1 | 3 | 7 | 8 | 9 | 4 | 2 |

**73**

| 6 | 9 | 2 | 1 | 3 | 4 | 8 | 7 | 5 |
|---|---|---|---|---|---|---|---|---|
| 4 | 7 | 1 | 8 | 9 | 5 | 2 | 6 | 3 |
| 3 | 8 | 5 | 7 | 6 | 2 | 4 | 9 | 1 |
| 9 | 6 | 4 | 5 | 2 | 3 | 1 | 8 | 7 |
| 8 | 5 | 3 | 9 | 1 | 7 | 6 | 2 | 4 |
| 2 | 1 | 7 | 4 | 8 | 6 | 5 | 3 | 9 |
| 7 | 3 | 6 | 2 | 5 | 1 | 9 | 4 | 8 |
| 5 | 4 | 8 | 6 | 7 | 9 | 3 | 1 | 2 |
| 1 | 2 | 9 | 3 | 4 | 8 | 7 | 5 | 6 |

**74**

| 4 | 7 | 6 | 2 | 3 | 8 | 9 | 5 | 1 |
|---|---|---|---|---|---|---|---|---|
| 9 | 8 | 3 | 5 | 4 | 1 | 7 | 2 | 6 |
| 2 | 1 | 5 | 7 | 9 | 6 | 3 | 8 | 4 |
| 6 | 5 | 2 | 9 | 8 | 7 | 1 | 4 | 3 |
| 3 | 4 | 8 | 6 | 1 | 5 | 2 | 7 | 9 |
| 7 | 9 | 1 | 3 | 2 | 4 | 5 | 6 | 8 |
| 5 | 3 | 9 | 4 | 6 | 2 | 8 | 1 | 7 |
| 8 | 6 | 7 | 1 | 5 | 9 | 4 | 3 | 2 |
| 1 | 2 | 4 | 8 | 7 | 3 | 6 | 9 | 5 |

**75**

| 7 | 2 | 8 | 9 | 5 | 1 | 3 | 6 | 4 |
|---|---|---|---|---|---|---|---|---|
| 9 | 6 | 5 | 7 | 3 | 4 | 1 | 8 | 2 |
| 4 | 3 | 1 | 2 | 6 | 8 | 5 | 9 | 7 |
| 3 | 5 | 6 | 8 | 2 | 7 | 4 | 1 | 9 |
| 1 | 4 | 2 | 5 | 9 | 6 | 8 | 7 | 3 |
| 8 | 9 | 7 | 1 | 4 | 3 | 2 | 5 | 6 |
| 2 | 1 | 4 | 6 | 7 | 5 | 9 | 3 | 8 |
| 6 | 8 | 3 | 4 | 1 | 9 | 7 | 2 | 5 |
| 5 | 7 | 9 | 3 | 8 | 2 | 6 | 4 | 1 |

**76**

| 7 | 9 | 6 | 8 | 3 | 5 | 4 | 1 | 2 |
|---|---|---|---|---|---|---|---|---|
| 8 | 2 | 3 | 4 | 6 | 1 | 5 | 9 | 7 |
| 4 | 1 | 5 | 9 | 2 | 7 | 8 | 6 | 3 |
| 3 | 5 | 1 | 6 | 8 | 4 | 7 | 2 | 9 |
| 6 | 7 | 9 | 1 | 5 | 2 | 3 | 8 | 4 |
| 2 | 4 | 8 | 7 | 9 | 3 | 1 | 5 | 6 |
| 9 | 3 | 4 | 2 | 1 | 8 | 6 | 7 | 5 |
| 1 | 6 | 7 | 5 | 4 | 9 | 2 | 3 | 8 |
| 5 | 8 | 2 | 3 | 7 | 6 | 9 | 4 | 1 |

**77**

| 6 | 4 | 9 | 7 | 1 | 5 | 3 | 8 | 2 |
|---|---|---|---|---|---|---|---|---|
| 2 | 8 | 5 | 9 | 4 | 3 | 1 | 7 | 6 |
| 7 | 3 | 1 | 6 | 2 | 8 | 5 | 9 | 4 |
| 5 | 6 | 7 | 1 | 8 | 2 | 4 | 3 | 9 |
| 8 | 9 | 4 | 5 | 3 | 6 | 2 | 1 | 7 |
| 3 | 1 | 2 | 4 | 7 | 9 | 6 | 5 | 8 |
| 4 | 7 | 3 | 2 | 9 | 1 | 8 | 6 | 5 |
| 1 | 2 | 6 | 8 | 5 | 7 | 9 | 4 | 3 |
| 9 | 5 | 8 | 3 | 6 | 4 | 7 | 2 | 1 |

**78**

| 1 | 2 | 7 | 3 | 9 | 4 | 6 | 5 | 8 |
|---|---|---|---|---|---|---|---|---|
| 5 | 4 | 9 | 7 | 6 | 8 | 2 | 3 | 1 |
| 3 | 6 | 8 | 5 | 2 | 1 | 7 | 9 | 4 |
| 7 | 9 | 3 | 2 | 8 | 5 | 4 | 1 | 6 |
| 4 | 8 | 6 | 9 | 1 | 7 | 5 | 2 | 3 |
| 2 | 5 | 1 | 6 | 4 | 3 | 8 | 7 | 9 |
| 8 | 1 | 2 | 4 | 5 | 9 | 3 | 6 | 7 |
| 6 | 7 | 4 | 1 | 3 | 2 | 9 | 8 | 5 |
| 9 | 3 | 5 | 8 | 7 | 6 | 1 | 4 | 2 |

**79**

| 2 | 1 | 9 | 6 | 3 | 7 | 8 | 4 | 5 |
|---|---|---|---|---|---|---|---|---|
| 6 | 4 | 8 | 2 | 9 | 5 | 3 | 1 | 7 |
| 5 | 7 | 3 | 8 | 4 | 1 | 9 | 2 | 6 |
| 3 | 8 | 2 | 5 | 7 | 4 | 1 | 6 | 9 |
| 4 | 6 | 5 | 1 | 2 | 9 | 7 | 8 | 3 |
| 1 | 9 | 7 | 3 | 6 | 8 | 2 | 5 | 4 |
| 8 | 5 | 4 | 9 | 1 | 3 | 6 | 7 | 2 |
| 9 | 2 | 1 | 7 | 5 | 6 | 4 | 3 | 8 |
| 7 | 3 | 6 | 4 | 8 | 2 | 5 | 9 | 1 |

**80**

| 2 | 8 | 9 | 5 | 7 | 4 | 1 | 6 | 3 |
|---|---|---|---|---|---|---|---|---|
| 1 | 4 | 3 | 8 | 6 | 2 | 5 | 9 | 7 |
| 7 | 5 | 6 | 3 | 1 | 9 | 2 | 4 | 8 |
| 8 | 6 | 1 | 7 | 4 | 3 | 9 | 2 | 5 |
| 5 | 9 | 4 | 2 | 8 | 6 | 3 | 7 | 1 |
| 3 | 7 | 2 | 1 | 9 | 5 | 6 | 8 | 4 |
| 9 | 3 | 5 | 4 | 2 | 8 | 7 | 1 | 6 |
| 4 | 2 | 7 | 6 | 3 | 1 | 8 | 5 | 9 |
| 6 | 1 | 8 | 9 | 5 | 7 | 4 | 3 | 2 |

## 8/1

| 7 | 3 | 9 | 2 | 1 | 5 | 8 | 6 | 4 |
|---|---|---|---|---|---|---|---|---|
| 2 | 8 | 1 | 6 | 7 | 4 | 3 | 9 | 5 |
| 6 | 4 | 5 | 8 | 9 | 3 | 7 | 1 | 2 |
| 9 | 7 | 3 | 4 | 8 | 2 | 1 | 5 | 6 |
| 5 | 6 | 8 | 1 | 3 | 9 | 4 | 2 | 7 |
| 1 | 2 | 4 | 7 | 5 | 6 | 9 | 3 | 8 |
| 3 | 9 | 7 | 5 | 6 | 8 | 2 | 4 | 1 |
| 4 | 1 | 6 | 9 | 2 | 7 | 5 | 8 | 3 |
| 8 | 5 | 2 | 3 | 4 | 1 | 6 | 7 | 9 |

## 8/2

| 1 | 3 | 9 | 5 | 4 | 8 | 2 | 7 | 6 |
|---|---|---|---|---|---|---|---|---|
| 6 | 2 | 8 | 7 | 9 | 1 | 4 | 3 | 5 |
| 4 | 5 | 7 | 6 | 3 | 2 | 1 | 8 | 9 |
| 9 | 6 | 2 | 3 | 5 | 4 | 8 | 1 | 7 |
| 8 | 4 | 1 | 9 | 2 | 7 | 6 | 5 | 3 |
| 5 | 7 | 3 | 8 | 1 | 6 | 9 | 4 | 2 |
| 7 | 1 | 6 | 2 | 8 | 3 | 5 | 9 | 4 |
| 3 | 8 | 5 | 4 | 6 | 9 | 7 | 2 | 1 |
| 2 | 9 | 4 | 1 | 7 | 5 | 3 | 6 | 8 |

## 8/3

| 8 | 7 | 6 | 5 | 3 | 4 | 2 | 9 | 1 |
|---|---|---|---|---|---|---|---|---|
| 9 | 1 | 3 | 7 | 8 | 2 | 4 | 6 | 5 |
| 2 | 5 | 4 | 6 | 1 | 9 | 8 | 3 | 7 |
| 7 | 9 | 1 | 3 | 5 | 8 | 6 | 4 | 2 |
| 4 | 3 | 2 | 9 | 6 | 1 | 7 | 5 | 8 |
| 6 | 8 | 5 | 2 | 4 | 7 | 9 | 1 | 3 |
| 5 | 4 | 7 | 8 | 9 | 3 | 1 | 2 | 6 |
| 1 | 6 | 8 | 4 | 2 | 5 | 3 | 7 | 9 |
| 3 | 2 | 9 | 1 | 7 | 6 | 5 | 8 | 4 |

## 8/4

| 6 | 9 | 3 | 5 | 8 | 4 | 1 | 2 | 7 |
|---|---|---|---|---|---|---|---|---|
| 8 | 2 | 5 | 9 | 7 | 1 | 3 | 6 | 4 |
| 7 | 1 | 4 | 2 | 3 | 6 | 9 | 8 | 5 |
| 4 | 7 | 8 | 3 | 2 | 9 | 5 | 1 | 6 |
| 5 | 6 | 2 | 1 | 4 | 7 | 8 | 9 | 3 |
| 1 | 3 | 9 | 6 | 5 | 8 | 7 | 4 | 2 |
| 3 | 4 | 6 | 8 | 9 | 5 | 2 | 7 | 1 |
| 2 | 8 | 1 | 7 | 6 | 3 | 4 | 5 | 9 |
| 9 | 5 | 7 | 4 | 1 | 2 | 6 | 3 | 8 |

## 8/5

| 1 | 5 | 8 | 6 | 2 | 7 | 4 | 9 | 3 |
|---|---|---|---|---|---|---|---|---|
| 6 | 2 | 9 | 3 | 1 | 4 | 8 | 7 | 5 |
| 3 | 4 | 7 | 5 | 9 | 8 | 1 | 6 | 2 |
| 9 | 3 | 5 | 1 | 8 | 6 | 2 | 4 | 7 |
| 2 | 6 | 1 | 7 | 4 | 5 | 9 | 3 | 8 |
| 7 | 8 | 4 | 2 | 3 | 9 | 6 | 5 | 1 |
| 5 | 7 | 2 | 4 | 6 | 1 | 3 | 8 | 9 |
| 4 | 9 | 3 | 8 | 5 | 2 | 7 | 1 | 6 |
| 8 | 1 | 6 | 9 | 7 | 3 | 5 | 2 | 4 |

## 8/6

| 9 | 2 | 3 | 6 | 4 | 8 | 7 | 5 | 1 |
|---|---|---|---|---|---|---|---|---|
| 7 | 5 | 1 | 2 | 3 | 9 | 8 | 6 | 4 |
| 6 | 8 | 4 | 5 | 1 | 7 | 2 | 9 | 3 |
| 8 | 3 | 2 | 1 | 6 | 4 | 5 | 7 | 9 |
| 1 | 9 | 6 | 8 | 7 | 5 | 3 | 4 | 2 |
| 5 | 4 | 7 | 3 | 9 | 2 | 6 | 1 | 8 |
| 4 | 7 | 8 | 9 | 2 | 6 | 1 | 3 | 5 |
| 3 | 6 | 5 | 4 | 8 | 1 | 9 | 2 | 7 |
| 2 | 1 | 9 | 7 | 5 | 3 | 4 | 8 | 6 |

## 8/7

| 9 | 8 | 1 | 2 | 6 | 4 | 3 | 7 | 5 |
|---|---|---|---|---|---|---|---|---|
| 4 | 6 | 5 | 8 | 7 | 3 | 1 | 9 | 2 |
| 2 | 3 | 7 | 9 | 1 | 5 | 4 | 6 | 8 |
| 1 | 2 | 8 | 3 | 9 | 7 | 6 | 5 | 4 |
| 6 | 5 | 4 | 1 | 2 | 8 | 9 | 3 | 7 |
| 3 | 7 | 9 | 5 | 4 | 6 | 2 | 8 | 1 |
| 7 | 1 | 2 | 6 | 5 | 9 | 8 | 4 | 3 |
| 5 | 9 | 3 | 4 | 8 | 1 | 7 | 2 | 6 |
| 8 | 4 | 6 | 7 | 3 | 2 | 5 | 1 | 9 |

## 8/8

| 5 | 8 | 9 | 3 | 2 | 7 | 4 | 6 | 1 |
|---|---|---|---|---|---|---|---|---|
| 4 | 7 | 1 | 6 | 9 | 8 | 5 | 3 | 2 |
| 3 | 6 | 2 | 1 | 4 | 5 | 7 | 8 | 9 |
| 7 | 1 | 6 | 9 | 5 | 4 | 8 | 2 | 3 |
| 9 | 2 | 3 | 8 | 7 | 6 | 1 | 5 | 4 |
| 8 | 4 | 5 | 2 | 3 | 1 | 6 | 9 | 7 |
| 2 | 5 | 7 | 4 | 6 | 3 | 9 | 1 | 8 |
| 1 | 3 | 4 | 5 | 8 | 9 | 2 | 7 | 6 |
| 6 | 9 | 8 | 7 | 1 | 2 | 3 | 4 | 5 |

**88/89**

| 3 | 8 | 6 | 4 | 1 | 7 | 2 | 9 | 5 |
|---|---|---|---|---|---|---|---|---|
| 4 | 5 | 9 | 3 | 6 | 2 | 8 | 1 | 7 |
| 7 | 1 | 2 | 9 | 8 | 5 | 3 | 4 | 6 |
| 6 | 9 | 4 | 5 | 7 | 3 | 1 | 8 | 2 |
| 8 | 7 | 5 | 2 | 9 | 1 | 6 | 3 | 4 |
| 2 | 3 | 1 | 6 | 4 | 8 | 5 | 7 | 9 |
| 1 | 4 | 3 | 7 | 2 | 6 | 9 | 5 | 8 |
| 5 | 6 | 7 | 8 | 3 | 9 | 4 | 2 | 1 |
| 9 | 2 | 8 | 1 | 5 | 4 | 7 | 6 | 3 |

**90**

| 4 | 7 | 2 | 6 | 9 | 3 | 1 | 8 | 5 |
|---|---|---|---|---|---|---|---|---|
| 9 | 8 | 5 | 4 | 7 | 1 | 3 | 2 | 6 |
| 3 | 6 | 1 | 2 | 5 | 8 | 4 | 9 | 7 |
| 8 | 2 | 7 | 3 | 6 | 9 | 5 | 4 | 1 |
| 5 | 1 | 4 | 7 | 8 | 2 | 6 | 3 | 9 |
| 6 | 3 | 9 | 1 | 4 | 5 | 2 | 7 | 8 |
| 7 | 9 | 6 | 5 | 2 | 4 | 8 | 1 | 3 |
| 1 | 4 | 8 | 9 | 3 | 6 | 7 | 5 | 2 |
| 2 | 5 | 3 | 8 | 1 | 7 | 9 | 6 | 4 |

**91**

| 9 | 5 | 6 | 1 | 2 | 4 | 3 | 8 | 7 |
|---|---|---|---|---|---|---|---|---|
| 8 | 7 | 4 | 9 | 6 | 3 | 5 | 2 | 1 |
| 1 | 2 | 3 | 8 | 7 | 5 | 9 | 4 | 6 |
| 3 | 9 | 2 | 4 | 8 | 7 | 6 | 1 | 5 |
| 7 | 8 | 1 | 2 | 5 | 6 | 4 | 3 | 9 |
| 4 | 6 | 5 | 3 | 9 | 1 | 2 | 7 | 8 |
| 6 | 3 | 9 | 7 | 4 | 8 | 1 | 5 | 2 |
| 2 | 4 | 8 | 5 | 1 | 9 | 7 | 6 | 3 |
| 5 | 1 | 7 | 6 | 3 | 2 | 8 | 9 | 4 |

**92**

| 4 | 2 | 1 | 8 | 9 | 6 | 3 | 7 | 5 |
|---|---|---|---|---|---|---|---|---|
| 6 | 9 | 8 | 3 | 7 | 5 | 4 | 2 | 1 |
| 7 | 3 | 5 | 1 | 2 | 4 | 6 | 9 | 8 |
| 5 | 4 | 3 | 7 | 6 | 2 | 1 | 8 | 9 |
| 8 | 7 | 6 | 5 | 1 | 9 | 2 | 3 | 4 |
| 2 | 1 | 9 | 4 | 8 | 3 | 5 | 6 | 7 |
| 3 | 5 | 2 | 9 | 4 | 8 | 7 | 1 | 6 |
| 1 | 8 | 4 | 6 | 3 | 7 | 9 | 5 | 2 |
| 9 | 6 | 7 | 2 | 5 | 1 | 8 | 4 | 3 |

**93**

| 8 | 2 | 4 | 9 | 3 | 5 | 1 | 6 | 7 |
|---|---|---|---|---|---|---|---|---|
| 1 | 3 | 5 | 2 | 7 | 6 | 9 | 4 | 8 |
| 7 | 9 | 6 | 4 | 1 | 8 | 3 | 5 | 2 |
| 5 | 7 | 9 | 6 | 8 | 4 | 2 | 3 | 1 |
| 4 | 8 | 3 | 1 | 5 | 2 | 6 | 7 | 9 |
| 6 | 1 | 2 | 7 | 9 | 3 | 5 | 8 | 4 |
| 2 | 5 | 1 | 3 | 4 | 7 | 8 | 9 | 6 |
| 9 | 4 | 8 | 5 | 6 | 1 | 7 | 2 | 3 |
| 3 | 6 | 7 | 8 | 2 | 9 | 4 | 1 | 5 |

**94**

| 6 | 1 | 5 | 4 | 7 | 3 | 8 | 9 | 2 |
|---|---|---|---|---|---|---|---|---|
| 4 | 2 | 7 | 1 | 8 | 9 | 5 | 3 | 6 |
| 8 | 3 | 9 | 6 | 2 | 5 | 7 | 1 | 4 |
| 5 | 7 | 6 | 9 | 4 | 1 | 3 | 2 | 8 |
| 3 | 9 | 2 | 7 | 5 | 8 | 4 | 6 | 1 |
| 1 | 4 | 8 | 3 | 6 | 2 | 9 | 7 | 5 |
| 9 | 8 | 3 | 2 | 1 | 4 | 6 | 5 | 7 |
| 7 | 5 | 1 | 8 | 9 | 6 | 2 | 4 | 3 |
| 2 | 6 | 4 | 5 | 3 | 7 | 1 | 8 | 9 |

**95**

| 2 | 3 | 8 | 5 | 4 | 7 | 1 | 9 | 6 |
|---|---|---|---|---|---|---|---|---|
| 9 | 7 | 1 | 8 | 2 | 6 | 3 | 5 | 4 |
| 6 | 5 | 4 | 1 | 9 | 3 | 2 | 7 | 8 |
| 7 | 4 | 6 | 9 | 1 | 5 | 8 | 3 | 2 |
| 1 | 9 | 2 | 7 | 3 | 8 | 4 | 6 | 5 |
| 5 | 8 | 3 | 2 | 6 | 4 | 9 | 1 | 7 |
| 3 | 1 | 5 | 6 | 8 | 2 | 7 | 4 | 9 |
| 4 | 2 | 7 | 3 | 5 | 9 | 6 | 8 | 1 |
| 8 | 6 | 9 | 4 | 7 | 1 | 5 | 2 | 3 |

**96**

| 2 | 9 | 5 | 6 | 1 | 3 | 7 | 4 | 8 |
|---|---|---|---|---|---|---|---|---|
| 4 | 7 | 3 | 9 | 8 | 2 | 6 | 5 | 1 |
| 8 | 1 | 6 | 4 | 5 | 7 | 9 | 2 | 3 |
| 1 | 6 | 2 | 8 | 3 | 9 | 4 | 7 | 5 |
| 7 | 4 | 9 | 5 | 6 | 1 | 3 | 8 | 2 |
| 5 | 3 | 8 | 7 | 2 | 4 | 1 | 9 | 6 |
| 3 | 5 | 7 | 1 | 9 | 8 | 2 | 6 | 4 |
| 6 | 2 | 4 | 3 | 7 | 5 | 8 | 1 | 9 |
| 9 | 8 | 1 | 2 | 4 | 6 | 5 | 3 | 7 |

**97**

| 4 | 9 | 3 | 8 | 6 | 5 | 2 | 7 | 1 |
|---|---|---|---|---|---|---|---|---|
| 5 | 7 | 6 | 9 | 1 | 2 | 3 | 8 | 4 |
| 8 | 2 | 1 | 7 | 4 | 3 | 5 | 9 | 6 |
| 1 | 6 | 7 | 5 | 8 | 4 | 9 | 3 | 2 |
| 2 | 3 | 8 | 6 | 9 | 7 | 4 | 1 | 5 |
| 9 | 5 | 4 | 3 | 2 | 1 | 7 | 6 | 8 |
| 3 | 8 | 2 | 4 | 7 | 6 | 1 | 5 | 9 |
| 6 | 1 | 5 | 2 | 3 | 9 | 8 | 4 | 7 |
| 7 | 4 | 9 | 1 | 5 | 8 | 6 | 2 | 3 |

**98**

| 1 | 4 | 7 | 2 | 8 | 5 | 9 | 3 | 6 |
|---|---|---|---|---|---|---|---|---|
| 8 | 3 | 5 | 4 | 6 | 9 | 2 | 7 | 1 |
| 9 | 2 | 6 | 1 | 7 | 3 | 8 | 5 | 4 |
| 5 | 6 | 9 | 3 | 1 | 2 | 7 | 4 | 8 |
| 3 | 8 | 1 | 9 | 4 | 7 | 6 | 2 | 5 |
| 4 | 7 | 2 | 8 | 5 | 6 | 1 | 9 | 3 |
| 6 | 1 | 3 | 7 | 9 | 4 | 5 | 8 | 2 |
| 2 | 9 | 8 | 5 | 3 | 1 | 4 | 6 | 7 |
| 7 | 5 | 4 | 6 | 2 | 8 | 3 | 1 | 9 |

**99**

| 9 | 7 | 1 | 2 | 4 | 6 | 8 | 5 | 3 |
|---|---|---|---|---|---|---|---|---|
| 5 | 6 | 4 | 8 | 3 | 9 | 2 | 7 | 1 |
| 3 | 2 | 8 | 1 | 5 | 7 | 4 | 6 | 9 |
| 6 | 9 | 7 | 3 | 1 | 4 | 5 | 8 | 2 |
| 8 | 3 | 2 | 7 | 9 | 5 | 1 | 4 | 6 |
| 1 | 4 | 5 | 6 | 2 | 8 | 3 | 9 | 7 |
| 7 | 8 | 3 | 5 | 6 | 1 | 9 | 2 | 4 |
| 2 | 5 | 9 | 4 | 7 | 3 | 6 | 1 | 8 |
| 4 | 1 | 6 | 9 | 8 | 2 | 7 | 3 | 5 |

**100**

| 6 | 7 | 1 | 9 | 2 | 5 | 4 | 3 | 8 |
|---|---|---|---|---|---|---|---|---|
| 3 | 9 | 4 | 7 | 8 | 1 | 2 | 6 | 5 |
| 5 | 8 | 2 | 6 | 3 | 4 | 7 | 9 | 1 |
| 2 | 1 | 9 | 8 | 4 | 7 | 6 | 5 | 3 |
| 7 | 5 | 8 | 1 | 6 | 3 | 9 | 4 | 2 |
| 4 | 3 | 6 | 5 | 9 | 2 | 1 | 8 | 7 |
| 8 | 4 | 7 | 3 | 1 | 6 | 5 | 2 | 9 |
| 9 | 2 | 5 | 4 | 7 | 8 | 3 | 1 | 6 |
| 1 | 6 | 3 | 2 | 5 | 9 | 8 | 7 | 4 |

**101**

| 1 | 5 | 8 | 4 | 6 | 3 | 7 | 9 | 2 |
|---|---|---|---|---|---|---|---|---|
| 4 | 2 | 3 | 7 | 1 | 9 | 8 | 6 | 5 |
| 9 | 6 | 7 | 8 | 2 | 5 | 3 | 1 | 4 |
| 2 | 8 | 9 | 3 | 7 | 6 | 4 | 5 | 1 |
| 5 | 1 | 4 | 9 | 8 | 2 | 6 | 7 | 3 |
| 3 | 7 | 6 | 5 | 4 | 1 | 2 | 8 | 9 |
| 6 | 4 | 5 | 2 | 9 | 8 | 1 | 3 | 7 |
| 7 | 3 | 1 | 6 | 5 | 4 | 9 | 2 | 8 |
| 8 | 9 | 2 | 1 | 3 | 7 | 5 | 4 | 6 |

**102**

| 5 | 2 | 7 | 8 | 3 | 9 | 6 | 4 | 1 |
|---|---|---|---|---|---|---|---|---|
| 3 | 1 | 4 | 5 | 6 | 2 | 8 | 9 | 7 |
| 6 | 8 | 9 | 7 | 4 | 1 | 3 | 2 | 5 |
| 2 | 9 | 6 | 4 | 7 | 3 | 1 | 5 | 8 |
| 4 | 3 | 1 | 2 | 8 | 5 | 7 | 6 | 9 |
| 8 | 7 | 5 | 9 | 1 | 6 | 2 | 3 | 4 |
| 1 | 6 | 8 | 3 | 5 | 4 | 9 | 7 | 2 |
| 7 | 4 | 2 | 6 | 9 | 8 | 5 | 1 | 3 |
| 9 | 5 | 3 | 1 | 2 | 7 | 4 | 8 | 6 |

**103**

| 5 | 9 | 4 | 7 | 3 | 8 | 2 | 6 | 1 |
|---|---|---|---|---|---|---|---|---|
| 8 | 2 | 6 | 5 | 9 | 1 | 7 | 3 | 4 |
| 1 | 3 | 7 | 2 | 4 | 6 | 8 | 9 | 5 |
| 2 | 4 | 3 | 9 | 5 | 7 | 1 | 8 | 6 |
| 6 | 8 | 9 | 4 | 1 | 3 | 5 | 2 | 7 |
| 7 | 1 | 5 | 8 | 6 | 2 | 3 | 4 | 9 |
| 9 | 7 | 1 | 3 | 8 | 4 | 6 | 5 | 2 |
| 3 | 5 | 2 | 6 | 7 | 9 | 4 | 1 | 8 |
| 4 | 6 | 8 | 1 | 2 | 5 | 9 | 7 | 3 |

**104**

| 1 | 2 | 3 | 4 | 5 | 9 | 8 | 6 | 7 |
|---|---|---|---|---|---|---|---|---|
| 9 | 7 | 8 | 6 | 1 | 2 | 3 | 4 | 5 |
| 5 | 6 | 4 | 3 | 7 | 8 | 1 | 2 | 9 |
| 2 | 1 | 6 | 9 | 3 | 7 | 5 | 8 | 4 |
| 4 | 5 | 7 | 8 | 6 | 1 | 9 | 3 | 2 |
| 3 | 8 | 9 | 5 | 2 | 4 | 7 | 1 | 6 |
| 7 | 3 | 5 | 2 | 8 | 6 | 4 | 9 | 1 |
| 8 | 4 | 2 | 1 | 9 | 5 | 6 | 7 | 3 |
| 6 | 9 | 1 | 7 | 4 | 3 | 2 | 5 | 8 |

## 105

| 2 | 7 | 3 | 8 | 1 | 5 | 4 | 9 | 6 |
|---|---|---|---|---|---|---|---|---|
| 5 | 9 | 1 | 7 | 6 | 4 | 2 | 8 | 3 |
| 4 | 8 | 6 | 9 | 3 | 2 | 7 | 5 | 1 |
| 8 | 6 | 5 | 4 | 2 | 1 | 9 | 3 | 7 |
| 7 | 4 | 2 | 5 | 9 | 3 | 6 | 1 | 8 |
| 1 | 3 | 9 | 6 | 7 | 8 | 5 | 2 | 4 |
| 3 | 1 | 7 | 2 | 5 | 6 | 8 | 4 | 9 |
| 9 | 2 | 8 | 3 | 4 | 7 | 1 | 6 | 5 |
| 6 | 5 | 4 | 1 | 8 | 9 | 3 | 7 | 2 |

## 106

| 4 | 7 | 8 | 3 | 1 | 9 | 5 | 2 | 6 |
|---|---|---|---|---|---|---|---|---|
| 2 | 6 | 3 | 5 | 7 | 8 | 9 | 4 | 1 |
| 1 | 5 | 9 | 4 | 6 | 2 | 8 | 7 | 3 |
| 8 | 2 | 7 | 9 | 5 | 1 | 3 | 6 | 4 |
| 9 | 1 | 5 | 6 | 4 | 3 | 2 | 8 | 7 |
| 6 | 3 | 4 | 8 | 2 | 7 | 1 | 5 | 9 |
| 5 | 4 | 1 | 2 | 9 | 6 | 7 | 3 | 8 |
| 7 | 8 | 6 | 1 | 3 | 5 | 4 | 9 | 2 |
| 3 | 9 | 2 | 7 | 8 | 4 | 6 | 1 | 5 |

## 107

| 3 | 4 | 9 | 2 | 7 | 8 | 6 | 1 | 5 |
|---|---|---|---|---|---|---|---|---|
| 8 | 1 | 6 | 9 | 4 | 5 | 3 | 2 | 7 |
| 7 | 2 | 5 | 6 | 3 | 1 | 9 | 4 | 8 |
| 2 | 5 | 3 | 4 | 9 | 7 | 1 | 8 | 6 |
| 6 | 7 | 1 | 5 | 8 | 3 | 2 | 9 | 4 |
| 4 | 9 | 8 | 1 | 6 | 2 | 7 | 5 | 3 |
| 1 | 6 | 7 | 8 | 5 | 9 | 4 | 3 | 2 |
| 9 | 8 | 4 | 3 | 2 | 6 | 5 | 7 | 1 |
| 5 | 3 | 2 | 7 | 1 | 4 | 8 | 6 | 9 |

## 108

| 2 | 5 | 3 | 6 | 4 | 7 | 8 | 1 | 9 |
|---|---|---|---|---|---|---|---|---|
| 1 | 9 | 4 | 3 | 8 | 2 | 5 | 6 | 7 |
| 6 | 8 | 7 | 1 | 5 | 9 | 4 | 2 | 3 |
| 8 | 6 | 1 | 2 | 7 | 3 | 9 | 4 | 5 |
| 7 | 3 | 2 | 4 | 9 | 5 | 1 | 8 | 6 |
| 9 | 4 | 5 | 8 | 1 | 6 | 3 | 7 | 2 |
| 3 | 1 | 6 | 9 | 2 | 8 | 7 | 5 | 4 |
| 4 | 7 | 9 | 5 | 6 | 1 | 2 | 3 | 8 |
| 5 | 2 | 8 | 7 | 3 | 4 | 6 | 9 | 1 |

## 109

| 3 | 1 | 5 | 2 | 8 | 9 | 6 | 4 | 7 |
|---|---|---|---|---|---|---|---|---|
| 9 | 6 | 7 | 1 | 5 | 4 | 3 | 2 | 8 |
| 2 | 8 | 4 | 6 | 3 | 7 | 5 | 9 | 1 |
| 6 | 7 | 2 | 3 | 4 | 5 | 1 | 8 | 9 |
| 5 | 4 | 3 | 8 | 9 | 1 | 2 | 7 | 6 |
| 1 | 9 | 8 | 7 | 6 | 2 | 4 | 3 | 5 |
| 7 | 2 | 6 | 4 | 1 | 8 | 9 | 5 | 3 |
| 4 | 5 | 1 | 9 | 7 | 3 | 8 | 6 | 2 |
| 8 | 3 | 9 | 5 | 2 | 6 | 7 | 1 | 4 |

## 110

| 7 | 8 | 3 | 4 | 1 | 9 | 6 | 2 | 5 |
|---|---|---|---|---|---|---|---|---|
| 4 | 2 | 9 | 7 | 5 | 6 | 8 | 3 | 1 |
| 6 | 1 | 5 | 2 | 3 | 8 | 7 | 4 | 9 |
| 9 | 6 | 4 | 1 | 7 | 5 | 2 | 8 | 3 |
| 8 | 7 | 1 | 3 | 6 | 2 | 9 | 5 | 4 |
| 3 | 5 | 2 | 9 | 8 | 4 | 1 | 7 | 6 |
| 2 | 4 | 6 | 8 | 9 | 3 | 5 | 1 | 7 |
| 5 | 3 | 7 | 6 | 2 | 1 | 4 | 9 | 8 |
| 1 | 9 | 8 | 5 | 4 | 7 | 3 | 6 | 2 |

## 111

| 3 | 8 | 7 | 4 | 2 | 1 | 5 | 6 | 9 |
|---|---|---|---|---|---|---|---|---|
| 1 | 6 | 9 | 8 | 7 | 5 | 2 | 4 | 3 |
| 4 | 5 | 2 | 9 | 3 | 6 | 7 | 1 | 8 |
| 6 | 4 | 3 | 7 | 9 | 2 | 8 | 5 | 1 |
| 5 | 9 | 8 | 6 | 1 | 3 | 4 | 7 | 2 |
| 2 | 7 | 1 | 5 | 4 | 8 | 3 | 9 | 6 |
| 7 | 1 | 5 | 3 | 8 | 9 | 6 | 2 | 4 |
| 8 | 2 | 4 | 1 | 6 | 7 | 9 | 3 | 5 |
| 9 | 3 | 6 | 2 | 5 | 4 | 1 | 8 | 7 |

## 112

| 9 | 7 | 8 | 3 | 1 | 5 | 6 | 2 | 4 |
|---|---|---|---|---|---|---|---|---|
| 5 | 3 | 6 | 9 | 2 | 4 | 7 | 1 | 8 |
| 2 | 4 | 1 | 6 | 7 | 8 | 9 | 3 | 5 |
| 7 | 2 | 3 | 5 | 6 | 1 | 8 | 4 | 9 |
| 6 | 1 | 5 | 8 | 4 | 9 | 3 | 7 | 2 |
| 4 | 8 | 9 | 2 | 3 | 7 | 5 | 6 | 1 |
| 1 | 5 | 2 | 7 | 9 | 3 | 4 | 8 | 6 |
| 3 | 9 | 4 | 1 | 8 | 6 | 2 | 5 | 7 |
| 8 | 6 | 7 | 4 | 5 | 2 | 1 | 9 | 3 |

**13**

| 2 | 4 | 5 | 9 | 8 | 6 | 7 | 1 | 3 |
|---|---|---|---|---|---|---|---|---|
| 3 | 8 | 6 | 4 | 7 | 1 | 9 | 5 | 2 |
| 1 | 7 | 9 | 2 | 3 | 5 | 4 | 6 | 8 |
| 9 | 5 | 8 | 7 | 2 | 4 | 6 | 3 | 1 |
| 6 | 1 | 4 | 8 | 5 | 3 | 2 | 9 | 7 |
| 7 | 2 | 3 | 6 | 1 | 9 | 5 | 8 | 4 |
| 8 | 9 | 1 | 5 | 4 | 7 | 3 | 2 | 6 |
| 5 | 3 | 7 | 1 | 6 | 2 | 8 | 4 | 9 |
| 4 | 6 | 2 | 3 | 9 | 8 | 1 | 7 | 5 |

**14**

| 6 | 4 | 2 | 8 | 5 | 1 | 9 | 3 | 7 |
|---|---|---|---|---|---|---|---|---|
| 3 | 1 | 7 | 4 | 2 | 9 | 6 | 5 | 8 |
| 9 | 8 | 5 | 3 | 7 | 6 | 4 | 2 | 1 |
| 7 | 3 | 6 | 2 | 9 | 5 | 1 | 8 | 4 |
| 2 | 9 | 8 | 6 | 1 | 4 | 3 | 7 | 5 |
| 4 | 5 | 1 | 7 | 3 | 8 | 2 | 6 | 9 |
| 5 | 7 | 4 | 1 | 6 | 3 | 8 | 9 | 2 |
| 8 | 2 | 3 | 9 | 4 | 7 | 5 | 1 | 6 |
| 1 | 6 | 9 | 5 | 8 | 2 | 7 | 4 | 3 |

**15**

| 9 | 8 | 6 | 5 | 2 | 4 | 7 | 3 | 1 |
|---|---|---|---|---|---|---|---|---|
| 7 | 4 | 3 | 8 | 9 | 1 | 5 | 6 | 2 |
| 1 | 2 | 5 | 7 | 3 | 6 | 8 | 9 | 4 |
| 5 | 1 | 9 | 2 | 6 | 8 | 3 | 4 | 7 |
| 4 | 3 | 7 | 1 | 5 | 9 | 2 | 8 | 6 |
| 8 | 6 | 2 | 4 | 7 | 3 | 1 | 5 | 9 |
| 2 | 7 | 8 | 9 | 4 | 5 | 6 | 1 | 3 |
| 3 | 5 | 4 | 6 | 1 | 7 | 9 | 2 | 8 |
| 6 | 9 | 1 | 3 | 8 | 2 | 4 | 7 | 5 |

**16**

| 9 | 3 | 5 | 6 | 2 | 8 | 4 | 7 | 1 |
|---|---|---|---|---|---|---|---|---|
| 2 | 4 | 6 | 5 | 1 | 7 | 8 | 9 | 3 |
| 8 | 1 | 7 | 3 | 4 | 9 | 2 | 6 | 5 |
| 5 | 6 | 4 | 2 | 9 | 3 | 7 | 1 | 8 |
| 7 | 8 | 2 | 4 | 6 | 1 | 3 | 5 | 9 |
| 1 | 9 | 3 | 8 | 7 | 5 | 6 | 2 | 4 |
| 3 | 5 | 1 | 7 | 8 | 2 | 9 | 4 | 6 |
| 4 | 7 | 8 | 9 | 5 | 6 | 1 | 3 | 2 |
| 6 | 2 | 9 | 1 | 3 | 4 | 5 | 8 | 7 |

**17**

| 7 | 4 | 9 | 3 | 5 | 2 | 8 | 1 | 6 |
|---|---|---|---|---|---|---|---|---|
| 5 | 3 | 2 | 8 | 1 | 6 | 7 | 9 | 4 |
| 6 | 1 | 8 | 4 | 9 | 7 | 2 | 5 | 3 |
| 4 | 2 | 7 | 6 | 3 | 1 | 9 | 8 | 5 |
| 1 | 8 | 6 | 5 | 2 | 9 | 3 | 4 | 7 |
| 3 | 9 | 5 | 7 | 8 | 4 | 6 | 2 | 1 |
| 9 | 7 | 1 | 2 | 4 | 3 | 5 | 6 | 8 |
| 8 | 6 | 4 | 9 | 7 | 5 | 1 | 3 | 2 |
| 2 | 5 | 3 | 1 | 6 | 8 | 4 | 7 | 9 |

**18**

| 9 | 5 | 3 | 2 | 7 | 6 | 1 | 4 | 8 |
|---|---|---|---|---|---|---|---|---|
| 7 | 2 | 4 | 3 | 8 | 1 | 6 | 9 | 5 |
| 6 | 1 | 8 | 9 | 5 | 4 | 3 | 2 | 7 |
| 8 | 6 | 1 | 7 | 2 | 5 | 4 | 3 | 9 |
| 5 | 3 | 9 | 4 | 1 | 8 | 2 | 7 | 6 |
| 2 | 4 | 7 | 6 | 3 | 9 | 5 | 8 | 1 |
| 3 | 9 | 6 | 1 | 4 | 7 | 8 | 5 | 2 |
| 1 | 8 | 2 | 5 | 9 | 3 | 7 | 6 | 4 |
| 4 | 7 | 5 | 8 | 6 | 2 | 9 | 1 | 3 |

**19**

| 4 | 9 | 7 | 3 | 8 | 6 | 5 | 1 | 2 |
|---|---|---|---|---|---|---|---|---|
| 3 | 2 | 8 | 1 | 7 | 5 | 4 | 6 | 9 |
| 1 | 6 | 5 | 9 | 4 | 2 | 8 | 3 | 7 |
| 9 | 3 | 6 | 7 | 2 | 4 | 1 | 8 | 5 |
| 8 | 7 | 4 | 5 | 6 | 1 | 9 | 2 | 3 |
| 5 | 1 | 2 | 8 | 9 | 3 | 7 | 4 | 6 |
| 6 | 5 | 1 | 4 | 3 | 9 | 2 | 7 | 8 |
| 7 | 4 | 3 | 2 | 5 | 8 | 6 | 9 | 1 |
| 2 | 8 | 9 | 6 | 1 | 7 | 3 | 5 | 4 |

**20**

| 5 | 8 | 4 | 7 | 1 | 3 | 9 | 2 | 6 |
|---|---|---|---|---|---|---|---|---|
| 1 | 7 | 2 | 4 | 9 | 6 | 5 | 3 | 8 |
| 6 | 3 | 9 | 2 | 8 | 5 | 7 | 1 | 4 |
| 2 | 1 | 3 | 9 | 7 | 8 | 4 | 6 | 5 |
| 7 | 4 | 5 | 1 | 6 | 2 | 3 | 8 | 9 |
| 9 | 6 | 8 | 3 | 5 | 4 | 1 | 7 | 2 |
| 8 | 9 | 1 | 6 | 4 | 7 | 2 | 5 | 3 |
| 3 | 5 | 7 | 8 | 2 | 9 | 6 | 4 | 1 |
| 4 | 2 | 6 | 5 | 3 | 1 | 8 | 9 | 7 |

**121**

| 1 | 8 | 7 | 3 | 5 | 4 | 6 | 2 | 9 |
|---|---|---|---|---|---|---|---|---|
| 2 | 3 | 5 | 6 | 7 | 9 | 8 | 1 | 4 |
| 6 | 4 | 9 | 1 | 8 | 2 | 5 | 7 | 3 |
| 4 | 6 | 1 | 9 | 2 | 7 | 3 | 8 | 5 |
| 3 | 9 | 8 | 4 | 1 | 5 | 7 | 6 | 2 |
| 5 | 7 | 2 | 8 | 3 | 6 | 9 | 4 | 1 |
| 7 | 5 | 4 | 2 | 9 | 8 | 1 | 3 | 6 |
| 8 | 1 | 6 | 5 | 4 | 3 | 2 | 9 | 7 |
| 9 | 2 | 3 | 7 | 6 | 1 | 4 | 5 | 8 |

**122**

| 8 | 2 | 3 | 4 | 1 | 7 | 5 | 9 | 6 |
|---|---|---|---|---|---|---|---|---|
| 7 | 5 | 9 | 8 | 6 | 3 | 2 | 4 | 1 |
| 6 | 4 | 1 | 9 | 5 | 2 | 8 | 7 | 3 |
| 3 | 7 | 5 | 2 | 8 | 1 | 9 | 6 | 4 |
| 2 | 6 | 8 | 7 | 4 | 9 | 1 | 3 | 5 |
| 9 | 1 | 4 | 6 | 3 | 5 | 7 | 8 | 2 |
| 1 | 9 | 7 | 3 | 2 | 6 | 4 | 5 | 8 |
| 5 | 8 | 6 | 1 | 9 | 4 | 3 | 2 | 7 |
| 4 | 3 | 2 | 5 | 7 | 8 | 6 | 1 | 9 |

**123**

| 7 | 8 | 5 | 9 | 6 | 1 | 3 | 2 | 4 |
|---|---|---|---|---|---|---|---|---|
| 9 | 2 | 1 | 8 | 3 | 4 | 6 | 7 | 5 |
| 3 | 6 | 4 | 5 | 2 | 7 | 1 | 8 | 9 |
| 4 | 9 | 2 | 1 | 5 | 6 | 7 | 3 | 8 |
| 6 | 1 | 3 | 7 | 9 | 8 | 5 | 4 | 2 |
| 5 | 7 | 8 | 3 | 4 | 2 | 9 | 6 | 1 |
| 2 | 4 | 7 | 6 | 1 | 5 | 8 | 9 | 3 |
| 8 | 5 | 9 | 2 | 7 | 3 | 4 | 1 | 6 |
| 1 | 3 | 6 | 4 | 8 | 9 | 2 | 5 | 7 |

**124**

| 1 | 8 | 5 | 6 | 9 | 3 | 2 | 7 | 4 |
|---|---|---|---|---|---|---|---|---|
| 6 | 2 | 4 | 8 | 7 | 5 | 1 | 9 | 3 |
| 9 | 7 | 3 | 2 | 4 | 1 | 5 | 6 | 8 |
| 3 | 1 | 6 | 4 | 8 | 7 | 9 | 2 | 5 |
| 4 | 9 | 7 | 1 | 5 | 2 | 8 | 3 | 6 |
| 8 | 5 | 2 | 9 | 3 | 6 | 4 | 1 | 7 |
| 2 | 4 | 8 | 3 | 6 | 9 | 7 | 5 | 1 |
| 5 | 3 | 9 | 7 | 1 | 4 | 6 | 8 | 2 |
| 7 | 6 | 1 | 5 | 2 | 8 | 3 | 4 | 9 |

**125**

| 9 | 2 | 4 | 7 | 6 | 5 | 1 | 3 | 8 |
|---|---|---|---|---|---|---|---|---|
| 1 | 8 | 6 | 3 | 4 | 2 | 9 | 7 | 5 |
| 5 | 3 | 7 | 8 | 9 | 1 | 2 | 4 | 6 |
| 8 | 4 | 2 | 6 | 3 | 7 | 5 | 1 | 9 |
| 7 | 9 | 3 | 1 | 5 | 8 | 4 | 6 | 2 |
| 6 | 1 | 5 | 9 | 2 | 4 | 7 | 8 | 3 |
| 4 | 5 | 8 | 2 | 1 | 6 | 3 | 9 | 7 |
| 3 | 6 | 1 | 5 | 7 | 9 | 8 | 2 | 4 |
| 2 | 7 | 9 | 4 | 8 | 3 | 6 | 5 | 1 |

**126**

| 8 | 9 | 7 | 2 | 5 | 3 | 4 | 1 | 6 |
|---|---|---|---|---|---|---|---|---|
| 1 | 5 | 6 | 8 | 4 | 9 | 3 | 7 | 2 |
| 3 | 4 | 2 | 6 | 1 | 7 | 8 | 9 | 5 |
| 9 | 3 | 5 | 7 | 2 | 6 | 1 | 8 | 4 |
| 2 | 6 | 1 | 3 | 8 | 4 | 7 | 5 | 9 |
| 7 | 8 | 4 | 1 | 9 | 5 | 6 | 2 | 3 |
| 5 | 1 | 8 | 4 | 6 | 2 | 9 | 3 | 7 |
| 4 | 2 | 3 | 9 | 7 | 8 | 5 | 6 | 1 |
| 6 | 7 | 9 | 5 | 3 | 1 | 2 | 4 | 8 |

**127**

| 2 | 1 | 3 | 6 | 8 | 5 | 7 | 4 | 9 |
|---|---|---|---|---|---|---|---|---|
| 7 | 9 | 6 | 3 | 4 | 2 | 1 | 5 | 8 |
| 4 | 8 | 5 | 1 | 9 | 7 | 2 | 6 | 3 |
| 9 | 4 | 8 | 7 | 3 | 6 | 5 | 2 | 1 |
| 5 | 7 | 2 | 4 | 1 | 8 | 3 | 9 | 6 |
| 6 | 3 | 1 | 2 | 5 | 9 | 4 | 8 | 7 |
| 8 | 6 | 4 | 5 | 7 | 3 | 9 | 1 | 2 |
| 3 | 5 | 9 | 8 | 2 | 1 | 6 | 7 | 4 |
| 1 | 2 | 7 | 9 | 6 | 4 | 8 | 3 | 5 |

**128**

| 3 | 5 | 4 | 8 | 1 | 2 | 9 | 7 | 6 |
|---|---|---|---|---|---|---|---|---|
| 8 | 6 | 1 | 9 | 4 | 7 | 5 | 2 | 3 |
| 2 | 7 | 9 | 6 | 5 | 3 | 4 | 8 | 1 |
| 9 | 3 | 2 | 5 | 6 | 8 | 7 | 1 | 4 |
| 4 | 8 | 6 | 1 | 7 | 9 | 2 | 3 | 5 |
| 7 | 1 | 5 | 3 | 2 | 4 | 8 | 6 | 9 |
| 6 | 4 | 8 | 2 | 9 | 1 | 3 | 5 | 7 |
| 1 | 9 | 3 | 7 | 8 | 5 | 6 | 4 | 2 |
| 5 | 2 | 7 | 4 | 3 | 6 | 1 | 9 | 8 |

**129**

| 2 | 7 | 4 | 8 | 3 | 9 | 6 | 5 | 1 |
| 8 | 3 | 1 | 7 | 5 | 6 | 4 | 2 | 9 |
| 5 | 9 | 6 | 1 | 2 | 4 | 7 | 3 | 8 |
| 4 | 6 | 9 | 2 | 7 | 8 | 3 | 1 | 5 |
| 7 | 2 | 3 | 9 | 1 | 5 | 8 | 4 | 6 |
| 1 | 5 | 8 | 6 | 4 | 3 | 2 | 9 | 7 |
| 3 | 1 | 2 | 5 | 8 | 7 | 9 | 6 | 4 |
| 6 | 4 | 7 | 3 | 9 | 1 | 5 | 8 | 2 |
| 9 | 8 | 5 | 4 | 6 | 2 | 1 | 7 | 3 |

**130**

| 8 | 6 | 4 | 3 | 2 | 5 | 1 | 9 | 7 |
| 3 | 2 | 9 | 8 | 1 | 7 | 6 | 4 | 5 |
| 7 | 5 | 1 | 6 | 9 | 4 | 3 | 8 | 2 |
| 6 | 9 | 3 | 7 | 5 | 2 | 8 | 1 | 4 |
| 4 | 7 | 5 | 9 | 8 | 1 | 2 | 6 | 3 |
| 2 | 1 | 8 | 4 | 6 | 3 | 7 | 5 | 9 |
| 9 | 3 | 6 | 2 | 4 | 8 | 5 | 7 | 1 |
| 1 | 8 | 2 | 5 | 7 | 9 | 4 | 3 | 6 |
| 5 | 4 | 7 | 1 | 3 | 6 | 9 | 2 | 8 |

**131**

| 6 | 4 | 5 | 9 | 8 | 7 | 1 | 2 | 3 |
| 8 | 9 | 7 | 1 | 2 | 3 | 4 | 5 | 6 |
| 3 | 1 | 2 | 6 | 5 | 4 | 7 | 8 | 9 |
| 9 | 2 | 3 | 5 | 7 | 6 | 8 | 4 | 1 |
| 7 | 5 | 6 | 8 | 4 | 1 | 3 | 9 | 2 |
| 1 | 8 | 4 | 2 | 3 | 9 | 6 | 7 | 5 |
| 5 | 6 | 9 | 7 | 1 | 8 | 2 | 3 | 4 |
| 2 | 3 | 8 | 4 | 6 | 5 | 9 | 1 | 7 |
| 4 | 7 | 1 | 3 | 9 | 2 | 5 | 6 | 8 |

**132**

| 3 | 1 | 5 | 8 | 7 | 9 | 6 | 2 | 4 |
| 7 | 8 | 9 | 4 | 2 | 6 | 3 | 5 | 1 |
| 6 | 2 | 4 | 3 | 1 | 5 | 7 | 8 | 9 |
| 1 | 3 | 6 | 2 | 9 | 4 | 8 | 7 | 5 |
| 4 | 7 | 2 | 5 | 8 | 3 | 9 | 1 | 6 |
| 9 | 5 | 8 | 1 | 6 | 7 | 4 | 3 | 2 |
| 2 | 4 | 7 | 6 | 5 | 8 | 1 | 9 | 3 |
| 5 | 9 | 3 | 7 | 4 | 1 | 2 | 6 | 8 |
| 8 | 6 | 1 | 9 | 3 | 2 | 5 | 4 | 7 |

**133**

| 7 | 4 | 1 | 9 | 6 | 8 | 5 | 2 | 3 |
| 8 | 6 | 3 | 1 | 2 | 5 | 4 | 9 | 7 |
| 2 | 9 | 5 | 3 | 4 | 7 | 1 | 8 | 6 |
| 1 | 5 | 4 | 8 | 3 | 9 | 7 | 6 | 2 |
| 3 | 8 | 7 | 6 | 1 | 2 | 9 | 4 | 5 |
| 6 | 2 | 9 | 7 | 5 | 4 | 8 | 3 | 1 |
| 5 | 3 | 2 | 4 | 9 | 1 | 6 | 7 | 8 |
| 4 | 7 | 6 | 5 | 8 | 3 | 2 | 1 | 9 |
| 9 | 1 | 8 | 2 | 7 | 6 | 3 | 5 | 4 |

**134**

| 7 | 8 | 5 | 4 | 3 | 1 | 2 | 6 | 9 |
| 2 | 9 | 6 | 5 | 8 | 7 | 4 | 3 | 1 |
| 4 | 3 | 1 | 9 | 2 | 6 | 5 | 7 | 8 |
| 5 | 7 | 9 | 6 | 1 | 3 | 8 | 4 | 2 |
| 6 | 2 | 3 | 8 | 5 | 4 | 9 | 1 | 7 |
| 1 | 4 | 8 | 2 | 7 | 9 | 6 | 5 | 3 |
| 8 | 1 | 4 | 7 | 9 | 5 | 3 | 2 | 6 |
| 9 | 6 | 7 | 3 | 4 | 2 | 1 | 8 | 5 |
| 3 | 5 | 2 | 1 | 6 | 8 | 7 | 9 | 4 |

**135**

| 8 | 7 | 9 | 3 | 4 | 6 | 5 | 2 | 1 |
| 1 | 5 | 4 | 8 | 2 | 9 | 6 | 3 | 7 |
| 6 | 3 | 2 | 5 | 7 | 1 | 4 | 9 | 8 |
| 5 | 6 | 7 | 1 | 9 | 2 | 8 | 4 | 3 |
| 9 | 4 | 3 | 7 | 6 | 8 | 1 | 5 | 2 |
| 2 | 1 | 8 | 4 | 3 | 5 | 9 | 7 | 6 |
| 4 | 9 | 6 | 2 | 8 | 7 | 3 | 1 | 5 |
| 3 | 2 | 1 | 6 | 5 | 4 | 7 | 8 | 9 |
| 7 | 8 | 5 | 9 | 1 | 3 | 2 | 6 | 4 |

**136**

| 5 | 6 | 3 | 1 | 9 | 2 | 4 | 7 | 8 |
| 9 | 8 | 7 | 6 | 5 | 4 | 3 | 1 | 2 |
| 1 | 2 | 4 | 7 | 8 | 3 | 6 | 5 | 9 |
| 3 | 1 | 8 | 5 | 4 | 7 | 2 | 9 | 6 |
| 2 | 5 | 9 | 8 | 1 | 6 | 7 | 4 | 3 |
| 4 | 7 | 6 | 2 | 3 | 9 | 5 | 8 | 1 |
| 7 | 9 | 1 | 3 | 6 | 5 | 8 | 2 | 4 |
| 8 | 3 | 5 | 4 | 2 | 1 | 9 | 6 | 7 |
| 6 | 4 | 2 | 9 | 7 | 8 | 1 | 3 | 5 |

**137**

| 2 | 8 | 7 | 3 | 1 | 5 | 6 | 4 | 9 |
|---|---|---|---|---|---|---|---|---|
| 9 | 5 | 3 | 7 | 4 | 6 | 2 | 8 | 1 |
| 4 | 1 | 6 | 9 | 8 | 2 | 3 | 7 | 5 |
| 3 | 9 | 5 | 1 | 7 | 8 | 4 | 6 | 2 |
| 8 | 6 | 1 | 2 | 3 | 4 | 5 | 9 | 7 |
| 7 | 2 | 4 | 6 | 5 | 9 | 8 | 1 | 3 |
| 6 | 4 | 9 | 5 | 2 | 7 | 1 | 3 | 8 |
| 5 | 3 | 8 | 4 | 9 | 1 | 7 | 2 | 6 |
| 1 | 7 | 2 | 8 | 6 | 3 | 9 | 5 | 4 |

**138**

| 6 | 4 | 9 | 2 | 1 | 5 | 3 | 7 | 8 |
|---|---|---|---|---|---|---|---|---|
| 2 | 8 | 7 | 3 | 9 | 6 | 4 | 5 | 1 |
| 1 | 5 | 3 | 7 | 8 | 4 | 2 | 6 | 9 |
| 9 | 6 | 5 | 1 | 2 | 3 | 7 | 8 | 4 |
| 7 | 1 | 4 | 8 | 5 | 9 | 6 | 3 | 2 |
| 3 | 2 | 8 | 6 | 4 | 7 | 1 | 9 | 5 |
| 5 | 7 | 1 | 9 | 3 | 2 | 8 | 4 | 6 |
| 4 | 3 | 2 | 5 | 6 | 8 | 9 | 1 | 7 |
| 8 | 9 | 6 | 4 | 7 | 1 | 5 | 2 | 3 |

**139**

| 8 | 3 | 2 | 5 | 1 | 7 | 6 | 9 | 4 |
|---|---|---|---|---|---|---|---|---|
| 1 | 7 | 9 | 4 | 8 | 6 | 5 | 3 | 2 |
| 6 | 4 | 5 | 9 | 3 | 2 | 8 | 1 | 7 |
| 7 | 1 | 8 | 3 | 6 | 9 | 4 | 2 | 5 |
| 3 | 9 | 6 | 2 | 4 | 5 | 1 | 7 | 8 |
| 5 | 2 | 4 | 1 | 7 | 8 | 3 | 6 | 9 |
| 4 | 6 | 7 | 8 | 2 | 3 | 9 | 5 | 1 |
| 2 | 5 | 1 | 6 | 9 | 4 | 7 | 8 | 3 |
| 9 | 8 | 3 | 7 | 5 | 1 | 2 | 4 | 6 |

**140**

| 2 | 3 | 9 | 7 | 5 | 8 | 1 | 6 | 4 |
|---|---|---|---|---|---|---|---|---|
| 5 | 7 | 8 | 6 | 1 | 4 | 2 | 9 | 3 |
| 6 | 1 | 4 | 9 | 3 | 2 | 5 | 8 | 7 |
| 9 | 5 | 2 | 3 | 8 | 6 | 4 | 7 | 1 |
| 3 | 4 | 1 | 5 | 7 | 9 | 6 | 2 | 8 |
| 7 | 8 | 6 | 4 | 2 | 1 | 9 | 3 | 5 |
| 1 | 6 | 3 | 8 | 9 | 5 | 7 | 4 | 2 |
| 8 | 9 | 5 | 2 | 4 | 7 | 3 | 1 | 6 |
| 4 | 2 | 7 | 1 | 6 | 3 | 8 | 5 | 9 |

**141**

| 3 | 9 | 7 | 8 | 5 | 1 | 4 | 6 | 2 |
|---|---|---|---|---|---|---|---|---|
| 2 | 6 | 5 | 7 | 3 | 4 | 9 | 1 | 8 |
| 4 | 1 | 8 | 2 | 9 | 6 | 7 | 3 | 5 |
| 5 | 2 | 1 | 4 | 6 | 8 | 3 | 7 | 9 |
| 6 | 7 | 9 | 1 | 2 | 3 | 8 | 5 | 4 |
| 8 | 4 | 3 | 5 | 7 | 9 | 6 | 2 | 1 |
| 1 | 3 | 6 | 9 | 8 | 5 | 2 | 4 | 7 |
| 7 | 8 | 4 | 3 | 1 | 2 | 5 | 9 | 6 |
| 9 | 5 | 2 | 6 | 4 | 7 | 1 | 8 | 3 |

**142**

| 2 | 9 | 7 | 8 | 3 | 1 | 5 | 4 | 6 |
|---|---|---|---|---|---|---|---|---|
| 5 | 8 | 3 | 7 | 6 | 4 | 9 | 2 | 1 |
| 1 | 4 | 6 | 5 | 9 | 2 | 7 | 8 | 3 |
| 7 | 3 | 5 | 9 | 4 | 6 | 8 | 1 | 2 |
| 6 | 1 | 9 | 2 | 5 | 8 | 4 | 3 | 7 |
| 4 | 2 | 8 | 3 | 1 | 7 | 6 | 9 | 5 |
| 8 | 5 | 1 | 4 | 7 | 3 | 2 | 6 | 9 |
| 9 | 6 | 2 | 1 | 8 | 5 | 3 | 7 | 4 |
| 3 | 7 | 4 | 6 | 2 | 9 | 1 | 5 | 8 |

**143**

| 7 | 1 | 6 | 8 | 9 | 3 | 4 | 2 | 5 |
|---|---|---|---|---|---|---|---|---|
| 9 | 5 | 2 | 4 | 6 | 7 | 8 | 1 | 3 |
| 3 | 4 | 8 | 5 | 2 | 1 | 9 | 7 | 6 |
| 5 | 3 | 7 | 9 | 8 | 2 | 1 | 6 | 4 |
| 1 | 6 | 4 | 7 | 3 | 5 | 2 | 8 | 9 |
| 2 | 8 | 9 | 1 | 4 | 6 | 3 | 5 | 7 |
| 8 | 2 | 3 | 6 | 7 | 4 | 5 | 9 | 1 |
| 6 | 9 | 5 | 3 | 1 | 8 | 7 | 4 | 2 |
| 4 | 7 | 1 | 2 | 5 | 9 | 6 | 3 | 8 |

**144**

| 8 | 5 | 6 | 1 | 2 | 9 | 4 | 3 | 7 |
|---|---|---|---|---|---|---|---|---|
| 9 | 2 | 4 | 7 | 8 | 3 | 6 | 1 | 5 |
| 7 | 3 | 1 | 6 | 4 | 5 | 2 | 8 | 9 |
| 5 | 8 | 3 | 9 | 6 | 2 | 1 | 7 | 4 |
| 2 | 4 | 9 | 8 | 1 | 7 | 5 | 6 | 3 |
| 6 | 1 | 7 | 5 | 3 | 4 | 8 | 9 | 2 |
| 1 | 9 | 2 | 3 | 5 | 8 | 7 | 4 | 6 |
| 3 | 6 | 5 | 4 | 7 | 1 | 9 | 2 | 8 |
| 4 | 7 | 8 | 2 | 9 | 6 | 3 | 5 | 1 |

**145**

| 8 | 3 | 9 | 2 | 6 | 4 | 7 | 5 | 1 |
|---|---|---|---|---|---|---|---|---|
| 1 | 4 | 6 | 3 | 5 | 7 | 9 | 8 | 2 |
| 2 | 5 | 7 | 9 | 1 | 8 | 6 | 4 | 3 |
| 9 | 7 | 5 | 6 | 4 | 1 | 3 | 2 | 8 |
| 6 | 8 | 1 | 5 | 2 | 3 | 4 | 9 | 7 |
| 4 | 2 | 3 | 8 | 7 | 9 | 5 | 1 | 6 |
| 5 | 6 | 8 | 7 | 9 | 2 | 1 | 3 | 4 |
| 3 | 9 | 4 | 1 | 8 | 6 | 2 | 7 | 5 |
| 7 | 1 | 2 | 4 | 3 | 5 | 8 | 6 | 9 |

**146**

| 7 | 8 | 4 | 6 | 1 | 9 | 5 | 2 | 3 |
|---|---|---|---|---|---|---|---|---|
| 9 | 5 | 1 | 8 | 2 | 3 | 7 | 6 | 4 |
| 3 | 2 | 6 | 7 | 5 | 4 | 8 | 9 | 1 |
| 2 | 7 | 8 | 4 | 6 | 5 | 3 | 1 | 9 |
| 6 | 9 | 3 | 2 | 8 | 1 | 4 | 7 | 5 |
| 1 | 4 | 5 | 3 | 9 | 7 | 2 | 8 | 6 |
| 4 | 1 | 7 | 9 | 3 | 8 | 6 | 5 | 2 |
| 5 | 3 | 2 | 1 | 7 | 6 | 9 | 4 | 8 |
| 8 | 6 | 9 | 5 | 4 | 2 | 1 | 3 | 7 |

**147**

| 3 | 4 | 1 | 9 | 6 | 5 | 8 | 7 | 2 |
|---|---|---|---|---|---|---|---|---|
| 9 | 7 | 2 | 4 | 8 | 3 | 5 | 1 | 6 |
| 5 | 6 | 8 | 1 | 2 | 7 | 9 | 3 | 4 |
| 7 | 5 | 4 | 8 | 3 | 9 | 2 | 6 | 1 |
| 1 | 8 | 3 | 6 | 5 | 2 | 7 | 4 | 9 |
| 2 | 9 | 6 | 7 | 1 | 4 | 3 | 5 | 8 |
| 4 | 1 | 5 | 2 | 7 | 8 | 6 | 9 | 3 |
| 6 | 2 | 7 | 3 | 9 | 1 | 4 | 8 | 5 |
| 8 | 3 | 9 | 5 | 4 | 6 | 1 | 2 | 7 |

**148**

| 8 | 4 | 9 | 6 | 1 | 5 | 3 | 7 | 2 |
|---|---|---|---|---|---|---|---|---|
| 5 | 7 | 1 | 3 | 4 | 2 | 8 | 9 | 6 |
| 2 | 3 | 6 | 8 | 9 | 7 | 1 | 4 | 5 |
| 9 | 8 | 3 | 5 | 6 | 4 | 7 | 2 | 1 |
| 7 | 2 | 5 | 9 | 3 | 1 | 6 | 8 | 4 |
| 1 | 6 | 4 | 7 | 2 | 8 | 9 | 5 | 3 |
| 3 | 5 | 8 | 2 | 7 | 6 | 4 | 1 | 9 |
| 6 | 1 | 2 | 4 | 8 | 9 | 5 | 3 | 7 |
| 4 | 9 | 7 | 1 | 5 | 3 | 2 | 6 | 8 |

**149**

| 9 | 2 | 5 | 7 | 8 | 3 | 1 | 4 | 6 |
|---|---|---|---|---|---|---|---|---|
| 4 | 8 | 1 | 2 | 9 | 6 | 5 | 7 | 3 |
| 6 | 3 | 7 | 5 | 4 | 1 | 2 | 9 | 8 |
| 3 | 9 | 4 | 6 | 7 | 2 | 8 | 1 | 5 |
| 7 | 1 | 8 | 3 | 5 | 9 | 4 | 6 | 2 |
| 5 | 6 | 2 | 8 | 1 | 4 | 9 | 3 | 7 |
| 2 | 7 | 9 | 1 | 6 | 5 | 3 | 8 | 4 |
| 1 | 5 | 6 | 4 | 3 | 8 | 7 | 2 | 9 |
| 8 | 4 | 3 | 9 | 2 | 7 | 6 | 5 | 1 |

**150**

| 1 | 4 | 7 | 6 | 9 | 8 | 2 | 3 | 5 |
|---|---|---|---|---|---|---|---|---|
| 3 | 2 | 8 | 4 | 7 | 5 | 9 | 6 | 1 |
| 9 | 6 | 5 | 3 | 2 | 1 | 7 | 8 | 4 |
| 5 | 8 | 3 | 7 | 6 | 2 | 4 | 1 | 9 |
| 6 | 9 | 2 | 8 | 1 | 4 | 5 | 7 | 3 |
| 4 | 7 | 1 | 5 | 3 | 9 | 6 | 2 | 8 |
| 2 | 3 | 4 | 9 | 8 | 7 | 1 | 5 | 6 |
| 7 | 5 | 6 | 1 | 4 | 3 | 8 | 9 | 2 |
| 8 | 1 | 9 | 2 | 5 | 6 | 3 | 4 | 7 |

**151**

| 8 | 5 | 4 | 6 | 7 | 2 | 9 | 1 | 3 |
|---|---|---|---|---|---|---|---|---|
| 6 | 7 | 2 | 1 | 3 | 9 | 8 | 5 | 4 |
| 9 | 3 | 1 | 8 | 4 | 5 | 2 | 6 | 7 |
| 1 | 6 | 3 | 4 | 5 | 8 | 7 | 2 | 9 |
| 7 | 4 | 8 | 2 | 9 | 6 | 5 | 3 | 1 |
| 2 | 9 | 5 | 3 | 1 | 7 | 4 | 8 | 6 |
| 5 | 1 | 9 | 7 | 8 | 3 | 6 | 4 | 2 |
| 4 | 8 | 6 | 9 | 2 | 1 | 3 | 7 | 5 |
| 3 | 2 | 7 | 5 | 6 | 4 | 1 | 9 | 8 |

**152**

| 3 | 4 | 9 | 8 | 2 | 5 | 1 | 6 | 7 |
|---|---|---|---|---|---|---|---|---|
| 5 | 1 | 7 | 3 | 4 | 6 | 9 | 8 | 2 |
| 6 | 2 | 8 | 1 | 7 | 9 | 3 | 5 | 4 |
| 2 | 8 | 6 | 5 | 9 | 4 | 7 | 3 | 1 |
| 9 | 7 | 3 | 6 | 8 | 1 | 4 | 2 | 5 |
| 1 | 5 | 4 | 7 | 3 | 2 | 6 | 9 | 8 |
| 8 | 6 | 1 | 9 | 5 | 7 | 2 | 4 | 3 |
| 7 | 3 | 2 | 4 | 6 | 8 | 5 | 1 | 9 |
| 4 | 9 | 5 | 2 | 1 | 3 | 8 | 7 | 6 |

## 153

| 9 | 3 | 6 | 4 | 1 | 2 | 7 | 5 | 8 |
|---|---|---|---|---|---|---|---|---|
| 1 | 2 | 8 | 5 | 9 | 7 | 3 | 6 | 4 |
| 5 | 4 | 7 | 3 | 6 | 8 | 2 | 9 | 1 |
| 4 | 5 | 1 | 9 | 2 | 3 | 6 | 8 | 7 |
| 7 | 6 | 2 | 1 | 8 | 5 | 4 | 3 | 9 |
| 8 | 9 | 3 | 7 | 4 | 6 | 1 | 2 | 5 |
| 6 | 1 | 9 | 8 | 3 | 4 | 5 | 7 | 2 |
| 3 | 8 | 5 | 2 | 7 | 1 | 9 | 4 | 6 |
| 2 | 7 | 4 | 6 | 5 | 9 | 8 | 1 | 3 |

## 154

| 5 | 7 | 9 | 1 | 4 | 3 | 6 | 8 | 2 |
|---|---|---|---|---|---|---|---|---|
| 6 | 4 | 8 | 7 | 5 | 2 | 1 | 3 | 9 |
| 3 | 1 | 2 | 9 | 8 | 6 | 7 | 4 | 5 |
| 2 | 3 | 1 | 8 | 7 | 4 | 9 | 5 | 6 |
| 9 | 5 | 6 | 3 | 2 | 1 | 4 | 7 | 8 |
| 4 | 8 | 7 | 5 | 6 | 9 | 2 | 1 | 3 |
| 1 | 6 | 4 | 2 | 3 | 5 | 8 | 9 | 7 |
| 7 | 9 | 3 | 6 | 1 | 8 | 5 | 2 | 4 |
| 8 | 2 | 5 | 4 | 9 | 7 | 3 | 6 | 1 |

## 155

| 7 | 4 | 6 | 2 | 3 | 9 | 8 | 5 | 1 |
|---|---|---|---|---|---|---|---|---|
| 1 | 8 | 3 | 5 | 7 | 4 | 6 | 2 | 9 |
| 2 | 9 | 5 | 6 | 8 | 1 | 4 | 7 | 3 |
| 9 | 1 | 8 | 7 | 4 | 3 | 5 | 6 | 2 |
| 4 | 3 | 2 | 9 | 5 | 6 | 1 | 8 | 7 |
| 5 | 6 | 7 | 1 | 2 | 8 | 3 | 9 | 4 |
| 6 | 5 | 9 | 3 | 1 | 7 | 2 | 4 | 8 |
| 8 | 2 | 1 | 4 | 9 | 5 | 7 | 3 | 6 |
| 3 | 7 | 4 | 8 | 6 | 2 | 9 | 1 | 5 |

## 156

| 1 | 3 | 9 | 5 | 7 | 6 | 2 | 4 | 8 |
|---|---|---|---|---|---|---|---|---|
| 2 | 7 | 4 | 8 | 3 | 1 | 9 | 6 | 5 |
| 5 | 8 | 6 | 9 | 4 | 2 | 7 | 3 | 1 |
| 9 | 4 | 8 | 6 | 1 | 7 | 5 | 2 | 3 |
| 7 | 5 | 1 | 3 | 2 | 9 | 4 | 8 | 6 |
| 3 | 6 | 2 | 4 | 5 | 8 | 1 | 9 | 7 |
| 6 | 1 | 3 | 7 | 9 | 4 | 8 | 5 | 2 |
| 8 | 9 | 7 | 2 | 6 | 5 | 3 | 1 | 4 |
| 4 | 2 | 5 | 1 | 8 | 3 | 6 | 7 | 9 |

## 157

| 8 | 6 | 4 | 3 | 5 | 2 | 7 | 1 | 9 |
|---|---|---|---|---|---|---|---|---|
| 9 | 5 | 2 | 8 | 1 | 7 | 4 | 3 | 6 |
| 1 | 3 | 7 | 4 | 6 | 9 | 2 | 8 | 5 |
| 4 | 1 | 6 | 5 | 2 | 3 | 9 | 7 | 8 |
| 3 | 9 | 5 | 6 | 7 | 8 | 1 | 2 | 4 |
| 7 | 2 | 8 | 9 | 4 | 1 | 6 | 5 | 3 |
| 6 | 4 | 1 | 2 | 8 | 5 | 3 | 9 | 7 |
| 2 | 8 | 9 | 7 | 3 | 6 | 5 | 4 | 1 |
| 5 | 7 | 3 | 1 | 9 | 4 | 8 | 6 | 2 |

## 158

| 5 | 6 | 7 | 2 | 3 | 8 | 1 | 4 | 9 |
|---|---|---|---|---|---|---|---|---|
| 2 | 8 | 1 | 5 | 9 | 4 | 6 | 3 | 7 |
| 4 | 3 | 9 | 1 | 6 | 7 | 8 | 5 | 2 |
| 6 | 7 | 2 | 4 | 1 | 3 | 9 | 8 | 5 |
| 3 | 1 | 5 | 9 | 8 | 2 | 7 | 6 | 4 |
| 8 | 9 | 4 | 6 | 7 | 5 | 2 | 1 | 3 |
| 1 | 4 | 6 | 7 | 5 | 9 | 3 | 2 | 8 |
| 9 | 2 | 8 | 3 | 4 | 6 | 5 | 7 | 1 |
| 7 | 5 | 3 | 8 | 2 | 1 | 4 | 9 | 6 |

## 159

| 6 | 4 | 9 | 3 | 7 | 8 | 2 | 1 | 5 |
|---|---|---|---|---|---|---|---|---|
| 2 | 8 | 7 | 4 | 1 | 5 | 6 | 3 | 9 |
| 5 | 3 | 1 | 9 | 2 | 6 | 8 | 7 | 4 |
| 9 | 2 | 4 | 5 | 6 | 3 | 1 | 8 | 7 |
| 7 | 1 | 3 | 2 | 8 | 9 | 5 | 4 | 6 |
| 8 | 5 | 6 | 7 | 4 | 1 | 3 | 9 | 2 |
| 1 | 9 | 8 | 6 | 5 | 4 | 7 | 2 | 3 |
| 4 | 6 | 2 | 8 | 3 | 7 | 9 | 5 | 1 |
| 3 | 7 | 5 | 1 | 9 | 2 | 4 | 6 | 8 |

## 160

| 4 | 9 | 3 | 7 | 2 | 5 | 6 | 1 | 8 |
|---|---|---|---|---|---|---|---|---|
| 6 | 8 | 2 | 1 | 3 | 4 | 5 | 9 | 7 |
| 5 | 7 | 1 | 9 | 8 | 6 | 4 | 3 | 2 |
| 9 | 6 | 8 | 4 | 7 | 1 | 3 | 2 | 5 |
| 3 | 4 | 7 | 5 | 9 | 2 | 8 | 6 | 1 |
| 2 | 1 | 5 | 3 | 6 | 8 | 9 | 7 | 4 |
| 8 | 2 | 4 | 6 | 1 | 3 | 7 | 5 | 9 |
| 1 | 3 | 9 | 8 | 5 | 7 | 2 | 4 | 6 |
| 7 | 5 | 6 | 2 | 4 | 9 | 1 | 8 | 3 |

**161**

| 9 | 2 | 1 | 7 | 6 | 8 | 3 | 5 | 4 |
|---|---|---|---|---|---|---|---|---|
| 8 | 4 | 3 | 5 | 1 | 2 | 7 | 6 | 9 |
| 6 | 7 | 5 | 9 | 3 | 4 | 2 | 8 | 1 |
| 7 | 6 | 8 | 1 | 2 | 3 | 4 | 9 | 5 |
| 4 | 3 | 2 | 6 | 9 | 5 | 8 | 1 | 7 |
| 5 | 1 | 9 | 8 | 4 | 7 | 6 | 2 | 3 |
| 3 | 5 | 6 | 4 | 8 | 9 | 1 | 7 | 2 |
| 2 | 8 | 7 | 3 | 5 | 1 | 9 | 4 | 6 |
| 1 | 9 | 4 | 2 | 7 | 6 | 5 | 3 | 8 |

**162**

| 5 | 4 | 6 | 1 | 2 | 8 | 3 | 7 | 9 |
|---|---|---|---|---|---|---|---|---|
| 7 | 2 | 9 | 5 | 6 | 3 | 1 | 4 | 8 |
| 8 | 3 | 1 | 4 | 7 | 9 | 2 | 5 | 6 |
| 4 | 7 | 8 | 2 | 5 | 6 | 9 | 3 | 1 |
| 1 | 9 | 2 | 8 | 3 | 7 | 4 | 6 | 5 |
| 6 | 5 | 3 | 9 | 1 | 4 | 7 | 8 | 2 |
| 9 | 6 | 5 | 3 | 4 | 1 | 8 | 2 | 7 |
| 3 | 8 | 7 | 6 | 9 | 2 | 5 | 1 | 4 |
| 2 | 1 | 4 | 7 | 8 | 5 | 6 | 9 | 3 |

**163**

| 1 | 2 | 3 | 4 | 6 | 5 | 7 | 8 | 9 |
|---|---|---|---|---|---|---|---|---|
| 6 | 5 | 4 | 9 | 7 | 8 | 2 | 3 | 1 |
| 7 | 8 | 9 | 1 | 2 | 3 | 4 | 5 | 6 |
| 3 | 7 | 2 | 8 | 5 | 1 | 6 | 9 | 4 |
| 8 | 1 | 6 | 2 | 4 | 9 | 5 | 7 | 3 |
| 4 | 9 | 5 | 7 | 3 | 6 | 8 | 1 | 2 |
| 5 | 6 | 8 | 3 | 1 | 2 | 9 | 4 | 7 |
| 9 | 3 | 7 | 6 | 8 | 4 | 1 | 2 | 5 |
| 2 | 4 | 1 | 5 | 9 | 7 | 3 | 6 | 8 |

**164**

| 7 | 5 | 9 | 2 | 4 | 1 | 3 | 8 | 6 |
|---|---|---|---|---|---|---|---|---|
| 4 | 3 | 6 | 7 | 5 | 8 | 1 | 2 | 9 |
| 8 | 2 | 1 | 3 | 9 | 6 | 4 | 5 | 7 |
| 5 | 6 | 3 | 1 | 7 | 4 | 8 | 9 | 2 |
| 2 | 8 | 4 | 5 | 3 | 9 | 6 | 7 | 1 |
| 1 | 9 | 7 | 6 | 8 | 2 | 5 | 4 | 3 |
| 6 | 4 | 2 | 9 | 1 | 5 | 7 | 3 | 8 |
| 3 | 1 | 5 | 8 | 2 | 7 | 9 | 6 | 4 |
| 9 | 7 | 8 | 4 | 6 | 3 | 2 | 1 | 5 |

**165**

| 7 | 5 | 6 | 4 | 2 | 9 | 8 | 3 | 1 |
|---|---|---|---|---|---|---|---|---|
| 2 | 1 | 3 | 8 | 5 | 7 | 4 | 9 | 6 |
| 9 | 8 | 4 | 6 | 3 | 1 | 7 | 2 | 5 |
| 1 | 7 | 8 | 9 | 4 | 2 | 6 | 5 | 3 |
| 6 | 9 | 2 | 3 | 7 | 5 | 1 | 8 | 4 |
| 4 | 3 | 5 | 1 | 8 | 6 | 9 | 7 | 2 |
| 3 | 4 | 7 | 5 | 1 | 8 | 2 | 6 | 9 |
| 5 | 2 | 9 | 7 | 6 | 4 | 3 | 1 | 8 |
| 8 | 6 | 1 | 2 | 9 | 3 | 5 | 4 | 7 |

**166**

| 5 | 7 | 9 | 6 | 2 | 4 | 1 | 3 | 8 |
|---|---|---|---|---|---|---|---|---|
| 1 | 8 | 3 | 9 | 5 | 7 | 4 | 6 | 2 |
| 6 | 2 | 4 | 1 | 3 | 8 | 9 | 5 | 7 |
| 3 | 6 | 7 | 2 | 9 | 1 | 5 | 8 | 4 |
| 8 | 4 | 1 | 3 | 7 | 5 | 2 | 9 | 6 |
| 2 | 9 | 5 | 8 | 4 | 6 | 7 | 1 | 3 |
| 7 | 3 | 8 | 4 | 1 | 9 | 6 | 2 | 5 |
| 9 | 5 | 6 | 7 | 8 | 2 | 3 | 4 | 1 |
| 4 | 1 | 2 | 5 | 6 | 3 | 8 | 7 | 9 |

**167**

| 2 | 6 | 8 | 5 | 1 | 9 | 7 | 4 | 3 |
|---|---|---|---|---|---|---|---|---|
| 5 | 1 | 3 | 4 | 2 | 7 | 6 | 8 | 9 |
| 4 | 7 | 9 | 8 | 6 | 3 | 1 | 5 | 2 |
| 1 | 5 | 6 | 7 | 3 | 8 | 2 | 9 | 4 |
| 8 | 2 | 7 | 6 | 9 | 4 | 5 | 3 | 1 |
| 9 | 3 | 4 | 2 | 5 | 1 | 8 | 7 | 6 |
| 3 | 9 | 2 | 1 | 7 | 5 | 4 | 6 | 8 |
| 7 | 4 | 1 | 9 | 8 | 6 | 3 | 2 | 5 |
| 6 | 8 | 5 | 3 | 4 | 2 | 9 | 1 | 7 |

**168**

| 3 | 8 | 4 | 2 | 7 | 6 | 9 | 1 | 5 |
|---|---|---|---|---|---|---|---|---|
| 7 | 5 | 2 | 9 | 3 | 1 | 6 | 4 | 8 |
| 6 | 1 | 9 | 5 | 8 | 4 | 7 | 2 | 3 |
| 8 | 6 | 3 | 4 | 5 | 9 | 1 | 7 | 2 |
| 5 | 4 | 7 | 1 | 2 | 3 | 8 | 6 | 9 |
| 2 | 9 | 1 | 8 | 6 | 7 | 5 | 3 | 4 |
| 1 | 2 | 5 | 6 | 4 | 8 | 3 | 9 | 7 |
| 4 | 3 | 6 | 7 | 9 | 5 | 2 | 8 | 1 |
| 9 | 7 | 8 | 3 | 1 | 2 | 4 | 5 | 6 |

## 169

| 6 | 1 | 7 | 3 | 5 | 8 | 9 | 4 | 2 |
| 4 | 3 | 9 | 6 | 2 | 1 | 8 | 7 | 5 |
| 8 | 5 | 2 | 9 | 7 | 4 | 3 | 1 | 6 |
| 2 | 6 | 3 | 1 | 4 | 5 | 7 | 8 | 9 |
| 1 | 4 | 5 | 7 | 8 | 9 | 6 | 2 | 3 |
| 9 | 7 | 8 | 2 | 6 | 3 | 1 | 5 | 4 |
| 3 | 9 | 4 | 5 | 1 | 7 | 2 | 6 | 8 |
| 7 | 8 | 6 | 4 | 3 | 2 | 5 | 9 | 1 |
| 5 | 2 | 1 | 8 | 9 | 6 | 4 | 3 | 7 |

## 170

| 9 | 7 | 2 | 8 | 4 | 1 | 5 | 6 | 3 |
| 8 | 1 | 4 | 6 | 3 | 5 | 9 | 7 | 2 |
| 6 | 3 | 5 | 7 | 2 | 9 | 8 | 1 | 4 |
| 7 | 5 | 1 | 2 | 9 | 8 | 3 | 4 | 6 |
| 4 | 8 | 6 | 1 | 7 | 3 | 2 | 9 | 5 |
| 2 | 9 | 3 | 4 | 5 | 6 | 1 | 8 | 7 |
| 5 | 2 | 8 | 9 | 6 | 7 | 4 | 3 | 1 |
| 1 | 4 | 7 | 3 | 8 | 2 | 6 | 5 | 9 |
| 3 | 6 | 9 | 5 | 1 | 4 | 7 | 2 | 8 |

## 171

| 9 | 1 | 6 | 7 | 8 | 5 | 3 | 2 | 4 |
| 2 | 7 | 8 | 4 | 3 | 9 | 5 | 1 | 6 |
| 3 | 5 | 4 | 1 | 2 | 6 | 9 | 7 | 8 |
| 4 | 2 | 1 | 8 | 7 | 3 | 6 | 9 | 5 |
| 6 | 8 | 5 | 9 | 1 | 4 | 2 | 3 | 7 |
| 7 | 3 | 9 | 5 | 6 | 2 | 8 | 4 | 1 |
| 8 | 6 | 2 | 3 | 4 | 1 | 7 | 5 | 9 |
| 5 | 4 | 7 | 2 | 9 | 8 | 1 | 6 | 3 |
| 1 | 9 | 3 | 6 | 5 | 7 | 4 | 8 | 2 |

## 172

| 2 | 1 | 4 | 9 | 6 | 8 | 3 | 7 | 5 |
| 9 | 8 | 6 | 5 | 3 | 7 | 1 | 4 | 2 |
| 3 | 7 | 5 | 1 | 2 | 4 | 6 | 8 | 9 |
| 6 | 5 | 8 | 3 | 7 | 2 | 4 | 9 | 1 |
| 4 | 2 | 1 | 8 | 5 | 9 | 7 | 3 | 6 |
| 7 | 9 | 3 | 6 | 4 | 1 | 2 | 5 | 8 |
| 8 | 6 | 2 | 4 | 9 | 3 | 5 | 1 | 7 |
| 5 | 3 | 9 | 7 | 1 | 6 | 8 | 2 | 4 |
| 1 | 4 | 7 | 2 | 8 | 5 | 9 | 6 | 3 |

## 173

| 4 | 3 | 6 | 8 | 7 | 9 | 1 | 5 | 2 |
| 5 | 7 | 8 | 3 | 1 | 2 | 9 | 6 | 4 |
| 9 | 1 | 2 | 6 | 5 | 4 | 7 | 8 | 3 |
| 8 | 6 | 1 | 2 | 3 | 5 | 4 | 9 | 7 |
| 7 | 4 | 9 | 1 | 6 | 8 | 2 | 3 | 5 |
| 3 | 2 | 5 | 4 | 9 | 7 | 6 | 1 | 8 |
| 6 | 9 | 7 | 5 | 4 | 3 | 8 | 2 | 1 |
| 1 | 8 | 3 | 7 | 2 | 6 | 5 | 4 | 9 |
| 2 | 5 | 4 | 9 | 8 | 1 | 3 | 7 | 6 |

## 174

| 4 | 6 | 2 | 8 | 5 | 7 | 3 | 9 | 1 |
| 7 | 8 | 1 | 3 | 4 | 9 | 5 | 2 | 6 |
| 9 | 5 | 3 | 6 | 1 | 2 | 7 | 4 | 8 |
| 2 | 7 | 8 | 1 | 3 | 6 | 9 | 5 | 4 |
| 1 | 9 | 5 | 2 | 7 | 4 | 6 | 8 | 3 |
| 6 | 3 | 4 | 9 | 8 | 5 | 2 | 1 | 7 |
| 3 | 4 | 9 | 5 | 6 | 8 | 1 | 7 | 2 |
| 5 | 1 | 7 | 4 | 2 | 3 | 8 | 6 | 9 |
| 8 | 2 | 6 | 7 | 9 | 1 | 4 | 3 | 5 |

## 175

| 3 | 1 | 8 | 7 | 5 | 6 | 2 | 4 | 9 |
| 4 | 7 | 6 | 2 | 1 | 9 | 3 | 8 | 5 |
| 2 | 5 | 9 | 4 | 8 | 3 | 1 | 6 | 7 |
| 8 | 2 | 3 | 9 | 7 | 5 | 6 | 1 | 4 |
| 6 | 9 | 5 | 3 | 4 | 1 | 7 | 2 | 8 |
| 7 | 4 | 1 | 8 | 6 | 2 | 9 | 5 | 3 |
| 1 | 6 | 7 | 5 | 9 | 4 | 8 | 3 | 2 |
| 9 | 3 | 4 | 6 | 2 | 8 | 5 | 7 | 1 |
| 5 | 8 | 2 | 1 | 3 | 7 | 4 | 9 | 6 |

## 176

| 4 | 1 | 9 | 2 | 6 | 5 | 8 | 3 | 7 |
| 7 | 8 | 6 | 9 | 3 | 1 | 2 | 5 | 4 |
| 2 | 5 | 3 | 8 | 4 | 7 | 9 | 1 | 6 |
| 1 | 9 | 4 | 3 | 7 | 8 | 6 | 2 | 5 |
| 8 | 3 | 5 | 6 | 2 | 4 | 7 | 9 | 1 |
| 6 | 7 | 2 | 5 | 1 | 9 | 4 | 8 | 3 |
| 3 | 4 | 8 | 1 | 9 | 6 | 5 | 7 | 2 |
| 9 | 6 | 1 | 7 | 5 | 2 | 3 | 4 | 8 |
| 5 | 2 | 7 | 4 | 8 | 3 | 1 | 6 | 9 |

**177**

| 5 | 8 | 3 | 2 | 7 | 1 | 9 | 6 | 4 |
|---|---|---|---|---|---|---|---|---|
| 4 | 9 | 6 | 5 | 3 | 8 | 2 | 1 | 7 |
| 2 | 1 | 7 | 6 | 4 | 9 | 5 | 8 | 3 |
| 1 | 3 | 4 | 8 | 5 | 6 | 7 | 2 | 9 |
| 8 | 6 | 5 | 7 | 9 | 2 | 4 | 3 | 1 |
| 9 | 7 | 2 | 3 | 1 | 4 | 6 | 5 | 8 |
| 3 | 4 | 9 | 1 | 2 | 5 | 8 | 7 | 6 |
| 6 | 2 | 1 | 9 | 8 | 7 | 3 | 4 | 5 |
| 7 | 5 | 8 | 4 | 6 | 3 | 1 | 9 | 2 |

**178**

| 7 | 3 | 8 | 9 | 4 | 6 | 2 | 5 | 1 |
|---|---|---|---|---|---|---|---|---|
| 9 | 2 | 5 | 7 | 3 | 1 | 8 | 4 | 6 |
| 1 | 4 | 6 | 2 | 8 | 5 | 3 | 7 | 9 |
| 3 | 6 | 7 | 1 | 5 | 9 | 4 | 8 | 2 |
| 8 | 1 | 9 | 4 | 2 | 3 | 5 | 6 | 7 |
| 4 | 5 | 2 | 8 | 6 | 7 | 9 | 1 | 3 |
| 2 | 8 | 1 | 6 | 9 | 4 | 7 | 3 | 5 |
| 6 | 9 | 3 | 5 | 7 | 8 | 1 | 2 | 4 |
| 5 | 7 | 4 | 3 | 1 | 2 | 6 | 9 | 8 |

**179**

| 7 | 1 | 2 | 5 | 4 | 6 | 8 | 9 | 3 |
|---|---|---|---|---|---|---|---|---|
| 8 | 5 | 6 | 3 | 9 | 1 | 7 | 4 | 2 |
| 4 | 9 | 3 | 2 | 7 | 8 | 1 | 5 | 6 |
| 3 | 4 | 8 | 9 | 5 | 7 | 6 | 2 | 1 |
| 9 | 6 | 5 | 1 | 3 | 2 | 4 | 8 | 7 |
| 1 | 2 | 7 | 8 | 6 | 4 | 9 | 3 | 5 |
| 2 | 7 | 9 | 4 | 1 | 5 | 3 | 6 | 8 |
| 6 | 8 | 4 | 7 | 2 | 3 | 5 | 1 | 9 |
| 5 | 3 | 1 | 6 | 8 | 9 | 2 | 7 | 4 |

**180**

| 2 | 8 | 1 | 3 | 4 | 7 | 9 | 5 | 6 |
|---|---|---|---|---|---|---|---|---|
| 6 | 4 | 3 | 1 | 5 | 9 | 2 | 7 | 8 |
| 5 | 9 | 7 | 2 | 8 | 6 | 3 | 4 | 1 |
| 7 | 6 | 9 | 5 | 2 | 8 | 4 | 1 | 3 |
| 4 | 5 | 8 | 6 | 3 | 1 | 7 | 2 | 9 |
| 1 | 3 | 2 | 9 | 7 | 4 | 8 | 6 | 5 |
| 8 | 1 | 6 | 4 | 9 | 2 | 5 | 3 | 7 |
| 3 | 7 | 4 | 8 | 6 | 5 | 1 | 9 | 2 |
| 9 | 2 | 5 | 7 | 1 | 3 | 6 | 8 | 4 |

**181**

| 7 | 2 | 5 | 9 | 4 | 6 | 8 | 3 | 1 |
|---|---|---|---|---|---|---|---|---|
| 1 | 6 | 9 | 2 | 3 | 8 | 7 | 5 | 4 |
| 3 | 8 | 4 | 5 | 1 | 7 | 9 | 6 | 2 |
| 5 | 7 | 2 | 8 | 9 | 1 | 6 | 4 | 3 |
| 4 | 1 | 8 | 3 | 6 | 2 | 5 | 7 | 9 |
| 6 | 9 | 3 | 4 | 7 | 5 | 2 | 1 | 8 |
| 9 | 5 | 7 | 1 | 2 | 4 | 3 | 8 | 6 |
| 2 | 4 | 6 | 7 | 8 | 3 | 1 | 9 | 5 |
| 8 | 3 | 1 | 6 | 5 | 9 | 4 | 2 | 7 |

**182**

| 2 | 7 | 9 | 8 | 3 | 4 | 5 | 6 | 1 |
|---|---|---|---|---|---|---|---|---|
| 1 | 3 | 4 | 5 | 9 | 6 | 2 | 7 | 8 |
| 6 | 8 | 5 | 2 | 7 | 1 | 9 | 4 | 3 |
| 5 | 2 | 6 | 4 | 1 | 9 | 3 | 8 | 7 |
| 8 | 4 | 7 | 3 | 2 | 5 | 1 | 9 | 6 |
| 9 | 1 | 3 | 6 | 8 | 7 | 4 | 5 | 2 |
| 7 | 5 | 1 | 9 | 6 | 3 | 8 | 2 | 4 |
| 3 | 9 | 8 | 7 | 4 | 2 | 6 | 1 | 5 |
| 4 | 6 | 2 | 1 | 5 | 8 | 7 | 3 | 9 |

**183**

| 8 | 9 | 7 | 1 | 4 | 6 | 5 | 2 | 3 |
|---|---|---|---|---|---|---|---|---|
| 3 | 5 | 2 | 8 | 7 | 9 | 1 | 4 | 6 |
| 6 | 1 | 4 | 2 | 3 | 5 | 7 | 8 | 9 |
| 9 | 6 | 3 | 4 | 1 | 2 | 8 | 5 | 7 |
| 7 | 2 | 1 | 6 | 5 | 8 | 9 | 3 | 4 |
| 4 | 8 | 5 | 3 | 9 | 7 | 2 | 6 | 1 |
| 2 | 4 | 6 | 9 | 8 | 1 | 3 | 7 | 5 |
| 1 | 7 | 8 | 5 | 6 | 3 | 4 | 9 | 2 |
| 5 | 3 | 9 | 7 | 2 | 4 | 6 | 1 | 8 |

**184**

| 4 | 1 | 8 | 3 | 6 | 2 | 7 | 5 | 9 |
|---|---|---|---|---|---|---|---|---|
| 2 | 3 | 9 | 5 | 8 | 7 | 1 | 4 | 6 |
| 5 | 7 | 6 | 9 | 4 | 1 | 8 | 2 | 3 |
| 3 | 6 | 7 | 8 | 9 | 5 | 4 | 1 | 2 |
| 1 | 9 | 4 | 7 | 2 | 3 | 6 | 8 | 5 |
| 8 | 2 | 5 | 6 | 1 | 4 | 9 | 3 | 7 |
| 6 | 8 | 1 | 2 | 3 | 9 | 5 | 7 | 4 |
| 7 | 4 | 3 | 1 | 5 | 6 | 2 | 9 | 8 |
| 9 | 5 | 2 | 4 | 7 | 8 | 3 | 6 | 1 |

## 185

| 5 | 6 | 2 | 7 | 1 | 8 | 9 | 4 | 3 |
|---|---|---|---|---|---|---|---|---|
| 8 | 7 | 1 | 9 | 3 | 4 | 5 | 2 | 6 |
| 4 | 3 | 9 | 2 | 6 | 5 | 7 | 8 | 1 |
| 2 | 1 | 7 | 3 | 8 | 6 | 4 | 9 | 5 |
| 9 | 5 | 4 | 1 | 7 | 2 | 3 | 6 | 8 |
| 3 | 8 | 6 | 4 | 5 | 9 | 1 | 7 | 2 |
| 1 | 2 | 8 | 5 | 9 | 7 | 6 | 3 | 4 |
| 7 | 4 | 5 | 6 | 2 | 3 | 8 | 1 | 9 |
| 6 | 9 | 3 | 8 | 4 | 1 | 2 | 5 | 7 |

## 186

| 8 | 4 | 3 | 7 | 1 | 6 | 5 | 2 | 9 |
|---|---|---|---|---|---|---|---|---|
| 1 | 5 | 6 | 4 | 2 | 9 | 3 | 7 | 8 |
| 9 | 2 | 7 | 8 | 3 | 5 | 4 | 6 | 1 |
| 3 | 1 | 8 | 2 | 7 | 4 | 6 | 9 | 5 |
| 4 | 9 | 5 | 1 | 6 | 8 | 7 | 3 | 2 |
| 6 | 7 | 2 | 5 | 9 | 3 | 1 | 8 | 4 |
| 5 | 6 | 1 | 3 | 8 | 2 | 9 | 4 | 7 |
| 2 | 3 | 4 | 9 | 5 | 7 | 8 | 1 | 6 |
| 7 | 8 | 9 | 6 | 4 | 1 | 2 | 5 | 3 |

## 187

| 5 | 3 | 4 | 6 | 7 | 9 | 1 | 2 | 8 |
|---|---|---|---|---|---|---|---|---|
| 8 | 2 | 9 | 3 | 1 | 5 | 4 | 7 | 6 |
| 1 | 7 | 6 | 2 | 4 | 8 | 5 | 9 | 3 |
| 9 | 5 | 8 | 4 | 6 | 7 | 2 | 3 | 1 |
| 2 | 1 | 7 | 8 | 5 | 3 | 6 | 4 | 9 |
| 6 | 4 | 3 | 1 | 9 | 2 | 7 | 8 | 5 |
| 4 | 9 | 1 | 7 | 3 | 6 | 8 | 5 | 2 |
| 7 | 8 | 5 | 9 | 2 | 1 | 3 | 6 | 4 |
| 3 | 6 | 2 | 5 | 8 | 4 | 9 | 1 | 7 |

## 188

| 1 | 3 | 8 | 6 | 2 | 4 | 9 | 5 | 7 |
|---|---|---|---|---|---|---|---|---|
| 4 | 5 | 2 | 7 | 8 | 9 | 6 | 3 | 1 |
| 6 | 9 | 7 | 5 | 3 | 1 | 8 | 2 | 4 |
| 3 | 2 | 6 | 9 | 7 | 8 | 1 | 4 | 5 |
| 7 | 4 | 1 | 2 | 6 | 5 | 3 | 9 | 8 |
| 9 | 8 | 5 | 4 | 1 | 3 | 7 | 6 | 2 |
| 2 | 7 | 9 | 1 | 4 | 6 | 5 | 8 | 3 |
| 5 | 1 | 3 | 8 | 9 | 2 | 4 | 7 | 6 |
| 8 | 6 | 4 | 3 | 5 | 7 | 2 | 1 | 9 |

## 189

| 9 | 3 | 6 | 7 | 5 | 2 | 8 | 4 | 1 |
|---|---|---|---|---|---|---|---|---|
| 5 | 2 | 1 | 3 | 4 | 8 | 9 | 6 | 7 |
| 4 | 8 | 7 | 9 | 6 | 1 | 2 | 3 | 5 |
| 7 | 4 | 9 | 6 | 2 | 5 | 3 | 1 | 8 |
| 8 | 5 | 2 | 1 | 3 | 9 | 6 | 7 | 4 |
| 1 | 6 | 3 | 8 | 7 | 4 | 5 | 2 | 9 |
| 3 | 1 | 4 | 5 | 9 | 6 | 7 | 8 | 2 |
| 2 | 7 | 5 | 4 | 8 | 3 | 1 | 9 | 6 |
| 6 | 9 | 8 | 2 | 1 | 7 | 4 | 5 | 3 |

## 190

| 9 | 3 | 1 | 6 | 2 | 5 | 4 | 8 | 7 |
|---|---|---|---|---|---|---|---|---|
| 8 | 2 | 7 | 9 | 3 | 4 | 5 | 6 | 1 |
| 4 | 5 | 6 | 8 | 1 | 7 | 9 | 3 | 2 |
| 1 | 8 | 5 | 3 | 9 | 6 | 2 | 7 | 4 |
| 3 | 9 | 4 | 2 | 7 | 1 | 6 | 5 | 8 |
| 6 | 7 | 2 | 4 | 5 | 8 | 3 | 1 | 9 |
| 7 | 6 | 9 | 5 | 8 | 2 | 1 | 4 | 3 |
| 2 | 4 | 8 | 1 | 6 | 3 | 7 | 9 | 5 |
| 5 | 1 | 3 | 7 | 4 | 9 | 8 | 2 | 6 |

## 191

| 5 | 8 | 2 | 9 | 3 | 1 | 7 | 6 | 4 |
|---|---|---|---|---|---|---|---|---|
| 3 | 1 | 7 | 2 | 6 | 4 | 5 | 9 | 8 |
| 6 | 9 | 4 | 5 | 8 | 7 | 2 | 1 | 3 |
| 1 | 7 | 9 | 4 | 2 | 6 | 8 | 3 | 5 |
| 2 | 4 | 6 | 8 | 5 | 3 | 1 | 7 | 9 |
| 8 | 5 | 3 | 7 | 1 | 9 | 4 | 2 | 6 |
| 4 | 3 | 5 | 6 | 7 | 2 | 9 | 8 | 1 |
| 7 | 6 | 8 | 1 | 9 | 5 | 3 | 4 | 2 |
| 9 | 2 | 1 | 3 | 4 | 8 | 6 | 5 | 7 |

## 192

| 3 | 6 | 7 | 1 | 8 | 9 | 5 | 4 | 2 |
|---|---|---|---|---|---|---|---|---|
| 5 | 9 | 2 | 3 | 4 | 7 | 8 | 6 | 1 |
| 1 | 8 | 4 | 5 | 6 | 2 | 7 | 3 | 9 |
| 9 | 1 | 5 | 4 | 2 | 6 | 3 | 7 | 8 |
| 6 | 7 | 8 | 9 | 1 | 3 | 4 | 2 | 5 |
| 4 | 2 | 3 | 8 | 7 | 5 | 9 | 1 | 6 |
| 2 | 3 | 6 | 7 | 5 | 8 | 1 | 9 | 4 |
| 7 | 5 | 1 | 2 | 9 | 4 | 6 | 8 | 3 |
| 8 | 4 | 9 | 6 | 3 | 1 | 2 | 5 | 7 |

**193**

| 3 | 7 | 6 | 8 | 2 | 5 | 9 | 1 | 4 |
|---|---|---|---|---|---|---|---|---|
| 5 | 2 | 1 | 7 | 9 | 4 | 6 | 8 | 3 |
| 4 | 9 | 8 | 3 | 1 | 6 | 2 | 5 | 7 |
| 9 | 4 | 2 | 6 | 5 | 1 | 7 | 3 | 8 |
| 8 | 1 | 7 | 4 | 3 | 9 | 5 | 6 | 2 |
| 6 | 3 | 5 | 2 | 7 | 8 | 4 | 9 | 1 |
| 2 | 8 | 9 | 1 | 6 | 7 | 3 | 4 | 5 |
| 1 | 6 | 3 | 5 | 4 | 2 | 8 | 7 | 9 |
| 7 | 5 | 4 | 9 | 8 | 3 | 1 | 2 | 6 |

**194**

| 1 | 8 | 3 | 6 | 7 | 2 | 4 | 5 | 9 |
|---|---|---|---|---|---|---|---|---|
| 2 | 7 | 9 | 4 | 5 | 3 | 6 | 8 | 1 |
| 4 | 5 | 6 | 1 | 8 | 9 | 3 | 7 | 2 |
| 5 | 1 | 2 | 8 | 4 | 6 | 9 | 3 | 7 |
| 9 | 3 | 8 | 7 | 2 | 5 | 1 | 4 | 6 |
| 7 | 6 | 4 | 3 | 9 | 1 | 5 | 2 | 8 |
| 3 | 4 | 1 | 2 | 6 | 8 | 7 | 9 | 5 |
| 6 | 2 | 5 | 9 | 3 | 7 | 8 | 1 | 4 |
| 8 | 9 | 7 | 5 | 1 | 4 | 2 | 6 | 3 |

**195**

| 4 | 2 | 3 | 5 | 7 | 1 | 9 | 6 | 8 |
|---|---|---|---|---|---|---|---|---|
| 6 | 7 | 1 | 9 | 4 | 8 | 3 | 2 | 5 |
| 5 | 9 | 8 | 6 | 3 | 2 | 1 | 7 | 4 |
| 8 | 3 | 5 | 4 | 2 | 7 | 6 | 1 | 9 |
| 2 | 6 | 9 | 3 | 1 | 5 | 4 | 8 | 7 |
| 7 | 1 | 4 | 8 | 9 | 6 | 2 | 5 | 3 |
| 3 | 8 | 7 | 1 | 6 | 9 | 5 | 4 | 2 |
| 1 | 4 | 2 | 7 | 5 | 3 | 8 | 9 | 6 |
| 9 | 5 | 6 | 2 | 8 | 4 | 7 | 3 | 1 |

**196**

| 5 | 7 | 2 | 6 | 4 | 9 | 3 | 1 | 8 |
|---|---|---|---|---|---|---|---|---|
| 9 | 4 | 8 | 3 | 2 | 1 | 7 | 5 | 6 |
| 1 | 6 | 3 | 5 | 7 | 8 | 4 | 2 | 9 |
| 3 | 5 | 6 | 7 | 1 | 4 | 8 | 9 | 2 |
| 2 | 1 | 9 | 8 | 3 | 5 | 6 | 7 | 4 |
| 4 | 8 | 7 | 9 | 6 | 2 | 1 | 3 | 5 |
| 7 | 3 | 4 | 2 | 5 | 6 | 9 | 8 | 1 |
| 8 | 2 | 1 | 4 | 9 | 7 | 5 | 6 | 3 |
| 6 | 9 | 5 | 1 | 8 | 3 | 2 | 4 | 7 |

**197**

| 9 | 6 | 1 | 5 | 3 | 8 | 2 | 7 | 4 |
|---|---|---|---|---|---|---|---|---|
| 5 | 3 | 2 | 4 | 9 | 7 | 1 | 8 | 6 |
| 8 | 4 | 7 | 6 | 2 | 1 | 9 | 5 | 3 |
| 4 | 8 | 9 | 1 | 5 | 2 | 3 | 6 | 7 |
| 7 | 5 | 6 | 3 | 4 | 9 | 8 | 2 | 1 |
| 2 | 1 | 3 | 7 | 8 | 6 | 4 | 9 | 5 |
| 1 | 2 | 5 | 9 | 6 | 4 | 7 | 3 | 8 |
| 3 | 7 | 8 | 2 | 1 | 5 | 6 | 4 | 9 |
| 6 | 9 | 4 | 8 | 7 | 3 | 5 | 1 | 2 |

**198**

| 9 | 5 | 6 | 2 | 8 | 1 | 7 | 3 | 4 |
|---|---|---|---|---|---|---|---|---|
| 3 | 8 | 7 | 5 | 4 | 9 | 2 | 6 | 1 |
| 1 | 2 | 4 | 3 | 6 | 7 | 9 | 5 | 8 |
| 4 | 6 | 8 | 9 | 7 | 5 | 3 | 1 | 2 |
| 2 | 7 | 1 | 6 | 3 | 8 | 4 | 9 | 5 |
| 5 | 3 | 9 | 4 | 1 | 2 | 6 | 8 | 7 |
| 8 | 4 | 2 | 1 | 9 | 3 | 5 | 7 | 6 |
| 7 | 9 | 5 | 8 | 2 | 6 | 1 | 4 | 3 |
| 6 | 1 | 3 | 7 | 5 | 4 | 8 | 2 | 9 |

**199**

| 7 | 3 | 2 | 9 | 8 | 1 | 6 | 4 | 5 |
|---|---|---|---|---|---|---|---|---|
| 1 | 5 | 9 | 4 | 6 | 7 | 8 | 3 | 2 |
| 8 | 6 | 4 | 2 | 3 | 5 | 9 | 1 | 7 |
| 2 | 8 | 6 | 5 | 1 | 3 | 4 | 7 | 9 |
| 3 | 1 | 5 | 7 | 4 | 9 | 2 | 8 | 6 |
| 9 | 4 | 7 | 8 | 2 | 6 | 1 | 5 | 3 |
| 4 | 9 | 1 | 3 | 7 | 2 | 5 | 6 | 8 |
| 5 | 7 | 8 | 6 | 9 | 4 | 3 | 2 | 1 |
| 6 | 2 | 3 | 1 | 5 | 8 | 7 | 9 | 4 |

**200**

| 8 | 1 | 9 | 3 | 7 | 2 | 4 | 6 | 5 |
|---|---|---|---|---|---|---|---|---|
| 4 | 5 | 6 | 1 | 9 | 8 | 7 | 3 | 2 |
| 3 | 7 | 2 | 4 | 6 | 5 | 1 | 9 | 8 |
| 9 | 8 | 5 | 2 | 1 | 3 | 6 | 4 | 7 |
| 1 | 6 | 3 | 7 | 8 | 4 | 5 | 2 | 9 |
| 2 | 4 | 7 | 6 | 5 | 9 | 8 | 1 | 3 |
| 5 | 9 | 4 | 8 | 3 | 1 | 2 | 7 | 6 |
| 6 | 2 | 8 | 9 | 4 | 7 | 3 | 5 | 1 |
| 7 | 3 | 1 | 5 | 2 | 6 | 9 | 8 | 4 |

**201**

| 1 | 8 | 5 | 7 | 2 | 3 | 4 | 6 | 9 |
|---|---|---|---|---|---|---|---|---|
| 3 | 7 | 2 | 9 | 6 | 4 | 5 | 1 | 8 |
| 9 | 4 | 6 | 1 | 8 | 5 | 2 | 7 | 3 |
| 5 | 6 | 9 | 2 | 7 | 8 | 3 | 4 | 1 |
| 8 | 2 | 4 | 5 | 3 | 1 | 7 | 9 | 6 |
| 7 | 3 | 1 | 4 | 9 | 6 | 8 | 2 | 5 |
| 6 | 5 | 7 | 3 | 4 | 9 | 1 | 8 | 2 |
| 2 | 1 | 8 | 6 | 5 | 7 | 9 | 3 | 4 |
| 4 | 9 | 3 | 8 | 1 | 2 | 6 | 5 | 7 |

**202**

| 2 | 5 | 3 | 6 | 7 | 4 | 9 | 1 | 8 |
|---|---|---|---|---|---|---|---|---|
| 1 | 6 | 8 | 3 | 2 | 9 | 5 | 7 | 4 |
| 7 | 4 | 9 | 5 | 1 | 8 | 6 | 3 | 2 |
| 3 | 2 | 7 | 4 | 8 | 6 | 1 | 9 | 5 |
| 9 | 8 | 6 | 1 | 3 | 5 | 4 | 2 | 7 |
| 5 | 1 | 4 | 2 | 9 | 7 | 3 | 8 | 6 |
| 4 | 9 | 2 | 8 | 6 | 1 | 7 | 5 | 3 |
| 6 | 3 | 1 | 7 | 5 | 2 | 8 | 4 | 9 |
| 8 | 7 | 5 | 9 | 4 | 3 | 2 | 6 | 1 |

**203**

| 5 | 1 | 2 | 9 | 7 | 6 | 8 | 3 | 4 |
|---|---|---|---|---|---|---|---|---|
| 6 | 9 | 3 | 4 | 1 | 8 | 2 | 5 | 7 |
| 4 | 8 | 7 | 2 | 3 | 5 | 1 | 6 | 9 |
| 1 | 4 | 5 | 8 | 6 | 2 | 9 | 7 | 3 |
| 2 | 7 | 8 | 5 | 9 | 3 | 6 | 4 | 1 |
| 3 | 6 | 9 | 1 | 4 | 7 | 5 | 2 | 8 |
| 7 | 2 | 1 | 3 | 5 | 9 | 4 | 8 | 6 |
| 8 | 3 | 4 | 6 | 2 | 1 | 7 | 9 | 5 |
| 9 | 5 | 6 | 7 | 8 | 4 | 3 | 1 | 2 |

**204**

| 5 | 7 | 6 | 4 | 3 | 8 | 1 | 2 | 9 |
|---|---|---|---|---|---|---|---|---|
| 4 | 8 | 3 | 1 | 2 | 9 | 6 | 5 | 7 |
| 2 | 1 | 9 | 7 | 6 | 5 | 4 | 8 | 3 |
| 8 | 9 | 1 | 6 | 4 | 7 | 5 | 3 | 2 |
| 7 | 5 | 4 | 2 | 9 | 3 | 8 | 1 | 6 |
| 6 | 3 | 2 | 5 | 8 | 1 | 9 | 7 | 4 |
| 1 | 4 | 5 | 3 | 7 | 6 | 2 | 9 | 8 |
| 3 | 2 | 8 | 9 | 5 | 4 | 7 | 6 | 1 |
| 9 | 6 | 7 | 8 | 1 | 2 | 3 | 4 | 5 |

**205**

| 6 | 5 | 1 | 7 | 9 | 4 | 3 | 2 | 8 |
|---|---|---|---|---|---|---|---|---|
| 8 | 7 | 9 | 5 | 3 | 2 | 1 | 4 | 6 |
| 2 | 3 | 4 | 1 | 6 | 8 | 9 | 5 | 7 |
| 5 | 9 | 2 | 3 | 4 | 7 | 6 | 8 | 1 |
| 3 | 8 | 7 | 2 | 1 | 6 | 4 | 9 | 5 |
| 4 | 1 | 6 | 8 | 5 | 9 | 7 | 3 | 2 |
| 1 | 6 | 3 | 4 | 8 | 5 | 2 | 7 | 9 |
| 7 | 4 | 5 | 9 | 2 | 1 | 8 | 6 | 3 |
| 9 | 2 | 8 | 6 | 7 | 3 | 5 | 1 | 4 |

**206**

| 8 | 5 | 9 | 3 | 6 | 7 | 1 | 4 | 2 |
|---|---|---|---|---|---|---|---|---|
| 3 | 4 | 7 | 9 | 1 | 2 | 8 | 5 | 6 |
| 6 | 1 | 2 | 8 | 5 | 4 | 3 | 7 | 9 |
| 7 | 8 | 1 | 5 | 4 | 9 | 6 | 2 | 3 |
| 2 | 9 | 4 | 7 | 3 | 6 | 5 | 1 | 8 |
| 5 | 3 | 6 | 1 | 2 | 8 | 7 | 9 | 4 |
| 4 | 2 | 3 | 6 | 7 | 5 | 9 | 8 | 1 |
| 9 | 6 | 5 | 2 | 8 | 1 | 4 | 3 | 7 |
| 1 | 7 | 8 | 4 | 9 | 3 | 2 | 6 | 5 |

**207**

| 2 | 3 | 1 | 9 | 4 | 7 | 5 | 8 | 6 |
|---|---|---|---|---|---|---|---|---|
| 9 | 8 | 6 | 5 | 1 | 3 | 2 | 4 | 7 |
| 7 | 5 | 4 | 8 | 6 | 2 | 3 | 1 | 9 |
| 6 | 4 | 2 | 3 | 9 | 8 | 1 | 7 | 5 |
| 3 | 1 | 8 | 7 | 5 | 4 | 6 | 9 | 2 |
| 5 | 7 | 9 | 6 | 2 | 1 | 4 | 3 | 8 |
| 4 | 2 | 5 | 1 | 7 | 9 | 8 | 6 | 3 |
| 1 | 9 | 3 | 2 | 8 | 6 | 7 | 5 | 4 |
| 8 | 6 | 7 | 4 | 3 | 5 | 9 | 2 | 1 |

**208**

| 1 | 3 | 9 | 2 | 7 | 8 | 5 | 6 | 4 |
|---|---|---|---|---|---|---|---|---|
| 7 | 4 | 6 | 3 | 5 | 1 | 8 | 2 | 9 |
| 8 | 5 | 2 | 4 | 9 | 6 | 1 | 3 | 7 |
| 2 | 8 | 7 | 5 | 6 | 9 | 3 | 4 | 1 |
| 3 | 6 | 4 | 1 | 2 | 7 | 9 | 5 | 8 |
| 9 | 1 | 5 | 8 | 3 | 4 | 2 | 7 | 6 |
| 4 | 9 | 3 | 6 | 8 | 2 | 7 | 1 | 5 |
| 5 | 7 | 1 | 9 | 4 | 3 | 6 | 8 | 2 |
| 6 | 2 | 8 | 7 | 1 | 5 | 4 | 9 | 3 |

## 209

| 8 | 3 | 5 | 4 | 7 | 1 | 9 | 2 | 6 |
|---|---|---|---|---|---|---|---|---|
| 9 | 1 | 7 | 2 | 3 | 6 | 5 | 4 | 8 |
| 6 | 4 | 2 | 5 | 9 | 8 | 3 | 7 | 1 |
| 7 | 5 | 6 | 8 | 2 | 9 | 1 | 3 | 4 |
| 3 | 8 | 9 | 1 | 5 | 4 | 7 | 6 | 2 |
| 4 | 2 | 1 | 3 | 6 | 7 | 8 | 5 | 9 |
| 2 | 6 | 8 | 7 | 1 | 5 | 4 | 9 | 3 |
| 5 | 9 | 4 | 6 | 8 | 3 | 2 | 1 | 7 |
| 1 | 7 | 3 | 9 | 4 | 2 | 6 | 8 | 5 |

## 210

| 3 | 2 | 9 | 5 | 1 | 4 | 8 | 7 | 6 |
|---|---|---|---|---|---|---|---|---|
| 6 | 4 | 5 | 9 | 8 | 7 | 2 | 3 | 1 |
| 7 | 1 | 8 | 2 | 6 | 3 | 5 | 4 | 9 |
| 4 | 5 | 1 | 6 | 9 | 2 | 3 | 8 | 7 |
| 2 | 9 | 6 | 3 | 7 | 8 | 4 | 1 | 5 |
| 8 | 7 | 3 | 4 | 5 | 1 | 6 | 9 | 2 |
| 5 | 3 | 7 | 1 | 4 | 6 | 9 | 2 | 8 |
| 9 | 8 | 2 | 7 | 3 | 5 | 1 | 6 | 4 |
| 1 | 6 | 4 | 8 | 2 | 9 | 7 | 5 | 3 |

## 211

| 4 | 6 | 9 | 3 | 5 | 2 | 8 | 1 | 7 |
|---|---|---|---|---|---|---|---|---|
| 3 | 8 | 7 | 6 | 1 | 4 | 9 | 2 | 5 |
| 2 | 1 | 5 | 8 | 9 | 7 | 4 | 6 | 3 |
| 1 | 3 | 8 | 9 | 7 | 5 | 6 | 4 | 2 |
| 6 | 5 | 2 | 4 | 8 | 1 | 7 | 3 | 9 |
| 9 | 7 | 4 | 2 | 3 | 6 | 5 | 8 | 1 |
| 7 | 9 | 3 | 1 | 4 | 8 | 2 | 5 | 6 |
| 5 | 4 | 6 | 7 | 2 | 3 | 1 | 9 | 8 |
| 8 | 2 | 1 | 5 | 6 | 9 | 3 | 7 | 4 |

## 212

| 6 | 9 | 8 | 3 | 7 | 2 | 1 | 4 | 5 |
|---|---|---|---|---|---|---|---|---|
| 5 | 1 | 2 | 6 | 4 | 8 | 3 | 9 | 7 |
| 7 | 4 | 3 | 9 | 1 | 5 | 2 | 6 | 8 |
| 4 | 6 | 9 | 1 | 8 | 3 | 5 | 7 | 2 |
| 1 | 8 | 5 | 4 | 2 | 7 | 6 | 3 | 9 |
| 3 | 2 | 7 | 5 | 9 | 6 | 4 | 8 | 1 |
| 2 | 7 | 1 | 8 | 3 | 4 | 9 | 5 | 6 |
| 9 | 3 | 6 | 7 | 5 | 1 | 8 | 2 | 4 |
| 8 | 5 | 4 | 2 | 6 | 9 | 7 | 1 | 3 |

## 213

| 7 | 3 | 1 | 6 | 5 | 4 | 9 | 8 | 2 |
|---|---|---|---|---|---|---|---|---|
| 8 | 2 | 9 | 3 | 1 | 7 | 6 | 5 | 4 |
| 5 | 6 | 4 | 8 | 2 | 9 | 7 | 3 | 1 |
| 2 | 7 | 5 | 4 | 9 | 6 | 8 | 1 | 3 |
| 4 | 8 | 6 | 2 | 3 | 1 | 5 | 7 | 9 |
| 1 | 9 | 3 | 5 | 7 | 8 | 2 | 4 | 6 |
| 3 | 4 | 8 | 7 | 6 | 2 | 1 | 9 | 5 |
| 6 | 1 | 7 | 9 | 4 | 5 | 3 | 2 | 8 |
| 9 | 5 | 2 | 1 | 8 | 3 | 4 | 6 | 7 |

## 214

| 7 | 3 | 8 | 6 | 5 | 4 | 9 | 2 | 1 |
|---|---|---|---|---|---|---|---|---|
| 6 | 5 | 4 | 2 | 9 | 1 | 8 | 7 | 3 |
| 9 | 1 | 2 | 7 | 8 | 3 | 5 | 6 | 4 |
| 2 | 9 | 3 | 8 | 4 | 6 | 1 | 5 | 7 |
| 5 | 7 | 6 | 9 | 1 | 2 | 4 | 3 | 8 |
| 8 | 4 | 1 | 5 | 3 | 7 | 2 | 9 | 6 |
| 3 | 8 | 5 | 1 | 7 | 9 | 6 | 4 | 2 |
| 1 | 6 | 7 | 4 | 2 | 5 | 3 | 8 | 9 |
| 4 | 2 | 9 | 3 | 6 | 8 | 7 | 1 | 5 |

## 215

| 6 | 9 | 7 | 1 | 4 | 3 | 8 | 2 | 5 |
|---|---|---|---|---|---|---|---|---|
| 8 | 4 | 3 | 7 | 2 | 5 | 1 | 9 | 6 |
| 5 | 1 | 2 | 8 | 9 | 6 | 4 | 3 | 7 |
| 1 | 7 | 8 | 5 | 3 | 9 | 2 | 6 | 4 |
| 9 | 5 | 6 | 2 | 7 | 4 | 3 | 8 | 1 |
| 2 | 3 | 4 | 6 | 8 | 1 | 7 | 5 | 9 |
| 4 | 2 | 1 | 9 | 6 | 8 | 5 | 7 | 3 |
| 3 | 8 | 9 | 4 | 5 | 7 | 6 | 1 | 2 |
| 7 | 6 | 5 | 3 | 1 | 2 | 9 | 4 | 8 |

## 216

| 7 | 3 | 8 | 6 | 1 | 4 | 2 | 9 | 5 |
|---|---|---|---|---|---|---|---|---|
| 5 | 4 | 2 | 9 | 3 | 8 | 7 | 6 | 1 |
| 6 | 1 | 9 | 2 | 7 | 5 | 4 | 8 | 3 |
| 4 | 5 | 3 | 8 | 6 | 1 | 9 | 2 | 7 |
| 2 | 6 | 7 | 3 | 5 | 9 | 8 | 1 | 4 |
| 8 | 9 | 1 | 7 | 4 | 2 | 3 | 5 | 6 |
| 3 | 8 | 5 | 1 | 9 | 7 | 6 | 4 | 2 |
| 9 | 7 | 4 | 5 | 2 | 6 | 1 | 3 | 8 |
| 1 | 2 | 6 | 4 | 8 | 3 | 5 | 7 | 9 |

**217**

| 9 | 7 | 3 | 6 | 8 | 2 | 1 | 4 | 5 |
|---|---|---|---|---|---|---|---|---|
| 1 | 4 | 8 | 9 | 5 | 7 | 2 | 3 | 6 |
| 5 | 6 | 2 | 4 | 1 | 3 | 9 | 8 | 7 |
| 2 | 5 | 4 | 1 | 6 | 9 | 8 | 7 | 3 |
| 6 | 3 | 1 | 5 | 7 | 8 | 4 | 2 | 9 |
| 7 | 8 | 9 | 2 | 3 | 4 | 5 | 6 | 1 |
| 4 | 1 | 5 | 7 | 2 | 6 | 3 | 9 | 8 |
| 8 | 2 | 6 | 3 | 9 | 5 | 7 | 1 | 4 |
| 3 | 9 | 7 | 8 | 4 | 1 | 6 | 5 | 2 |

**218**

| 5 | 4 | 7 | 6 | 8 | 1 | 2 | 9 | 3 |
|---|---|---|---|---|---|---|---|---|
| 9 | 6 | 2 | 7 | 4 | 3 | 8 | 1 | 5 |
| 3 | 8 | 1 | 9 | 5 | 2 | 4 | 7 | 6 |
| 1 | 3 | 6 | 4 | 9 | 5 | 7 | 8 | 2 |
| 2 | 5 | 8 | 1 | 6 | 7 | 9 | 3 | 4 |
| 4 | 7 | 9 | 3 | 2 | 8 | 6 | 5 | 1 |
| 7 | 2 | 5 | 8 | 3 | 4 | 1 | 6 | 9 |
| 6 | 1 | 3 | 2 | 7 | 9 | 5 | 4 | 8 |
| 8 | 9 | 4 | 5 | 1 | 6 | 3 | 2 | 7 |

**219**

| 4 | 5 | 9 | 1 | 6 | 8 | 7 | 2 | 3 |
|---|---|---|---|---|---|---|---|---|
| 7 | 6 | 1 | 3 | 5 | 2 | 4 | 9 | 8 |
| 8 | 3 | 2 | 7 | 4 | 9 | 1 | 6 | 5 |
| 6 | 2 | 3 | 5 | 1 | 7 | 9 | 8 | 4 |
| 5 | 4 | 8 | 2 | 9 | 6 | 3 | 7 | 1 |
| 1 | 9 | 7 | 8 | 3 | 4 | 6 | 5 | 2 |
| 2 | 1 | 5 | 6 | 7 | 3 | 8 | 4 | 9 |
| 9 | 8 | 6 | 4 | 2 | 1 | 5 | 3 | 7 |
| 3 | 7 | 4 | 9 | 8 | 5 | 2 | 1 | 6 |

**220**

| 9 | 2 | 1 | 3 | 7 | 4 | 6 | 8 | 5 |
|---|---|---|---|---|---|---|---|---|
| 6 | 7 | 3 | 5 | 1 | 8 | 9 | 2 | 4 |
| 8 | 4 | 5 | 2 | 6 | 9 | 1 | 7 | 3 |
| 3 | 6 | 4 | 8 | 9 | 1 | 2 | 5 | 7 |
| 2 | 8 | 9 | 6 | 5 | 7 | 3 | 4 | 1 |
| 1 | 5 | 7 | 4 | 2 | 3 | 8 | 6 | 9 |
| 4 | 9 | 8 | 7 | 3 | 6 | 5 | 1 | 2 |
| 5 | 3 | 6 | 1 | 4 | 2 | 7 | 9 | 8 |
| 7 | 1 | 2 | 9 | 8 | 5 | 4 | 3 | 6 |

**221**

| 7 | 1 | 6 | 9 | 2 | 3 | 5 | 4 | 8 |
|---|---|---|---|---|---|---|---|---|
| 5 | 3 | 8 | 7 | 1 | 4 | 6 | 9 | 2 |
| 4 | 2 | 9 | 8 | 6 | 5 | 1 | 3 | 7 |
| 2 | 5 | 4 | 1 | 8 | 7 | 3 | 6 | 9 |
| 8 | 7 | 3 | 4 | 9 | 6 | 2 | 1 | 5 |
| 6 | 9 | 1 | 5 | 3 | 2 | 7 | 8 | 4 |
| 9 | 4 | 5 | 6 | 7 | 1 | 8 | 2 | 3 |
| 1 | 8 | 2 | 3 | 5 | 9 | 4 | 7 | 6 |
| 3 | 6 | 7 | 2 | 4 | 8 | 9 | 5 | 1 |

**222**

| 9 | 5 | 6 | 1 | 8 | 3 | 2 | 4 | 7 |
|---|---|---|---|---|---|---|---|---|
| 1 | 4 | 3 | 9 | 7 | 2 | 6 | 5 | 8 |
| 2 | 7 | 8 | 5 | 4 | 6 | 1 | 3 | 9 |
| 6 | 8 | 2 | 3 | 1 | 4 | 9 | 7 | 5 |
| 3 | 9 | 5 | 7 | 6 | 8 | 4 | 1 | 2 |
| 4 | 1 | 7 | 2 | 5 | 9 | 3 | 8 | 6 |
| 8 | 6 | 1 | 4 | 2 | 7 | 5 | 9 | 3 |
| 5 | 2 | 9 | 8 | 3 | 1 | 7 | 6 | 4 |
| 7 | 3 | 4 | 6 | 9 | 5 | 8 | 2 | 1 |

**223**

| 7 | 4 | 1 | 8 | 5 | 2 | 3 | 6 | 9 |
|---|---|---|---|---|---|---|---|---|
| 6 | 5 | 2 | 9 | 1 | 3 | 8 | 4 | 7 |
| 3 | 9 | 8 | 6 | 4 | 7 | 1 | 5 | 2 |
| 9 | 7 | 3 | 2 | 8 | 4 | 6 | 1 | 5 |
| 1 | 8 | 4 | 5 | 9 | 6 | 7 | 2 | 3 |
| 5 | 2 | 6 | 7 | 3 | 1 | 9 | 8 | 4 |
| 4 | 6 | 9 | 3 | 2 | 8 | 5 | 7 | 1 |
| 8 | 1 | 5 | 4 | 7 | 9 | 2 | 3 | 6 |
| 2 | 3 | 7 | 1 | 6 | 5 | 4 | 9 | 8 |

**224**

| 7 | 3 | 9 | 5 | 2 | 4 | 1 | 6 | 8 |
|---|---|---|---|---|---|---|---|---|
| 2 | 4 | 1 | 8 | 3 | 6 | 9 | 7 | 5 |
| 6 | 5 | 8 | 7 | 9 | 1 | 4 | 3 | 2 |
| 9 | 7 | 4 | 6 | 8 | 3 | 2 | 5 | 1 |
| 1 | 6 | 5 | 4 | 7 | 2 | 8 | 9 | 3 |
| 3 | 8 | 2 | 1 | 5 | 9 | 6 | 4 | 7 |
| 4 | 9 | 3 | 2 | 1 | 7 | 5 | 8 | 6 |
| 5 | 2 | 6 | 3 | 4 | 8 | 7 | 1 | 9 |
| 8 | 1 | 7 | 9 | 6 | 5 | 3 | 2 | 4 |

**25**

| 3 | 6 | 9 | 2 | 1 | 4 | 5 | 7 | 8 |
|---|---|---|---|---|---|---|---|---|
| 4 | 2 | 1 | 5 | 8 | 7 | 6 | 3 | 9 |
| 8 | 7 | 5 | 3 | 9 | 6 | 4 | 1 | 2 |
| 2 | 8 | 7 | 9 | 3 | 5 | 1 | 4 | 6 |
| 5 | 4 | 6 | 8 | 7 | 1 | 9 | 2 | 3 |
| 9 | 1 | 3 | 4 | 6 | 2 | 7 | 8 | 5 |
| 1 | 3 | 4 | 6 | 2 | 9 | 8 | 5 | 7 |
| 6 | 5 | 8 | 7 | 4 | 3 | 2 | 9 | 1 |
| 7 | 9 | 2 | 1 | 5 | 8 | 3 | 6 | 4 |

**26**

| 7 | 8 | 6 | 9 | 4 | 3 | 2 | 1 | 5 |
|---|---|---|---|---|---|---|---|---|
| 4 | 5 | 2 | 6 | 7 | 1 | 8 | 3 | 9 |
| 1 | 3 | 9 | 8 | 2 | 5 | 7 | 6 | 4 |
| 5 | 2 | 7 | 4 | 9 | 6 | 3 | 8 | 1 |
| 6 | 9 | 3 | 5 | 1 | 8 | 4 | 2 | 7 |
| 8 | 4 | 1 | 2 | 3 | 7 | 9 | 5 | 6 |
| 9 | 1 | 8 | 7 | 5 | 2 | 6 | 4 | 3 |
| 2 | 7 | 5 | 3 | 6 | 4 | 1 | 9 | 8 |
| 3 | 6 | 4 | 1 | 8 | 9 | 5 | 7 | 2 |

**27**

| 1 | 3 | 4 | 5 | 9 | 8 | 2 | 7 | 6 |
|---|---|---|---|---|---|---|---|---|
| 7 | 5 | 2 | 6 | 4 | 1 | 3 | 9 | 8 |
| 6 | 8 | 9 | 2 | 7 | 3 | 4 | 1 | 5 |
| 3 | 9 | 6 | 7 | 5 | 2 | 8 | 4 | 1 |
| 4 | 1 | 8 | 3 | 6 | 9 | 7 | 5 | 2 |
| 5 | 2 | 7 | 8 | 1 | 4 | 6 | 3 | 9 |
| 8 | 7 | 5 | 1 | 3 | 6 | 9 | 2 | 4 |
| 2 | 4 | 1 | 9 | 8 | 7 | 5 | 6 | 3 |
| 9 | 6 | 3 | 4 | 2 | 5 | 1 | 8 | 7 |

**28**

| 6 | 8 | 3 | 2 | 1 | 7 | 9 | 4 | 5 |
|---|---|---|---|---|---|---|---|---|
| 5 | 4 | 2 | 6 | 9 | 8 | 3 | 1 | 7 |
| 1 | 7 | 9 | 3 | 5 | 4 | 6 | 8 | 2 |
| 8 | 6 | 7 | 5 | 4 | 3 | 2 | 9 | 1 |
| 2 | 1 | 4 | 8 | 7 | 9 | 5 | 6 | 3 |
| 9 | 3 | 5 | 1 | 2 | 6 | 4 | 7 | 8 |
| 4 | 5 | 1 | 9 | 8 | 2 | 7 | 3 | 6 |
| 3 | 9 | 8 | 7 | 6 | 5 | 1 | 2 | 4 |
| 7 | 2 | 6 | 4 | 3 | 1 | 8 | 5 | 9 |

**29**

| 6 | 5 | 8 | 9 | 3 | 2 | 7 | 1 | 4 |
|---|---|---|---|---|---|---|---|---|
| 4 | 7 | 3 | 6 | 5 | 1 | 9 | 2 | 8 |
| 1 | 2 | 9 | 7 | 8 | 4 | 5 | 6 | 3 |
| 7 | 6 | 2 | 5 | 9 | 8 | 3 | 4 | 1 |
| 3 | 8 | 4 | 1 | 7 | 6 | 2 | 9 | 5 |
| 9 | 1 | 5 | 4 | 2 | 3 | 6 | 8 | 7 |
| 5 | 4 | 7 | 8 | 6 | 9 | 1 | 3 | 2 |
| 8 | 3 | 6 | 2 | 1 | 5 | 4 | 7 | 9 |
| 2 | 9 | 1 | 3 | 4 | 7 | 8 | 5 | 6 |

**30**

| 6 | 2 | 4 | 7 | 5 | 1 | 3 | 9 | 8 |
|---|---|---|---|---|---|---|---|---|
| 3 | 8 | 1 | 6 | 2 | 9 | 4 | 7 | 5 |
| 7 | 5 | 9 | 3 | 8 | 4 | 6 | 2 | 1 |
| 2 | 3 | 8 | 5 | 1 | 6 | 9 | 4 | 7 |
| 1 | 4 | 7 | 2 | 9 | 3 | 8 | 5 | 6 |
| 9 | 6 | 5 | 4 | 7 | 8 | 1 | 3 | 2 |
| 4 | 1 | 2 | 9 | 6 | 5 | 7 | 8 | 3 |
| 8 | 7 | 3 | 1 | 4 | 2 | 5 | 6 | 9 |
| 5 | 9 | 6 | 8 | 3 | 7 | 2 | 1 | 4 |

**31**

| 4 | 3 | 1 | 2 | 6 | 5 | 9 | 7 | 8 |
|---|---|---|---|---|---|---|---|---|
| 7 | 8 | 9 | 4 | 1 | 3 | 2 | 6 | 5 |
| 6 | 2 | 5 | 8 | 7 | 9 | 3 | 1 | 4 |
| 9 | 7 | 4 | 6 | 5 | 8 | 1 | 3 | 2 |
| 5 | 6 | 3 | 9 | 2 | 1 | 8 | 4 | 7 |
| 2 | 1 | 8 | 7 | 3 | 4 | 5 | 9 | 6 |
| 3 | 4 | 6 | 5 | 9 | 2 | 7 | 8 | 1 |
| 8 | 9 | 2 | 1 | 4 | 7 | 6 | 5 | 3 |
| 1 | 5 | 7 | 3 | 8 | 6 | 4 | 2 | 9 |

**32**

| 2 | 4 | 8 | 7 | 6 | 1 | 9 | 5 | 3 |
|---|---|---|---|---|---|---|---|---|
| 9 | 6 | 7 | 2 | 5 | 3 | 1 | 8 | 4 |
| 5 | 1 | 3 | 4 | 8 | 9 | 2 | 7 | 6 |
| 1 | 3 | 4 | 5 | 7 | 8 | 6 | 2 | 9 |
| 8 | 7 | 9 | 3 | 2 | 6 | 4 | 1 | 5 |
| 6 | 5 | 2 | 9 | 1 | 4 | 7 | 3 | 8 |
| 7 | 2 | 6 | 8 | 4 | 5 | 3 | 9 | 1 |
| 3 | 8 | 1 | 6 | 9 | 2 | 5 | 4 | 7 |
| 4 | 9 | 5 | 1 | 3 | 7 | 8 | 6 | 2 |

## 233

| 8 | 2 | 1 | 5 | 7 | 9 | 4 | 3 | 6 |
|---|---|---|---|---|---|---|---|---|
| 9 | 4 | 7 | 3 | 2 | 6 | 5 | 1 | 8 |
| 3 | 5 | 6 | 4 | 8 | 1 | 7 | 2 | 9 |
| 2 | 8 | 3 | 6 | 1 | 4 | 9 | 5 | 7 |
| 6 | 1 | 9 | 7 | 3 | 5 | 8 | 4 | 2 |
| 4 | 7 | 5 | 8 | 9 | 2 | 1 | 6 | 3 |
| 7 | 3 | 2 | 1 | 4 | 8 | 6 | 9 | 5 |
| 1 | 6 | 8 | 9 | 5 | 3 | 2 | 7 | 4 |
| 5 | 9 | 4 | 2 | 6 | 7 | 3 | 8 | 1 |

## 234

| 2 | 8 | 9 | 4 | 6 | 1 | 3 | 7 | 5 |
|---|---|---|---|---|---|---|---|---|
| 4 | 1 | 7 | 5 | 9 | 3 | 6 | 2 | 8 |
| 6 | 5 | 3 | 8 | 2 | 7 | 9 | 4 | 1 |
| 9 | 2 | 4 | 1 | 7 | 8 | 5 | 3 | 6 |
| 8 | 3 | 6 | 9 | 5 | 4 | 2 | 1 | 7 |
| 1 | 7 | 5 | 6 | 3 | 2 | 8 | 9 | 4 |
| 7 | 4 | 2 | 3 | 8 | 5 | 1 | 6 | 9 |
| 3 | 6 | 8 | 7 | 1 | 9 | 4 | 5 | 2 |
| 5 | 9 | 1 | 2 | 4 | 6 | 7 | 8 | 3 |

## 235

| 9 | 1 | 8 | 2 | 3 | 7 | 4 | 5 | 6 |
|---|---|---|---|---|---|---|---|---|
| 6 | 4 | 5 | 1 | 8 | 9 | 2 | 7 | 3 |
| 2 | 3 | 7 | 6 | 5 | 4 | 8 | 1 | 9 |
| 5 | 2 | 9 | 3 | 1 | 8 | 7 | 6 | 4 |
| 7 | 8 | 4 | 5 | 9 | 6 | 3 | 2 | 1 |
| 1 | 6 | 3 | 4 | 7 | 2 | 5 | 9 | 8 |
| 4 | 5 | 6 | 9 | 2 | 3 | 1 | 8 | 7 |
| 8 | 9 | 2 | 7 | 4 | 1 | 6 | 3 | 5 |
| 3 | 7 | 1 | 8 | 6 | 5 | 9 | 4 | 2 |

## 236

| 5 | 2 | 6 | 8 | 9 | 4 | 3 | 7 | 1 |
|---|---|---|---|---|---|---|---|---|
| 9 | 8 | 1 | 7 | 6 | 3 | 4 | 5 | 2 |
| 7 | 3 | 4 | 5 | 2 | 1 | 6 | 8 | 9 |
| 4 | 1 | 7 | 6 | 3 | 8 | 9 | 2 | 5 |
| 2 | 5 | 9 | 1 | 4 | 7 | 8 | 6 | 3 |
| 3 | 6 | 8 | 9 | 5 | 2 | 7 | 1 | 4 |
| 8 | 7 | 5 | 4 | 1 | 9 | 2 | 3 | 6 |
| 6 | 9 | 3 | 2 | 8 | 5 | 1 | 4 | 7 |
| 1 | 4 | 2 | 3 | 7 | 6 | 5 | 9 | 8 |

## 237

| 6 | 9 | 2 | 7 | 1 | 4 | 3 | 5 | 8 |
|---|---|---|---|---|---|---|---|---|
| 8 | 7 | 5 | 3 | 2 | 9 | 4 | 1 | 6 |
| 4 | 3 | 1 | 5 | 6 | 8 | 2 | 9 | 7 |
| 3 | 6 | 7 | 8 | 5 | 2 | 1 | 4 | 9 |
| 2 | 5 | 4 | 1 | 9 | 6 | 8 | 7 | 3 |
| 1 | 8 | 9 | 4 | 7 | 3 | 5 | 6 | 2 |
| 5 | 2 | 6 | 9 | 8 | 1 | 7 | 3 | 4 |
| 9 | 1 | 3 | 2 | 4 | 7 | 6 | 8 | 5 |
| 7 | 4 | 8 | 6 | 3 | 5 | 9 | 2 | 1 |

## 238

| 4 | 3 | 6 | 9 | 7 | 2 | 8 | 5 | 1 |
|---|---|---|---|---|---|---|---|---|
| 5 | 8 | 9 | 3 | 1 | 4 | 2 | 6 | 7 |
| 7 | 1 | 2 | 6 | 8 | 5 | 9 | 4 | 3 |
| 9 | 5 | 4 | 2 | 3 | 7 | 1 | 8 | 6 |
| 2 | 6 | 8 | 4 | 5 | 1 | 3 | 7 | 9 |
| 3 | 7 | 1 | 8 | 9 | 6 | 4 | 2 | 5 |
| 1 | 2 | 7 | 5 | 4 | 9 | 6 | 3 | 8 |
| 8 | 4 | 5 | 1 | 6 | 3 | 7 | 9 | 2 |
| 6 | 9 | 3 | 7 | 2 | 8 | 5 | 1 | 4 |

## 239

| 1 | 4 | 6 | 3 | 8 | 9 | 7 | 5 | 2 |
|---|---|---|---|---|---|---|---|---|
| 2 | 5 | 7 | 1 | 6 | 4 | 3 | 8 | 9 |
| 3 | 8 | 9 | 7 | 2 | 5 | 6 | 1 | 4 |
| 8 | 6 | 2 | 4 | 3 | 1 | 5 | 9 | 7 |
| 9 | 7 | 4 | 2 | 5 | 8 | 1 | 6 | 3 |
| 5 | 1 | 3 | 6 | 9 | 7 | 4 | 2 | 8 |
| 6 | 9 | 1 | 8 | 7 | 3 | 2 | 4 | 5 |
| 4 | 3 | 8 | 5 | 1 | 2 | 9 | 7 | 6 |
| 7 | 2 | 5 | 9 | 4 | 6 | 8 | 3 | 1 |

## 240

| 7 | 6 | 5 | 3 | 2 | 1 | 9 | 8 | 4 |
|---|---|---|---|---|---|---|---|---|
| 2 | 9 | 4 | 5 | 8 | 7 | 3 | 1 | 6 |
| 8 | 1 | 3 | 9 | 4 | 6 | 7 | 5 | 2 |
| 3 | 2 | 6 | 1 | 7 | 5 | 4 | 9 | 8 |
| 9 | 8 | 1 | 2 | 3 | 4 | 5 | 6 | 7 |
| 4 | 5 | 7 | 8 | 6 | 9 | 1 | 2 | 3 |
| 6 | 4 | 9 | 7 | 5 | 8 | 2 | 3 | 1 |
| 5 | 3 | 8 | 4 | 1 | 2 | 6 | 7 | 9 |
| 1 | 7 | 2 | 6 | 9 | 3 | 8 | 4 | 5 |

**241**

| 6 | 7 | 1 | 4 | 9 | 3 | 2 | 8 | 5 |
|---|---|---|---|---|---|---|---|---|
| 2 | 3 | 9 | 8 | 6 | 5 | 1 | 4 | 7 |
| 8 | 5 | 4 | 7 | 1 | 2 | 9 | 6 | 3 |
| 3 | 6 | 5 | 1 | 2 | 8 | 7 | 9 | 4 |
| 9 | 4 | 2 | 5 | 3 | 7 | 6 | 1 | 8 |
| 1 | 8 | 7 | 6 | 4 | 9 | 3 | 5 | 2 |
| 7 | 2 | 6 | 9 | 5 | 4 | 8 | 3 | 1 |
| 5 | 9 | 8 | 3 | 7 | 1 | 4 | 2 | 6 |
| 4 | 1 | 3 | 2 | 8 | 6 | 5 | 7 | 9 |

**242**

| 5 | 3 | 6 | 2 | 7 | 1 | 9 | 4 | 8 |
|---|---|---|---|---|---|---|---|---|
| 4 | 1 | 2 | 8 | 3 | 9 | 5 | 6 | 7 |
| 8 | 9 | 7 | 6 | 5 | 4 | 3 | 1 | 2 |
| 1 | 5 | 9 | 7 | 2 | 8 | 4 | 3 | 6 |
| 2 | 8 | 3 | 5 | 4 | 6 | 1 | 7 | 9 |
| 7 | 6 | 4 | 9 | 1 | 3 | 8 | 2 | 5 |
| 9 | 2 | 1 | 4 | 8 | 7 | 6 | 5 | 3 |
| 3 | 7 | 8 | 1 | 6 | 5 | 2 | 9 | 4 |
| 6 | 4 | 5 | 3 | 9 | 2 | 7 | 8 | 1 |

**243**

| 3 | 8 | 9 | 1 | 6 | 2 | 4 | 7 | 5 |
|---|---|---|---|---|---|---|---|---|
| 4 | 7 | 2 | 9 | 3 | 5 | 1 | 6 | 8 |
| 5 | 1 | 6 | 7 | 4 | 8 | 2 | 9 | 3 |
| 9 | 3 | 1 | 2 | 7 | 6 | 8 | 5 | 4 |
| 8 | 4 | 7 | 5 | 1 | 3 | 9 | 2 | 6 |
| 2 | 6 | 5 | 4 | 8 | 9 | 3 | 1 | 7 |
| 1 | 2 | 3 | 6 | 5 | 4 | 7 | 8 | 9 |
| 6 | 9 | 4 | 8 | 2 | 7 | 5 | 3 | 1 |
| 7 | 5 | 8 | 3 | 9 | 1 | 6 | 4 | 2 |

**244**

| 6 | 4 | 3 | 7 | 8 | 1 | 2 | 5 | 9 |
|---|---|---|---|---|---|---|---|---|
| 2 | 5 | 9 | 6 | 3 | 4 | 8 | 7 | 1 |
| 8 | 7 | 1 | 9 | 5 | 2 | 4 | 6 | 3 |
| 5 | 8 | 7 | 3 | 6 | 9 | 1 | 2 | 4 |
| 1 | 2 | 6 | 5 | 4 | 8 | 3 | 9 | 7 |
| 3 | 9 | 4 | 1 | 2 | 7 | 5 | 8 | 6 |
| 4 | 3 | 5 | 8 | 9 | 6 | 7 | 1 | 2 |
| 7 | 6 | 2 | 4 | 1 | 5 | 9 | 3 | 8 |
| 9 | 1 | 8 | 2 | 7 | 3 | 6 | 4 | 5 |

**245**

| 8 | 7 | 4 | 6 | 2 | 3 | 5 | 9 | 1 |
|---|---|---|---|---|---|---|---|---|
| 9 | 1 | 6 | 4 | 5 | 8 | 7 | 3 | 2 |
| 5 | 3 | 2 | 7 | 9 | 1 | 6 | 8 | 4 |
| 6 | 9 | 5 | 8 | 1 | 7 | 4 | 2 | 3 |
| 4 | 8 | 1 | 5 | 3 | 2 | 9 | 7 | 6 |
| 7 | 2 | 3 | 9 | 4 | 6 | 8 | 1 | 5 |
| 1 | 4 | 7 | 2 | 8 | 5 | 3 | 6 | 9 |
| 2 | 5 | 8 | 3 | 6 | 9 | 1 | 4 | 7 |
| 3 | 6 | 9 | 1 | 7 | 4 | 2 | 5 | 8 |

**246**

| 1 | 6 | 7 | 5 | 8 | 4 | 2 | 3 | 9 |
|---|---|---|---|---|---|---|---|---|
| 4 | 2 | 3 | 9 | 1 | 6 | 7 | 5 | 8 |
| 5 | 8 | 9 | 3 | 2 | 7 | 4 | 1 | 6 |
| 3 | 1 | 8 | 6 | 5 | 2 | 9 | 4 | 7 |
| 7 | 5 | 2 | 4 | 3 | 9 | 8 | 6 | 1 |
| 9 | 4 | 6 | 8 | 7 | 1 | 5 | 2 | 3 |
| 2 | 7 | 5 | 1 | 9 | 3 | 6 | 8 | 4 |
| 8 | 3 | 4 | 7 | 6 | 5 | 1 | 9 | 2 |
| 6 | 9 | 1 | 2 | 4 | 8 | 3 | 7 | 5 |

**247**

| 7 | 5 | 3 | 9 | 4 | 8 | 1 | 2 | 6 |
|---|---|---|---|---|---|---|---|---|
| 2 | 8 | 1 | 3 | 6 | 5 | 4 | 9 | 7 |
| 9 | 6 | 4 | 1 | 2 | 7 | 8 | 5 | 3 |
| 1 | 4 | 6 | 5 | 3 | 2 | 9 | 7 | 8 |
| 5 | 7 | 9 | 6 | 8 | 1 | 3 | 4 | 2 |
| 8 | 3 | 2 | 7 | 9 | 4 | 5 | 6 | 1 |
| 4 | 9 | 7 | 2 | 1 | 3 | 6 | 8 | 5 |
| 3 | 2 | 8 | 4 | 5 | 6 | 7 | 1 | 9 |
| 6 | 1 | 5 | 8 | 7 | 9 | 2 | 3 | 4 |

**248**

| 3 | 9 | 2 | 5 | 7 | 8 | 6 | 4 | 1 |
|---|---|---|---|---|---|---|---|---|
| 7 | 8 | 6 | 9 | 1 | 4 | 3 | 2 | 5 |
| 5 | 4 | 1 | 2 | 6 | 3 | 8 | 7 | 9 |
| 6 | 3 | 8 | 4 | 9 | 7 | 1 | 5 | 2 |
| 9 | 5 | 4 | 1 | 8 | 2 | 7 | 3 | 6 |
| 2 | 1 | 7 | 6 | 3 | 5 | 9 | 8 | 4 |
| 8 | 6 | 5 | 7 | 4 | 9 | 2 | 1 | 3 |
| 4 | 7 | 9 | 3 | 2 | 1 | 5 | 6 | 8 |
| 1 | 2 | 3 | 8 | 5 | 6 | 4 | 9 | 7 |

**249**

| 9 | 3 | 6 | 8 | 4 | 2 | 5 | 7 | 1 |
|---|---|---|---|---|---|---|---|---|
| 2 | 4 | 5 | 6 | 7 | 1 | 8 | 3 | 9 |
| 1 | 8 | 7 | 3 | 9 | 5 | 2 | 4 | 6 |
| 5 | 9 | 2 | 4 | 8 | 7 | 6 | 1 | 3 |
| 4 | 7 | 8 | 1 | 6 | 3 | 9 | 2 | 5 |
| 6 | 1 | 3 | 5 | 2 | 9 | 7 | 8 | 4 |
| 3 | 2 | 1 | 9 | 5 | 8 | 4 | 6 | 7 |
| 8 | 5 | 4 | 7 | 1 | 6 | 3 | 9 | 2 |
| 7 | 6 | 9 | 2 | 3 | 4 | 1 | 5 | 8 |

**250**

| 5 | 2 | 1 | 8 | 4 | 9 | 3 | 7 | 6 |
|---|---|---|---|---|---|---|---|---|
| 7 | 9 | 8 | 3 | 6 | 1 | 5 | 2 | 4 |
| 4 | 6 | 3 | 7 | 2 | 5 | 8 | 1 | 9 |
| 9 | 4 | 7 | 6 | 1 | 8 | 2 | 3 | 5 |
| 6 | 1 | 2 | 9 | 5 | 3 | 7 | 4 | 8 |
| 3 | 8 | 5 | 2 | 7 | 4 | 9 | 6 | 1 |
| 1 | 3 | 6 | 5 | 9 | 7 | 4 | 8 | 2 |
| 8 | 5 | 4 | 1 | 3 | 2 | 6 | 9 | 7 |
| 2 | 7 | 9 | 4 | 8 | 6 | 1 | 5 | 3 |

**251**

| 3 | 4 | 2 | 9 | 1 | 8 | 7 | 5 | 6 |
|---|---|---|---|---|---|---|---|---|
| 9 | 6 | 8 | 5 | 4 | 7 | 2 | 1 | 3 |
| 5 | 1 | 7 | 6 | 3 | 2 | 4 | 8 | 9 |
| 4 | 2 | 3 | 7 | 9 | 5 | 8 | 6 | 1 |
| 1 | 7 | 5 | 4 | 8 | 6 | 9 | 3 | 2 |
| 6 | 8 | 9 | 1 | 2 | 3 | 5 | 4 | 7 |
| 7 | 5 | 1 | 8 | 6 | 9 | 3 | 2 | 4 |
| 8 | 3 | 4 | 2 | 7 | 1 | 6 | 9 | 5 |
| 2 | 9 | 6 | 3 | 5 | 4 | 1 | 7 | 8 |

**252**

| 9 | 8 | 4 | 7 | 6 | 3 | 5 | 2 | 1 |
|---|---|---|---|---|---|---|---|---|
| 1 | 5 | 6 | 2 | 8 | 4 | 9 | 3 | 7 |
| 7 | 2 | 3 | 5 | 1 | 9 | 4 | 6 | 8 |
| 4 | 7 | 5 | 1 | 9 | 6 | 2 | 8 | 3 |
| 3 | 9 | 1 | 4 | 2 | 8 | 7 | 5 | 6 |
| 2 | 6 | 8 | 3 | 5 | 7 | 1 | 9 | 4 |
| 6 | 1 | 7 | 9 | 3 | 2 | 8 | 4 | 5 |
| 5 | 3 | 2 | 8 | 4 | 1 | 6 | 7 | 9 |
| 8 | 4 | 9 | 6 | 7 | 5 | 3 | 1 | 2 |

**253**

| 4 | 7 | 6 | 5 | 2 | 8 | 9 | 3 | 1 |
|---|---|---|---|---|---|---|---|---|
| 5 | 2 | 9 | 4 | 3 | 1 | 7 | 6 | 8 |
| 1 | 8 | 3 | 7 | 6 | 9 | 4 | 5 | 2 |
| 2 | 3 | 7 | 8 | 9 | 5 | 6 | 1 | 4 |
| 6 | 5 | 8 | 3 | 1 | 4 | 2 | 9 | 7 |
| 9 | 1 | 4 | 6 | 7 | 2 | 5 | 8 | 3 |
| 8 | 9 | 1 | 2 | 4 | 6 | 3 | 7 | 5 |
| 3 | 4 | 5 | 9 | 8 | 7 | 1 | 2 | 6 |
| 7 | 6 | 2 | 1 | 5 | 3 | 8 | 4 | 9 |

**254**

| 3 | 5 | 2 | 7 | 4 | 6 | 1 | 8 | 9 |
|---|---|---|---|---|---|---|---|---|
| 6 | 9 | 4 | 2 | 8 | 1 | 3 | 7 | 5 |
| 1 | 7 | 8 | 9 | 5 | 3 | 4 | 2 | 6 |
| 9 | 2 | 5 | 8 | 7 | 4 | 6 | 3 | 1 |
| 7 | 6 | 3 | 1 | 2 | 9 | 8 | 5 | 4 |
| 8 | 4 | 1 | 6 | 3 | 5 | 2 | 9 | 7 |
| 4 | 3 | 9 | 5 | 1 | 2 | 7 | 6 | 8 |
| 5 | 1 | 7 | 3 | 6 | 8 | 9 | 4 | 2 |
| 2 | 8 | 6 | 4 | 9 | 7 | 5 | 1 | 3 |

**255**

| 1 | 7 | 2 | 9 | 3 | 6 | 4 | 8 | 5 |
|---|---|---|---|---|---|---|---|---|
| 6 | 8 | 4 | 1 | 2 | 5 | 7 | 9 | 3 |
| 5 | 3 | 9 | 7 | 8 | 4 | 6 | 2 | 1 |
| 9 | 6 | 1 | 3 | 4 | 7 | 2 | 5 | 8 |
| 7 | 4 | 8 | 2 | 5 | 1 | 9 | 3 | 6 |
| 2 | 5 | 3 | 6 | 9 | 8 | 1 | 7 | 4 |
| 8 | 9 | 7 | 4 | 1 | 3 | 5 | 6 | 2 |
| 3 | 1 | 6 | 5 | 7 | 2 | 8 | 4 | 9 |
| 4 | 2 | 5 | 8 | 6 | 9 | 3 | 1 | 7 |

**256**

| 3 | 9 | 6 | 2 | 4 | 5 | 8 | 1 | 7 |
|---|---|---|---|---|---|---|---|---|
| 7 | 2 | 5 | 1 | 6 | 8 | 4 | 3 | 9 |
| 8 | 4 | 1 | 7 | 3 | 9 | 2 | 6 | 5 |
| 2 | 8 | 9 | 6 | 5 | 3 | 1 | 7 | 4 |
| 6 | 5 | 4 | 8 | 1 | 7 | 3 | 9 | 2 |
| 1 | 7 | 3 | 9 | 2 | 4 | 6 | 5 | 8 |
| 4 | 3 | 2 | 5 | 7 | 6 | 9 | 8 | 1 |
| 9 | 1 | 7 | 3 | 8 | 2 | 5 | 4 | 6 |
| 5 | 6 | 8 | 4 | 9 | 1 | 7 | 2 | 3 |

**257**

| 5 | 6 | 4 | 9 | 3 | 8 | 2 | 7 | 1 |
|---|---|---|---|---|---|---|---|---|
| 2 | 1 | 7 | 5 | 6 | 4 | 3 | 9 | 8 |
| 9 | 3 | 8 | 7 | 2 | 1 | 4 | 5 | 6 |
| 7 | 5 | 2 | 1 | 9 | 3 | 6 | 8 | 4 |
| 1 | 9 | 6 | 8 | 4 | 7 | 5 | 2 | 3 |
| 4 | 8 | 3 | 2 | 5 | 6 | 7 | 1 | 9 |
| 6 | 7 | 1 | 4 | 8 | 5 | 9 | 3 | 2 |
| 8 | 4 | 9 | 3 | 7 | 2 | 1 | 6 | 5 |
| 3 | 2 | 5 | 6 | 1 | 9 | 8 | 4 | 7 |

**258**

| 6 | 8 | 5 | 2 | 3 | 4 | 1 | 7 | 9 |
|---|---|---|---|---|---|---|---|---|
| 7 | 1 | 4 | 8 | 9 | 6 | 2 | 5 | 3 |
| 9 | 3 | 2 | 1 | 7 | 5 | 4 | 8 | 6 |
| 3 | 7 | 6 | 9 | 8 | 2 | 5 | 1 | 4 |
| 2 | 4 | 8 | 3 | 5 | 1 | 9 | 6 | 7 |
| 5 | 9 | 1 | 6 | 4 | 7 | 3 | 2 | 8 |
| 8 | 6 | 3 | 5 | 1 | 9 | 7 | 4 | 2 |
| 1 | 2 | 7 | 4 | 6 | 3 | 8 | 9 | 5 |
| 4 | 5 | 9 | 7 | 2 | 8 | 6 | 3 | 1 |

**259**

| 2 | 8 | 4 | 1 | 3 | 9 | 5 | 7 | 6 |
|---|---|---|---|---|---|---|---|---|
| 3 | 9 | 5 | 6 | 7 | 2 | 1 | 8 | 4 |
| 1 | 7 | 6 | 8 | 5 | 4 | 2 | 3 | 9 |
| 8 | 6 | 7 | 9 | 2 | 5 | 4 | 1 | 3 |
| 9 | 2 | 3 | 7 | 4 | 1 | 8 | 6 | 5 |
| 4 | 5 | 1 | 3 | 6 | 8 | 9 | 2 | 7 |
| 7 | 1 | 2 | 5 | 9 | 3 | 6 | 4 | 8 |
| 5 | 3 | 8 | 4 | 1 | 6 | 7 | 9 | 2 |
| 6 | 4 | 9 | 2 | 8 | 7 | 3 | 5 | 1 |

**260**

| 1 | 2 | 7 | 3 | 5 | 9 | 8 | 4 | 6 |
|---|---|---|---|---|---|---|---|---|
| 5 | 3 | 9 | 6 | 8 | 4 | 7 | 1 | 2 |
| 4 | 8 | 6 | 7 | 1 | 2 | 5 | 9 | 3 |
| 9 | 6 | 3 | 8 | 4 | 7 | 1 | 2 | 5 |
| 2 | 7 | 5 | 9 | 3 | 1 | 6 | 8 | 4 |
| 8 | 1 | 4 | 2 | 6 | 5 | 3 | 7 | 9 |
| 6 | 4 | 1 | 5 | 2 | 8 | 9 | 3 | 7 |
| 7 | 5 | 2 | 1 | 9 | 3 | 4 | 6 | 8 |
| 3 | 9 | 8 | 4 | 7 | 6 | 2 | 5 | 1 |

**261**

| 3 | 7 | 9 | 1 | 6 | 5 | 8 | 2 | 4 |
|---|---|---|---|---|---|---|---|---|
| 1 | 6 | 4 | 9 | 2 | 8 | 5 | 7 | 3 |
| 8 | 2 | 5 | 7 | 4 | 3 | 6 | 1 | 9 |
| 7 | 9 | 3 | 2 | 5 | 1 | 4 | 6 | 8 |
| 5 | 8 | 2 | 6 | 3 | 4 | 7 | 9 | 1 |
| 6 | 4 | 1 | 8 | 9 | 7 | 3 | 5 | 2 |
| 2 | 5 | 8 | 3 | 1 | 6 | 9 | 4 | 7 |
| 9 | 3 | 6 | 4 | 7 | 2 | 1 | 8 | 5 |
| 4 | 1 | 7 | 5 | 8 | 9 | 2 | 3 | 6 |

**262**

| 6 | 1 | 9 | 4 | 8 | 7 | 3 | 2 | 5 |
|---|---|---|---|---|---|---|---|---|
| 7 | 3 | 4 | 2 | 1 | 5 | 9 | 6 | 8 |
| 5 | 8 | 2 | 9 | 3 | 6 | 7 | 1 | 4 |
| 8 | 6 | 7 | 5 | 2 | 3 | 1 | 4 | 9 |
| 1 | 4 | 3 | 6 | 7 | 9 | 5 | 8 | 2 |
| 2 | 9 | 5 | 8 | 4 | 1 | 6 | 3 | 7 |
| 9 | 7 | 8 | 1 | 6 | 2 | 4 | 5 | 3 |
| 3 | 2 | 6 | 7 | 5 | 4 | 8 | 9 | 1 |
| 4 | 5 | 1 | 3 | 9 | 8 | 2 | 7 | 6 |

**263**

| 1 | 4 | 3 | 9 | 7 | 2 | 6 | 8 | 5 |
|---|---|---|---|---|---|---|---|---|
| 8 | 6 | 7 | 5 | 3 | 1 | 2 | 9 | 4 |
| 9 | 2 | 5 | 8 | 6 | 4 | 1 | 7 | 3 |
| 3 | 5 | 2 | 7 | 4 | 9 | 8 | 6 | 1 |
| 7 | 8 | 1 | 2 | 5 | 6 | 3 | 4 | 9 |
| 6 | 9 | 4 | 1 | 8 | 3 | 7 | 5 | 2 |
| 5 | 1 | 6 | 4 | 2 | 7 | 9 | 3 | 8 |
| 2 | 3 | 8 | 6 | 9 | 5 | 4 | 1 | 7 |
| 4 | 7 | 9 | 3 | 1 | 8 | 5 | 2 | 6 |

**264**

| 4 | 2 | 9 | 7 | 8 | 1 | 6 | 3 | 5 |
|---|---|---|---|---|---|---|---|---|
| 6 | 5 | 7 | 4 | 9 | 3 | 1 | 2 | 8 |
| 3 | 1 | 8 | 6 | 2 | 5 | 9 | 7 | 4 |
| 5 | 9 | 3 | 8 | 1 | 4 | 7 | 6 | 2 |
| 8 | 6 | 4 | 3 | 7 | 2 | 5 | 1 | 9 |
| 2 | 7 | 1 | 9 | 5 | 6 | 4 | 8 | 3 |
| 1 | 4 | 6 | 5 | 3 | 8 | 2 | 9 | 7 |
| 9 | 8 | 2 | 1 | 4 | 7 | 3 | 5 | 6 |
| 7 | 3 | 5 | 2 | 6 | 9 | 8 | 4 | 1 |

## 265

| 5 | 1 | 6 | 2 | 8 | 4 | 3 | 7 | 9 |
|---|---|---|---|---|---|---|---|---|
| 4 | 3 | 8 | 9 | 1 | 7 | 5 | 2 | 6 |
| 2 | 9 | 7 | 6 | 5 | 3 | 1 | 8 | 4 |
| 1 | 8 | 9 | 4 | 2 | 6 | 7 | 5 | 3 |
| 3 | 7 | 2 | 1 | 9 | 5 | 6 | 4 | 8 |
| 6 | 5 | 4 | 3 | 7 | 8 | 2 | 9 | 1 |
| 7 | 6 | 3 | 5 | 4 | 9 | 8 | 1 | 2 |
| 8 | 4 | 1 | 7 | 3 | 2 | 9 | 6 | 5 |
| 9 | 2 | 5 | 8 | 6 | 1 | 4 | 3 | 7 |

## 266

| 1 | 2 | 9 | 8 | 5 | 4 | 7 | 3 | 6 |
|---|---|---|---|---|---|---|---|---|
| 8 | 4 | 6 | 9 | 3 | 7 | 5 | 1 | 2 |
| 7 | 3 | 5 | 6 | 1 | 2 | 4 | 8 | 9 |
| 4 | 9 | 8 | 1 | 7 | 5 | 2 | 6 | 3 |
| 2 | 6 | 1 | 4 | 9 | 3 | 8 | 5 | 7 |
| 3 | 5 | 7 | 2 | 8 | 6 | 1 | 9 | 4 |
| 6 | 1 | 4 | 3 | 2 | 8 | 9 | 7 | 5 |
| 5 | 8 | 3 | 7 | 4 | 9 | 6 | 2 | 1 |
| 9 | 7 | 2 | 5 | 6 | 1 | 3 | 4 | 8 |

## 267

| 9 | 3 | 5 | 6 | 2 | 7 | 8 | 1 | 4 |
|---|---|---|---|---|---|---|---|---|
| 7 | 1 | 2 | 8 | 4 | 3 | 9 | 5 | 6 |
| 8 | 4 | 6 | 5 | 9 | 1 | 7 | 2 | 3 |
| 1 | 2 | 7 | 3 | 5 | 8 | 4 | 6 | 9 |
| 4 | 9 | 8 | 2 | 7 | 6 | 5 | 3 | 1 |
| 5 | 6 | 3 | 9 | 1 | 4 | 2 | 8 | 7 |
| 2 | 5 | 1 | 4 | 3 | 9 | 6 | 7 | 8 |
| 3 | 8 | 4 | 7 | 6 | 5 | 1 | 9 | 2 |
| 6 | 7 | 9 | 1 | 8 | 2 | 3 | 4 | 5 |

## 268

| 9 | 1 | 6 | 5 | 7 | 8 | 3 | 4 | 2 |
|---|---|---|---|---|---|---|---|---|
| 3 | 4 | 7 | 9 | 6 | 2 | 1 | 5 | 8 |
| 5 | 2 | 8 | 3 | 4 | 1 | 9 | 7 | 6 |
| 4 | 7 | 3 | 6 | 9 | 5 | 8 | 2 | 1 |
| 2 | 6 | 5 | 8 | 1 | 7 | 4 | 9 | 3 |
| 8 | 9 | 1 | 2 | 3 | 4 | 7 | 6 | 5 |
| 1 | 8 | 4 | 7 | 2 | 6 | 5 | 3 | 9 |
| 7 | 3 | 2 | 1 | 5 | 9 | 6 | 8 | 4 |
| 6 | 5 | 9 | 4 | 8 | 3 | 2 | 1 | 7 |

## 269

| 7 | 3 | 1 | 8 | 4 | 5 | 9 | 2 | 6 |
|---|---|---|---|---|---|---|---|---|
| 4 | 5 | 9 | 7 | 6 | 2 | 1 | 8 | 3 |
| 8 | 6 | 2 | 9 | 1 | 3 | 4 | 5 | 7 |
| 5 | 1 | 4 | 3 | 9 | 8 | 6 | 7 | 2 |
| 3 | 2 | 6 | 4 | 5 | 7 | 8 | 9 | 1 |
| 9 | 7 | 8 | 6 | 2 | 1 | 5 | 3 | 4 |
| 6 | 9 | 7 | 5 | 3 | 4 | 2 | 1 | 8 |
| 2 | 4 | 3 | 1 | 8 | 9 | 7 | 6 | 5 |
| 1 | 8 | 5 | 2 | 7 | 6 | 3 | 4 | 9 |

## 270

| 5 | 2 | 3 | 8 | 1 | 4 | 6 | 7 | 9 |
|---|---|---|---|---|---|---|---|---|
| 9 | 6 | 4 | 5 | 7 | 3 | 2 | 1 | 8 |
| 7 | 8 | 1 | 6 | 2 | 9 | 4 | 3 | 5 |
| 2 | 5 | 6 | 1 | 8 | 7 | 3 | 9 | 4 |
| 4 | 7 | 8 | 3 | 9 | 6 | 1 | 5 | 2 |
| 1 | 3 | 9 | 2 | 4 | 5 | 7 | 8 | 6 |
| 3 | 4 | 5 | 7 | 6 | 8 | 9 | 2 | 1 |
| 8 | 9 | 2 | 4 | 3 | 1 | 5 | 6 | 7 |
| 6 | 1 | 7 | 9 | 5 | 2 | 8 | 4 | 3 |

## 271

| 6 | 1 | 5 | 4 | 7 | 9 | 8 | 2 | 3 |
|---|---|---|---|---|---|---|---|---|
| 9 | 7 | 8 | 2 | 1 | 3 | 4 | 5 | 6 |
| 4 | 2 | 3 | 6 | 5 | 8 | 1 | 9 | 7 |
| 7 | 8 | 2 | 5 | 3 | 4 | 9 | 6 | 1 |
| 1 | 3 | 4 | 8 | 9 | 6 | 5 | 7 | 2 |
| 5 | 6 | 9 | 1 | 2 | 7 | 3 | 4 | 8 |
| 2 | 9 | 6 | 3 | 8 | 5 | 7 | 1 | 4 |
| 3 | 5 | 1 | 7 | 4 | 2 | 6 | 8 | 9 |
| 8 | 4 | 7 | 9 | 6 | 1 | 2 | 3 | 5 |

## 272

| 2 | 1 | 8 | 3 | 4 | 6 | 7 | 5 | 9 |
|---|---|---|---|---|---|---|---|---|
| 4 | 6 | 7 | 1 | 9 | 5 | 8 | 3 | 2 |
| 3 | 9 | 5 | 7 | 8 | 2 | 6 | 4 | 1 |
| 9 | 5 | 3 | 4 | 1 | 8 | 2 | 6 | 7 |
| 7 | 4 | 1 | 6 | 2 | 3 | 5 | 9 | 8 |
| 6 | 8 | 2 | 9 | 5 | 7 | 4 | 1 | 3 |
| 8 | 2 | 6 | 5 | 3 | 9 | 1 | 7 | 4 |
| 5 | 3 | 4 | 8 | 7 | 1 | 9 | 2 | 6 |
| 1 | 7 | 9 | 2 | 6 | 4 | 3 | 8 | 5 |

**273**

| | | | | | | | | |
|---|---|---|---|---|---|---|---|---|
| 3 | 9 | 4 | 6 | 7 | 8 | 1 | 5 | 2 |
| 6 | 7 | 2 | 1 | 4 | 5 | 9 | 8 | 3 |
| 5 | 1 | 8 | 2 | 3 | 9 | 6 | 4 | 7 |
| 4 | 3 | 6 | 9 | 5 | 2 | 7 | 1 | 8 |
| 2 | 8 | 1 | 4 | 6 | 7 | 5 | 3 | 9 |
| 7 | 5 | 9 | 3 | 8 | 1 | 4 | 2 | 6 |
| 1 | 4 | 3 | 8 | 9 | 6 | 2 | 7 | 5 |
| 8 | 6 | 7 | 5 | 2 | 4 | 3 | 9 | 1 |
| 9 | 2 | 5 | 7 | 1 | 3 | 8 | 6 | 4 |

**274**

| | | | | | | | | |
|---|---|---|---|---|---|---|---|---|
| 7 | 9 | 6 | 2 | 4 | 5 | 1 | 3 | 8 |
| 4 | 3 | 1 | 9 | 7 | 8 | 2 | 6 | 5 |
| 2 | 8 | 5 | 1 | 3 | 6 | 7 | 4 | 9 |
| 3 | 5 | 4 | 6 | 1 | 2 | 9 | 8 | 7 |
| 8 | 7 | 2 | 5 | 9 | 3 | 6 | 1 | 4 |
| 6 | 1 | 9 | 4 | 8 | 7 | 3 | 5 | 2 |
| 1 | 6 | 8 | 7 | 5 | 9 | 4 | 2 | 3 |
| 9 | 4 | 3 | 8 | 2 | 1 | 5 | 7 | 6 |
| 5 | 2 | 7 | 3 | 6 | 4 | 8 | 9 | 1 |

**275**

| | | | | | | | | |
|---|---|---|---|---|---|---|---|---|
| 9 | 1 | 2 | 8 | 6 | 7 | 3 | 5 | 4 |
| 4 | 7 | 8 | 1 | 5 | 3 | 2 | 6 | 9 |
| 6 | 3 | 5 | 4 | 2 | 9 | 1 | 7 | 8 |
| 8 | 6 | 9 | 3 | 7 | 4 | 5 | 1 | 2 |
| 3 | 4 | 1 | 2 | 8 | 5 | 7 | 9 | 6 |
| 5 | 2 | 7 | 6 | 9 | 1 | 4 | 8 | 3 |
| 7 | 8 | 3 | 5 | 4 | 6 | 9 | 2 | 1 |
| 2 | 9 | 4 | 7 | 1 | 8 | 6 | 3 | 5 |
| 1 | 5 | 6 | 9 | 3 | 2 | 8 | 4 | 7 |

**276**

| | | | | | | | | |
|---|---|---|---|---|---|---|---|---|
| 7 | 6 | 9 | 1 | 5 | 4 | 2 | 8 | 3 |
| 5 | 4 | 2 | 3 | 7 | 8 | 1 | 9 | 6 |
| 8 | 1 | 3 | 2 | 6 | 9 | 7 | 4 | 5 |
| 6 | 8 | 4 | 7 | 9 | 1 | 5 | 3 | 2 |
| 1 | 3 | 5 | 6 | 8 | 2 | 9 | 7 | 4 |
| 2 | 9 | 7 | 5 | 4 | 3 | 6 | 1 | 8 |
| 3 | 2 | 6 | 8 | 1 | 7 | 4 | 5 | 9 |
| 4 | 5 | 1 | 9 | 3 | 6 | 8 | 2 | 7 |
| 9 | 7 | 8 | 4 | 2 | 5 | 3 | 6 | 1 |

**277**

| | | | | | | | | |
|---|---|---|---|---|---|---|---|---|
| 1 | 9 | 8 | 6 | 2 | 4 | 5 | 3 | 7 |
| 2 | 5 | 4 | 9 | 7 | 3 | 6 | 1 | 8 |
| 3 | 6 | 7 | 1 | 8 | 5 | 4 | 2 | 9 |
| 6 | 7 | 1 | 3 | 9 | 2 | 8 | 4 | 5 |
| 9 | 4 | 5 | 7 | 1 | 8 | 3 | 6 | 2 |
| 8 | 3 | 2 | 5 | 4 | 6 | 9 | 7 | 1 |
| 4 | 8 | 3 | 2 | 5 | 1 | 7 | 9 | 6 |
| 7 | 2 | 6 | 8 | 3 | 9 | 1 | 5 | 4 |
| 5 | 1 | 9 | 4 | 6 | 7 | 2 | 8 | 3 |

**278**

| | | | | | | | | |
|---|---|---|---|---|---|---|---|---|
| 6 | 1 | 3 | 5 | 7 | 2 | 8 | 4 | 9 |
| 9 | 5 | 2 | 1 | 8 | 4 | 6 | 3 | 7 |
| 7 | 8 | 4 | 3 | 9 | 6 | 5 | 2 | 1 |
| 2 | 4 | 1 | 8 | 3 | 5 | 7 | 9 | 6 |
| 5 | 3 | 6 | 9 | 4 | 7 | 1 | 8 | 2 |
| 8 | 9 | 7 | 2 | 6 | 1 | 4 | 5 | 3 |
| 3 | 2 | 5 | 7 | 1 | 8 | 9 | 6 | 4 |
| 1 | 6 | 9 | 4 | 5 | 3 | 2 | 7 | 8 |
| 4 | 7 | 8 | 6 | 2 | 9 | 3 | 1 | 5 |

**279**

| | | | | | | | | |
|---|---|---|---|---|---|---|---|---|
| 9 | 5 | 8 | 3 | 6 | 2 | 7 | 4 | 1 |
| 2 | 6 | 1 | 9 | 7 | 4 | 3 | 8 | 5 |
| 3 | 4 | 7 | 5 | 8 | 1 | 2 | 6 | 9 |
| 4 | 8 | 3 | 7 | 2 | 5 | 9 | 1 | 6 |
| 5 | 9 | 6 | 8 | 1 | 3 | 4 | 7 | 2 |
| 7 | 1 | 2 | 4 | 9 | 6 | 5 | 3 | 8 |
| 1 | 3 | 9 | 2 | 4 | 8 | 6 | 5 | 7 |
| 6 | 7 | 4 | 1 | 5 | 9 | 8 | 2 | 3 |
| 8 | 2 | 5 | 6 | 3 | 7 | 1 | 9 | 4 |

**280**

| | | | | | | | | |
|---|---|---|---|---|---|---|---|---|
| 7 | 5 | 8 | 3 | 1 | 9 | 6 | 2 | 4 |
| 1 | 2 | 3 | 6 | 4 | 5 | 9 | 8 | 7 |
| 4 | 9 | 6 | 7 | 8 | 2 | 3 | 5 | 1 |
| 3 | 7 | 4 | 2 | 6 | 1 | 8 | 9 | 5 |
| 6 | 8 | 2 | 5 | 9 | 7 | 1 | 4 | 3 |
| 9 | 1 | 5 | 4 | 3 | 8 | 2 | 7 | 6 |
| 2 | 4 | 9 | 1 | 5 | 3 | 7 | 6 | 8 |
| 8 | 6 | 1 | 9 | 7 | 4 | 5 | 3 | 2 |
| 5 | 3 | 7 | 8 | 2 | 6 | 4 | 1 | 9 |

**Puzzle 281**

| 9 | 5 | 3 | 1 | 6 | 8 | 4 | 7 | 2 |
|---|---|---|---|---|---|---|---|---|
| 8 | 1 | 7 | 3 | 2 | 4 | 9 | 6 | 5 |
| 2 | 4 | 6 | 7 | 9 | 5 | 1 | 8 | 3 |
| 1 | 3 | 4 | 2 | 5 | 6 | 8 | 9 | 7 |
| 7 | 8 | 5 | 4 | 1 | 9 | 2 | 3 | 6 |
| 6 | 9 | 2 | 8 | 7 | 3 | 5 | 4 | 1 |
| 5 | 7 | 9 | 6 | 8 | 1 | 3 | 2 | 4 |
| 4 | 6 | 1 | 9 | 3 | 2 | 7 | 5 | 8 |
| 3 | 2 | 8 | 5 | 4 | 7 | 6 | 1 | 9 |

**Puzzle 282**

| 7 | 4 | 8 | 6 | 3 | 9 | 5 | 2 | 1 |
|---|---|---|---|---|---|---|---|---|
| 3 | 2 | 6 | 4 | 1 | 5 | 7 | 8 | 9 |
| 1 | 9 | 5 | 7 | 2 | 8 | 6 | 3 | 4 |
| 4 | 5 | 7 | 8 | 9 | 3 | 1 | 6 | 2 |
| 2 | 6 | 9 | 5 | 4 | 1 | 3 | 7 | 8 |
| 8 | 1 | 3 | 2 | 6 | 7 | 4 | 9 | 5 |
| 6 | 7 | 4 | 9 | 5 | 2 | 8 | 1 | 3 |
| 5 | 3 | 2 | 1 | 8 | 6 | 9 | 4 | 7 |
| 9 | 8 | 1 | 3 | 7 | 4 | 2 | 5 | 6 |

**Puzzle 283**

| 8 | 9 | 6 | 3 | 1 | 5 | 7 | 4 | 2 |
|---|---|---|---|---|---|---|---|---|
| 5 | 1 | 4 | 7 | 8 | 2 | 9 | 6 | 3 |
| 3 | 7 | 2 | 6 | 4 | 9 | 1 | 8 | 5 |
| 2 | 4 | 5 | 1 | 7 | 8 | 6 | 3 | 9 |
| 6 | 3 | 7 | 9 | 2 | 4 | 5 | 1 | 8 |
| 9 | 8 | 1 | 5 | 3 | 6 | 4 | 2 | 7 |
| 1 | 2 | 3 | 4 | 9 | 7 | 8 | 5 | 6 |
| 7 | 5 | 8 | 2 | 6 | 1 | 3 | 9 | 4 |
| 4 | 6 | 9 | 8 | 5 | 3 | 2 | 7 | 1 |

**Puzzle 284**

| 6 | 9 | 8 | 4 | 7 | 2 | 3 | 5 | 1 |
|---|---|---|---|---|---|---|---|---|
| 3 | 4 | 2 | 8 | 5 | 1 | 7 | 9 | 6 |
| 7 | 1 | 5 | 6 | 9 | 3 | 4 | 2 | 8 |
| 1 | 8 | 7 | 3 | 4 | 9 | 2 | 6 | 5 |
| 9 | 3 | 6 | 1 | 2 | 5 | 8 | 4 | 7 |
| 5 | 2 | 4 | 7 | 6 | 8 | 1 | 3 | 9 |
| 4 | 6 | 9 | 2 | 8 | 7 | 5 | 1 | 3 |
| 8 | 5 | 3 | 9 | 1 | 4 | 6 | 7 | 2 |
| 2 | 7 | 1 | 5 | 3 | 6 | 9 | 8 | 4 |

**Puzzle 285**

| 7 | 8 | 1 | 5 | 4 | 3 | 6 | 9 | 2 |
|---|---|---|---|---|---|---|---|---|
| 4 | 9 | 3 | 6 | 1 | 2 | 7 | 5 | 8 |
| 6 | 2 | 5 | 7 | 9 | 8 | 4 | 3 | 1 |
| 3 | 7 | 4 | 1 | 6 | 5 | 8 | 2 | 9 |
| 1 | 5 | 2 | 8 | 7 | 9 | 3 | 4 | 6 |
| 9 | 6 | 8 | 3 | 2 | 4 | 5 | 1 | 7 |
| 5 | 1 | 6 | 2 | 3 | 7 | 9 | 8 | 4 |
| 2 | 3 | 9 | 4 | 8 | 6 | 1 | 7 | 5 |
| 8 | 4 | 7 | 9 | 5 | 1 | 2 | 6 | 3 |

**Puzzle 286**

| 5 | 8 | 1 | 9 | 3 | 2 | 7 | 6 | 4 |
|---|---|---|---|---|---|---|---|---|
| 6 | 2 | 4 | 1 | 7 | 8 | 9 | 3 | 5 |
| 9 | 7 | 3 | 4 | 6 | 5 | 8 | 1 | 2 |
| 1 | 4 | 2 | 6 | 9 | 3 | 5 | 8 | 7 |
| 3 | 9 | 5 | 7 | 8 | 1 | 4 | 2 | 6 |
| 7 | 6 | 8 | 2 | 5 | 4 | 3 | 9 | 1 |
| 8 | 5 | 7 | 3 | 2 | 6 | 1 | 4 | 9 |
| 4 | 3 | 6 | 5 | 1 | 9 | 2 | 7 | 8 |
| 2 | 1 | 9 | 8 | 4 | 7 | 6 | 5 | 3 |

**Puzzle 287**

| 1 | 8 | 9 | 7 | 3 | 2 | 4 | 6 | 5 |
|---|---|---|---|---|---|---|---|---|
| 6 | 3 | 7 | 1 | 4 | 5 | 2 | 9 | 8 |
| 2 | 5 | 4 | 9 | 8 | 6 | 3 | 7 | 1 |
| 5 | 6 | 2 | 4 | 1 | 8 | 9 | 3 | 7 |
| 9 | 1 | 8 | 6 | 7 | 3 | 5 | 2 | 4 |
| 4 | 7 | 3 | 2 | 5 | 9 | 8 | 1 | 6 |
| 8 | 4 | 6 | 3 | 9 | 1 | 7 | 5 | 2 |
| 7 | 9 | 1 | 5 | 2 | 4 | 6 | 8 | 3 |
| 3 | 2 | 5 | 8 | 6 | 7 | 1 | 4 | 9 |

**Puzzle 288**

| 4 | 9 | 5 | 3 | 7 | 1 | 8 | 6 | 2 |
|---|---|---|---|---|---|---|---|---|
| 8 | 7 | 6 | 2 | 4 | 5 | 9 | 1 | 3 |
| 2 | 3 | 1 | 6 | 9 | 8 | 4 | 5 | 7 |
| 5 | 6 | 4 | 9 | 3 | 7 | 2 | 8 | 1 |
| 1 | 8 | 3 | 4 | 5 | 2 | 6 | 7 | 9 |
| 9 | 2 | 7 | 1 | 8 | 6 | 5 | 3 | 4 |
| 7 | 5 | 2 | 8 | 1 | 9 | 3 | 4 | 6 |
| 6 | 4 | 8 | 7 | 2 | 3 | 1 | 9 | 5 |
| 3 | 1 | 9 | 5 | 6 | 4 | 7 | 2 | 8 |

**289**

| 5 | 3 | 2 | 6 | 9 | 4 | 1 | 7 | 8 |
|---|---|---|---|---|---|---|---|---|
| 7 | 8 | 1 | 5 | 3 | 2 | 9 | 6 | 4 |
| 6 | 4 | 9 | 7 | 1 | 8 | 2 | 3 | 5 |
| 9 | 6 | 8 | 3 | 2 | 1 | 4 | 5 | 7 |
| 1 | 5 | 3 | 4 | 7 | 9 | 6 | 8 | 2 |
| 2 | 7 | 4 | 8 | 6 | 5 | 3 | 1 | 9 |
| 3 | 9 | 5 | 2 | 8 | 6 | 7 | 4 | 1 |
| 8 | 2 | 6 | 1 | 4 | 7 | 5 | 9 | 3 |
| 4 | 1 | 7 | 9 | 5 | 3 | 8 | 2 | 6 |

**290**

| 9 | 5 | 6 | 3 | 8 | 2 | 7 | 4 | 1 |
|---|---|---|---|---|---|---|---|---|
| 1 | 2 | 8 | 6 | 4 | 7 | 9 | 5 | 3 |
| 4 | 3 | 7 | 5 | 1 | 9 | 8 | 6 | 2 |
| 2 | 6 | 3 | 4 | 5 | 8 | 1 | 7 | 9 |
| 5 | 7 | 4 | 1 | 9 | 3 | 2 | 8 | 6 |
| 8 | 9 | 1 | 7 | 2 | 6 | 5 | 3 | 4 |
| 6 | 8 | 2 | 9 | 3 | 5 | 4 | 1 | 7 |
| 3 | 1 | 9 | 8 | 7 | 4 | 6 | 2 | 5 |
| 7 | 4 | 5 | 2 | 6 | 1 | 3 | 9 | 8 |

**291**

| 7 | 8 | 2 | 5 | 3 | 4 | 6 | 9 | 1 |
|---|---|---|---|---|---|---|---|---|
| 5 | 4 | 6 | 1 | 2 | 9 | 8 | 3 | 7 |
| 3 | 9 | 1 | 6 | 7 | 8 | 5 | 4 | 2 |
| 6 | 2 | 8 | 9 | 5 | 1 | 4 | 7 | 3 |
| 4 | 7 | 3 | 2 | 8 | 6 | 9 | 1 | 5 |
| 1 | 5 | 9 | 3 | 4 | 7 | 2 | 8 | 6 |
| 8 | 6 | 7 | 4 | 1 | 5 | 3 | 2 | 9 |
| 2 | 1 | 5 | 8 | 9 | 3 | 7 | 6 | 4 |
| 9 | 3 | 4 | 7 | 6 | 2 | 1 | 5 | 8 |

**292**

| 9 | 2 | 4 | 7 | 6 | 3 | 1 | 5 | 8 |
|---|---|---|---|---|---|---|---|---|
| 1 | 6 | 7 | 5 | 4 | 8 | 3 | 2 | 9 |
| 3 | 8 | 5 | 1 | 9 | 2 | 4 | 7 | 6 |
| 4 | 7 | 8 | 2 | 1 | 5 | 6 | 9 | 3 |
| 6 | 9 | 1 | 3 | 7 | 4 | 2 | 8 | 5 |
| 2 | 5 | 3 | 9 | 8 | 6 | 7 | 1 | 4 |
| 7 | 3 | 2 | 4 | 5 | 9 | 8 | 6 | 1 |
| 8 | 4 | 9 | 6 | 2 | 1 | 5 | 3 | 7 |
| 5 | 1 | 6 | 8 | 3 | 7 | 9 | 4 | 2 |

**293**

| 9 | 1 | 3 | 6 | 2 | 8 | 7 | 4 | 5 |
|---|---|---|---|---|---|---|---|---|
| 2 | 7 | 5 | 1 | 3 | 4 | 6 | 8 | 9 |
| 6 | 4 | 8 | 7 | 9 | 5 | 2 | 1 | 3 |
| 8 | 5 | 2 | 9 | 6 | 7 | 4 | 3 | 1 |
| 1 | 3 | 7 | 5 | 4 | 2 | 9 | 6 | 8 |
| 4 | 6 | 9 | 3 | 8 | 1 | 5 | 7 | 2 |
| 7 | 2 | 4 | 8 | 5 | 3 | 1 | 9 | 6 |
| 5 | 8 | 6 | 4 | 1 | 9 | 3 | 2 | 7 |
| 3 | 9 | 1 | 2 | 7 | 6 | 8 | 5 | 4 |

**294**

| 1 | 9 | 4 | 6 | 7 | 3 | 5 | 2 | 8 |
|---|---|---|---|---|---|---|---|---|
| 6 | 7 | 8 | 1 | 5 | 2 | 3 | 4 | 9 |
| 2 | 3 | 5 | 4 | 9 | 8 | 6 | 7 | 1 |
| 3 | 1 | 7 | 2 | 6 | 4 | 9 | 8 | 5 |
| 5 | 6 | 2 | 9 | 8 | 7 | 1 | 3 | 4 |
| 4 | 8 | 9 | 3 | 1 | 5 | 7 | 6 | 2 |
| 7 | 4 | 6 | 5 | 2 | 9 | 8 | 1 | 3 |
| 9 | 2 | 1 | 8 | 3 | 6 | 4 | 5 | 7 |
| 8 | 5 | 3 | 7 | 4 | 1 | 2 | 9 | 6 |

**295**

| 9 | 2 | 3 | 4 | 7 | 1 | 6 | 5 | 8 |
|---|---|---|---|---|---|---|---|---|
| 4 | 5 | 6 | 3 | 8 | 9 | 7 | 2 | 1 |
| 8 | 1 | 7 | 6 | 5 | 2 | 3 | 4 | 9 |
| 7 | 6 | 1 | 8 | 3 | 5 | 2 | 9 | 4 |
| 5 | 9 | 4 | 7 | 2 | 6 | 8 | 1 | 3 |
| 3 | 8 | 2 | 9 | 1 | 4 | 5 | 6 | 7 |
| 2 | 7 | 9 | 5 | 4 | 3 | 1 | 8 | 6 |
| 6 | 3 | 5 | 1 | 9 | 8 | 4 | 7 | 2 |
| 1 | 4 | 8 | 2 | 6 | 7 | 9 | 3 | 5 |

**296**

| 1 | 8 | 5 | 7 | 6 | 3 | 2 | 4 | 9 |
|---|---|---|---|---|---|---|---|---|
| 6 | 9 | 3 | 4 | 2 | 8 | 1 | 7 | 5 |
| 2 | 7 | 4 | 9 | 1 | 5 | 6 | 3 | 8 |
| 4 | 6 | 2 | 8 | 9 | 7 | 5 | 1 | 3 |
| 3 | 1 | 9 | 2 | 5 | 6 | 4 | 8 | 7 |
| 8 | 5 | 7 | 3 | 4 | 1 | 9 | 6 | 2 |
| 9 | 4 | 8 | 1 | 7 | 2 | 3 | 5 | 6 |
| 7 | 2 | 6 | 5 | 3 | 4 | 8 | 9 | 1 |
| 5 | 3 | 1 | 6 | 8 | 9 | 7 | 2 | 4 |

**297**

| 4 | 3 | 7 | 2 | 6 | 9 | 1 | 5 | 8 |
| 9 | 2 | 6 | 1 | 8 | 5 | 4 | 3 | 7 |
| 8 | 1 | 5 | 4 | 7 | 3 | 6 | 2 | 9 |
| 5 | 8 | 1 | 9 | 2 | 7 | 3 | 4 | 6 |
| 7 | 6 | 9 | 5 | 3 | 4 | 8 | 1 | 2 |
| 3 | 4 | 2 | 6 | 1 | 8 | 7 | 9 | 5 |
| 2 | 7 | 3 | 8 | 5 | 1 | 9 | 6 | 4 |
| 6 | 9 | 8 | 3 | 4 | 2 | 5 | 7 | 1 |
| 1 | 5 | 4 | 7 | 9 | 6 | 2 | 8 | 3 |

**298**

| 8 | 6 | 4 | 7 | 2 | 9 | 3 | 1 | 5 |
| 7 | 9 | 3 | 5 | 1 | 4 | 6 | 2 | 8 |
| 2 | 5 | 1 | 3 | 8 | 6 | 7 | 9 | 4 |
| 5 | 1 | 2 | 4 | 3 | 7 | 8 | 6 | 9 |
| 3 | 8 | 6 | 9 | 5 | 1 | 4 | 7 | 2 |
| 9 | 4 | 7 | 2 | 6 | 8 | 1 | 5 | 3 |
| 4 | 7 | 5 | 1 | 9 | 3 | 2 | 8 | 6 |
| 6 | 3 | 9 | 8 | 7 | 2 | 5 | 4 | 1 |
| 1 | 2 | 8 | 6 | 4 | 5 | 9 | 3 | 7 |

**299**

| 3 | 7 | 9 | 1 | 2 | 5 | 6 | 8 | 4 |
| 4 | 6 | 8 | 7 | 9 | 3 | 2 | 1 | 5 |
| 2 | 5 | 1 | 8 | 4 | 6 | 7 | 3 | 9 |
| 7 | 8 | 6 | 3 | 1 | 4 | 9 | 5 | 2 |
| 9 | 2 | 5 | 6 | 7 | 8 | 1 | 4 | 3 |
| 1 | 3 | 4 | 2 | 5 | 9 | 8 | 7 | 6 |
| 5 | 4 | 2 | 9 | 8 | 1 | 3 | 6 | 7 |
| 8 | 9 | 3 | 5 | 6 | 7 | 4 | 2 | 1 |
| 6 | 1 | 7 | 4 | 3 | 2 | 5 | 9 | 8 |

**300**

| 7 | 5 | 8 | 2 | 1 | 4 | 9 | 3 | 6 |
| 1 | 3 | 9 | 7 | 6 | 8 | 5 | 2 | 4 |
| 6 | 2 | 4 | 9 | 5 | 3 | 1 | 8 | 7 |
| 2 | 7 | 6 | 8 | 9 | 1 | 3 | 4 | 5 |
| 8 | 1 | 3 | 4 | 7 | 5 | 6 | 9 | 2 |
| 4 | 9 | 5 | 3 | 2 | 6 | 7 | 1 | 8 |
| 3 | 6 | 1 | 5 | 8 | 2 | 4 | 7 | 9 |
| 5 | 8 | 7 | 1 | 4 | 9 | 2 | 6 | 3 |
| 9 | 4 | 2 | 6 | 3 | 7 | 8 | 5 | 1 |